Packed with q
from girls about
with boys – fr
coping with yo
written book gives sensible, down to earth
advice about relationships.

Carol Weston

Girltalk about Guys: Honest Answers to Candid Questions

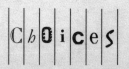

First published in the USA 1988
First published in Great Britain in 1989
by Lions Choices

Lions Choices is an imprint of
the Children's Division, part of
the Collins Publishing Group,
8 Grafton Street, London W1X 3LA

Printed and bound in Great Britain by
William Collins Sons & Co. Ltd, Glasgow

Dedicated to the first guys in my life:
my older brothers, Mark and Eric

Acknowledgements

What would I do without my family and friends? I thank:

Robert Ackerman, my husband, who read this book not once, not twice, but again and again, and whose suggestions for the manuscript were as good as the dinners he cooked to keep us going.

Marybeth Weston, an editor, an author, and most of all, my mother. She marked up my rough draft with the same care and insight with which she used to edit my first junior high compositions.

Janet Goldstein, my ebullient editor, who helped shape this book and who set me straight when I began to feel overwhelmed.

The Harper & Row team – Bill Shinker, Dan Harvey, Joe Montebello, Lisa Kitei, Scott Manning and Martin Weaver – for their hard work, high spirits and faith in me.

Sally Ackerman, Susan Sánchez, Seth Aidinoff and Patty Dann who went beyond the call of friendship and looked over certain chapters with a sharp eye and a sharp pencil.

Nina Kallen, Jennifer Sachs and Kim Gladman, Yale students who, thanks to Yale's externship programme, spent part of their vacations hard at work in my office.

Connie Clausen, my enthusiastic agent.

Dr. Hakim Elahi and Amy Sutnick of Planned Parenthood of New York City and Beth Fredrick of the Alan Guttmacher Institute for answering endless questions.

My ob/gyns, Dr. Suzanne Yale and Dr. Adam Romoff, and their staff, for answering still more questions.

Yosef M. Shimron of Tower Copy at Amsterdam and 85th for his good cheer and fast photocopies.

My cat Chanda because I've loved her for seventeen years.

And all the *Girltalk* readers who wrote me funny, poignant and surprising letters. This book is for you.

Grateful acknowledgement is made for permission to reprint an adaptation of "What Guys Like (and Hate) About Girls", first published in *Young Miss* magazine, August 1986.

Contents

Hello

What I like about advice books is that they get right to the point. You can't ask your mum how to French-kiss because a) you'd be too embarrassed, b) she might not tell, c) she'd want to know why you want to know and d) she might, heaven forbid, repeat the question at a family reunion. Even your friends don't always give the best advice. Mindy likes you too much to tell you that your boyfriend is a jerk, Tammy doesn't know any more about contraception than you do, and Jen and you have a crush on the same guy so forget asking her for help!

Since I wrote my first book *Girltalk*, I've received over a thousand letters from teenage girls and I've answered every one myself. Perhaps because you don't know me personally, you wrote me superpersonal questions. Because I don't know you, I wrote you no-nonsense

15

answers. But here's what surprised me: most of your letters addressed the same subject – boys, boys, boys.

One girl wrote, 'My friends all have boyfriends. When I'm walking through the school and see guys kissing girls, it makes me feel lonesome and terrible.' Another asked, 'What am I doing wrong? I'm pretty, I'm not a snob and I act like myself around guys, but I've never had a real boyfriend and I'm sick of hearing, "Your turn will come." ' A third wrote, 'I have a ton of questions about boys. I dream about them all night and I think about them all day. I feel I need someone to hug now and then, and I don't mean my parents.'

Fair enough. If it's boys you want, it's boys you'll get. You'll hear from girls in every stage of a relationship, from breaking up with one guy to meeting someone new. And I'll tell you about overcoming shyness, flirting, juggling friends and boyfriends and surviving your first date, first kiss and first fight. I'll give you ten reasons to say no to sex as well as ways to protect yourself when you some day decide to say yes.

This book includes quizzes, tips, advice and a lot of our correspondence. The variety of voices – and the similarity of situations – may amaze you. I bet each of you will recognize your own predicament in some letters; I hope all of you will recognize your own good fortune in others.

Whether you are 11, 18 or in between, you're about to get a better perspective on your own passions and problems. If you're a younger teenager, you may not need all the nitty-gritty facts about contraception and sexually transmitted disease, but it's nice to know that Chapter 7 is there when you are ready for it. If you're an older teenager, you may come across some letters that seem young, especially in the beginning of the book, but they will make you smile and will remind you of how far you've come. You'll all learn as much from other girls' questions as you will from my comments and answers.

The letters are in italics. I shortened some of them, but I didn't make any up, honest.

By the way, I don't mean to suggest that having a boyfriend is the be-all and end-all, or that boyfriends are more important than family, friends or schoolwork. We all know there's more to life than boys. But liking a guy who likes you is fun and good for your self-esteem. Don't let anyone tease you for being interested in guys. Believe me, they are interested in you too.

1

Do You Wish You Had a Boyfriend?

Today's mail brought this letter:

> *Lately I have found that I really want a boyfriend. Last night I had a very strange dream. I was sitting on a swing with a boy and his arm was around me, but he didn't have a face. Could you please figure this out for me?*

If you look at the photo on the inside jacket of this book, you'll see I don't look a bit like Sigmund Freud. But it doesn't take a beard or a doctor's degree to analyze this dream. She's deciphered it herself: she wants a boyfriend.

Lots of teenage girls are taken with the idea of a boyfriend in the abstract – faceless, perhaps, but flawless too. So how do you turn dream into reality? This chapter can get you started. It will help you figure out your best qualities and determine what kind of guy you're looking for. Do you think you'll never get any guy? Read the section on attitude. Are you too shy to say hi? Read about starting a conversation and do the shyness quiz. Do you want to get to know some new boys? Find out how to meet them – in school and out.

Ready? Set? Wait! Before you plunge into pages and pages of girltalk, how about a quick glimpse at the male point of view?

WHAT BOYS LIKE AND DISLIKE MOST ABOUT GIRLS

To research an article I recently wrote for a teenage magazine, I asked 14- to 19-year-old guys all over America what they liked and loathed about girls. Their answers are as varied as the guys themselves, but the survey showed some patterns.

> *My ideal girl friend is someone who is interesting and funny and likes to dance and have a good time.*
> *—Mark, Perkiomenville, Pennsylvania*

I hate girls who are obsessed with popular-
ity and are overly concerned with material
possessions.

–Bryan, Lincoln, Nebraska

I like energetic girls who are into sports,
but are still feminine – no bodybuilders!
–Charlie, Joliet, Illinois

WHAT GUYS CAN'T RESIST

A Winning Personality

If you are friendly, good-natured and a good listener, step right up – there are thousands of guys who'd like to meet you. In the recipe for romance, guys say a well-rounded personality is more important than a well-rounded figure.

But guys define personality in different ways. John, of Lafayette, Indiana, likes a girl 'who has a really good sense of humour and goes crazy sometimes.' Scott, of Honaker, Virginia, goes for girls 'who are considerate and who always have time to help people'.

Are you free-spirited or tied to the crowd? Dirk, of Harlan, Iowa, respects a girl 'who is not heavily influenced by her peers and who is able to be herself.' For Victor, of Longview,

Texas, confidence is key. 'I like a girl who can love herself and me.'

Just as girls gravitate towards guys with big smiles and big hearts, guys like girls who are, well, likable.

Eye-catching Looks

After personality, appearance comes in a close second on a guy's priority list, according to the *Young Miss* survey. Guys like girls they consider 'sexy', 'pretty', 'cute' and 'well-built'. Does that mean you have to be 36-24-36? No! Opinions differ on just what makes a girl sexy and what makes a guy do a double-take.

Some guys gravitate toward brunettes. Others go for freckled redheads. Others describe their fantasy girl friend as a blue-eyed blonde with shoulder-length hair. And many shrug their shoulders and say that eye and hair colour make no difference. Dylan, of Brooklyn, New York, says that stylish hair is a plus, but 'some girls think it's a crisis if one hair is out of place'.

As for fingernails, guys don't care if they're polished, but they do agree, hands down, that nails shouldn't be nibbled. And makeup? 'Less is more,' says the majority.

Boys also like girls who are medium weight. 'I don't like girls who are skinny and anaemic-looking. I like girls with more to them,' says Matthew, of Long Island. In Evanston, Illinois, Chris says he hates 'girls who are obsessive about their weight. They look fine but are constantly dieting and saying, "I'm so fat", and making a big deal of it. A lot of girls put too much emphasis on having the perfect body.'

And what do you wear on that body? According to the survey, if you sport the latest styles, about half the guys will think it's great and the other half will barely notice. Boys like everything from 'preppy clothes', 'classic dresses', 'jeans' and 'sweatshirts' to 'short skirts' and 'fuzzy sweaters' – it depends on the guy and on the situation.

If you're fairly traditional, you'd go well with someone like Brady, from Montesano, Washington, who likes clothes that are 'conservative and not too flashy'. If you're more unconventional, you might be a match for someone like Bob, from Santa Monica, California; he likes 'creative girls who aren't afraid to wear way-out styles and who don't dress like everybody else'. And then there's the easygoing type like Roy, a junior in Hunt, West Virginia, who believes anything goes 'as long as it's neat and appropriate'. A word of caution from Adam, of Armonk, New York: 'Don't be overly appearance-conscious, always worrying about looking the right way and saying the right thing. It shows when someone is trying too hard.'

Sounds like a Catch-22, doesn't it? You're supposed to look like a million – without looking like you care.

Intelligence

Could you wear the T-shirt that reads 'All this and brains too'? That's what guys hope. The days of the beautiful bimbo are behind us; today's guy is attracted to college- and career-oriented girls with ambition. Believe it or not, the guys polled were more impressed with a girl who's getting straight A's than with a girl who's popular or rumoured to be fast.

Adam says he likes 'girls who can hold a good conversation. A lot of girls can spend hours talking on the phone, but they aren't really saying anything. I like girls who can go beyond small talk.'

That doesn't mean you should turn every breezy conversation into an interview. Nathan, of Roslyn, New York, says, 'I hate it when girls ask embarrassing questions that I'm not sure I want to answer. Like: "Are you a virgin?" Sometimes I'd rather talk about the weather!'

So don't be a detective but don't play dumb. Like you, guys enjoy witty, sensitive and sensible girls with whom they share common interests.

If a good personality, good looks and a good mind are what boys like, then what's the flip side?

What Guys Can't Stand

'Girls who flirt with every boy they see,' 'girls who spread rumours,' 'girls who get mad over the tiniest things,' 'girls who steal other people's boyfriends,' 'girls who are two-faced,' 'moody,' 'obnoxious,' 'gossipy,' 'phony,' 'possessive' – and that's just for starters! You'd think guys had been waiting their whole lives for someone to come along and ask what they hate most about girls!

What are their biggest gripes? The envelope, please:

Girls Who Smoke

Cigarettes may have earned girls points in the past, but nearly nine out of ten of the boys surveyed think smoking is a drag. Drug use and excessive drinking leave most guys cold too. Says Doug, in Fresno, California, 'A girl who drinks, smokes, is "loose" and brags about her experiences has no self-respect, so why should I respect her?' Sure there is always the minority of guys who go for promiscuous pot-heads, but are they the kind of guys *you* want to attract?

24

Girls Who Are Stuck-up

Again the male message is loud and clear: Stuck-up girls are the pits. Greg, of Austin, Texas, hates 'girls who act superior, like they own the world'. Jeff, of Toms River, New Jersey, loathes 'girls who constantly put people down and think they are better than anyone else'. Jody, of Tylertown, Mississippi, is sick of 'girls who think that everybody is "hot" for them'. And John reports from Plymouth, North Carolina, that he dislikes 'girls who tell everybody about your personal relationship and then ignore you when they're around their friends'. If being stuck-up is the opposite of being friendly, Ed, of Philadelphia, makes his point more plainly than anybody: 'I hate girls who hate me.'

Slobs and Blobs

Slobs and blobs? Where do these guys get off? But then geeks with rings around their collars and cuffs probably don't make your heart skip a beat either. So maybe you can't blame guys for veering away from girls who do nothing to take care of themselves or to bring out their best. 'A girl who is dirty and is not well-groomed is a real turn-off,' says Charlie, of Joliet, Illinois. 'Girls who are vulgar and curse a lot and are always chewing gum aren't my type,' says Rick, of Alexandria, Virginia. Other guys' pet peeves are 'girls with yellow teeth and bad breath', 'girls who burp,' and 'girls who don't brush their teeth and are scuzzy messy dirtbags'. You heard it here! And I know *you* don't fit into this gross group.)

So much for slobs. What about blobs? 'A blob is someone who is dull. She has no sense of humour and nothing to say,' explains Jason, of Santa Barbara, California. Guys agree that going out with a girl who 'is always complaining about herself,' can also be a snooze. 'And if she wants to know everything I tell anyone else and bugs me to death until I tell her – forget it,' says Terry, of Channahon, Illinois.

What does all this mean? On the one hand, while guys are picky, picky, picky, on the other hand, they, like you, are simply on the lookout for someone who is outgoing, attractive and bright, whose company they can enjoy and who can offer friendship as well as romance. That's not too unreasonable. And that could be you!

BEYOND NICE: FIVE GOOD REASONS A GUY SHOULD FALL FOR YOU

The guy I like is going with another girl in my class. I don't have the faintest idea what he sees in her. I'm so confused. I've never had a boyfriend and I'm a nice person. I just wish guys would give me a chance and see how nice I am.

Nice is nice. But is nice enough? What are the best qualities? Are you upbeat? Offbeat? What is it about you that can pique a guy's interest?

1. You have spark.

Are you fun to be with? Do you like to laugh? Do you have a positive outlook? Do you make things happen? Girls with spark don't mope around whining that there's nothing to do over the weekend, they round up the gang and have everybody meet at a store, amusement park, museum, pizza parlour or in somebody's home.

At school, a charismatic girl can turn lunch into a party. She's apt to get everybody telling jokes or funny pet stories or laughing about their most embarrassing moment or the day they learned the truth about Santa Claus. She might lean forward and whisper, 'Let's take a vote. Which guy has the sexiest smile in the cafeteria?' Or she might suggest a game of verbal volleyball by saying, 'Let's go around the table and name famous living couples. Whoever can't think of one has to wink at a boy in front of the rest of us.' Sounds silly? Maybe it is. But girls with spark are lively and spirited, and there's nothing silly about that.

2. You have talent.

What could be more magnetic than skill and accomplishment? If you have a beautiful voice, show it off in the school musical. If you are a gifted dancer, let loose at the party. If you read palms, read palms. Can you play the piano? Knit sweaters? Walk on your hands? Wield a mean tennis racket? Whip up a delicious brunch? Are you an amateur photographer or rock climber or computer whiz? Are you phenomenal on skates?

Talent is captivating. A guy who scarcely notices you now might read your editorial in the school paper or see your painting hanging in the art room, and suddenly find you fascinating. If you have no accent in English and he overhears you speaking Japanese, Spanish or Ukrainian on the phone, he may be awestruck.

Do you have a talent you take for granted?

If you can't think of a skill that gives you confidence and wins you attention, it's never too late to develop one.

3. You're interesting

Do you stand out in a crowd? Some girls are shallow conformists; others, refreshing individualists. There's more to you than meets the eye, so show it. Make your conversation engaging. Defend your ideas. If you loved a movie, say so and say why – even if the person you're with hated it. In English class, offer your interpretation of a Robert Frost poem – even if the teacher's is far different.

Interesting girls look at things through a unique perspective and always have their eyes and ears open for surprising statistics or thought-provoking news to share. If you know facts (without acting like a know-it-all) and have ideas (without sounding opinionated), then your friends are fortunate: being with you is never dull.

4. You're attractive

Okay, okay, so maybe your hairstyle is still growing in and your figure is still taking shape. You do your best to look your best, don't you? Do you stand up straight and smile readily? Are your clothes well cared-for and becoming (or is your closet crammed with last year's fashion fads)? If you have an unusual feature (you're a fiery redhead or a long-legged 5'11"), do you take pride in what sets you apart rather than feeling self-conscious or apologetic about it?

What if your complexion is a mess? A dermatologist came to my rescue – and reminded me that boys' skin problems tend to be worse than girls'. What if you're flat (as I was) or more buxom than you wished? Relax. If you accept your curves and like yourself, guys will like you too. Whether or not you're model material, if you carry yourself well and exercise to stay fit and trim, heads will turn.

5. You're thoughtful

Can a guy assume that if you turn him down for a date, you won't do it rudely or make him a laughingstock around school? Do you make other people feel good by being generous with your time and your compliments? Are you trustworthy? Tactful? If a new person in school walked past your lunch table and sat down alone, would you be intimidated or snooty, or would you simply say, 'Want to sit with us?'

Guys find considerate girls friendly and sincere – and a welcome change from self-absorbed girls who play games and make themselves nearly impossible to read, and from bitchy girls who make a point of putting others down. So don't be merely nice – be as warm and well-mannered as possible.

The list could go on. How many of these winning characteristics apply to you? Two? Three? Can you come up with five reasons of your own why a guy might single you out?

'Five?' you ask. Yes, five. I know you can do it.

Think about your stellar qualities. Your honesty? Creativity? Intelligence? Wit? Sound advice? Sense of adventure? Concern for others? If you're coming up blank, it's not against the law to ask your friend (or sister or mum) for a rah-rah speech. Today she can spur you on with a pep talk full of praise and cheers. Tomorrow it may be your turn to lift her spirits or fortify her sagging ego. (You could also agree to give each other honest gentle feedback on any not-so-splendid mannerisms that can be changed.)

Once you've taken stock of your strong points, give yourself a hearty pat on the back – there's no point in being modest all the time. But don't become too self-satisfied. Continue developing your best traits and talents, and continue putting your best foot forward. Do it for yourself, not just the guys.

BEYOND CUTE: WHAT MAKES A GUY CATCH YOUR EYE?

> *I'm in love with this totally gorgeous 17-year-old. What a babe! He's about five foot ten, blond, a wrestler and totally gorgeous. I think he's the cutest guy in the whole entire world. He is so cute!*

Girls often write me about how cute their crushes are. But how much should cuteness count?

It's a fine fringe benefit if the guy you like happens to be tall, blond and handsome, but isn't it even better if he is lively, talented and thoughtful?

Try to figure out why you melt at the mere thought of him. Is it because he's a sporty type? An artist? Is it because he's funny? Or smooth? Or involved in tons of projects?

If you like him simply because he's cute, you may wind up disappointed. First of all, he probably already has a dozen doe-eyed admirers to choose from and that lessens your odds of becoming his one and only. And second, if he does ask you out, you may find that he doesn't have quite as much going for him as you had imagined.

Don't get me wrong. A few guys have it all: they're sexy, smart, sensitive – and their parents have an Olympic-size backyard swimming pool. But have-it-alls are few and far between. Many other head turners bank on their good looks and don't work hard enough to develop their minds and personalities.

When I think back on the guys I would have died for when I was at high school, I'm amazed. Hugh. Rod. Stan. What did I have in common with them? Nothing. Sure, they were cute and popular, but our goals, hobbies and friends were completely different. I wanted to be accepted by them, but we could never even get beyond small talk because they weren't interested in French, writing and animals (as I was) and I wasn't interested in cars, sports and beer (as they were). If I actually had started going with any of them, I might have stopped counting my lucky stars by the third date.

Yet back then, I didn't have the guts or the foresight to pay attention to some of the undiscovered kids in my school. Not only might they have been surprised and delighted if a girl ever smiled their way, but many turned out to be incredible catches. A late bloomer whom most girls hardly noticed grew up to be a gorgeous and successful Broadway star. An odd-looking short guy became a brain surgeon – with uncanny rhythm on the dance floor and a crackerjack sense of humour. My own husband admits that when he was in high school, he had a horrible complexion; today he's a dapper and handsome (not to mention intelligent and charming) adult – and I'm not just saying that because he reads every word I write.

Look for intellect, ambition, athletic prowess, enthusiasm, musical ability, style, compassion, whatever you like. But don't just look for looks. You know how you feel about guys who judge girls only on how pretty they are. Besides, if you like a guy, you'll start finding him more and more attractive. And if he likes you back, he'll actually become cuter. Not because love is blind (although it can be myopic), but because people who are in love often seem happier and more radiant than usual and start taking extra care of themselves and their appearance.

HOW'S YOUR ATTITUDE?

I started liking boys when I was three. Young, right?

Yup, that's young. Now that you're older, how do *you* feel about boys? Some girls wonder why they are so fickle. Others feel left out because they never have crushes. Truth is, you're not crazy if you're boy-crazy, and it's also okay to be indifferent about guys for a while.

Many girls can't wait to fall in love, not because love is rich and meaningful and fulfilling, but because they want a boyfriend to complete their lives or to make them feel they belong.

> *I feel like I have a hole in my life that I am trying to fill with romance novels and my imagination. We just read* Romeo and Juliet *in English and I think I'm in love with love.*

> *I feel like I'm not 'in' if I don't have a boyfriend. I want so much to be in love, but it just seems that I have an unlucky spell or something. What's wrong with me?*

If you've been questioning your luck, remind yourself that most of your classmates aren't blissfully paired off and you can be 'in' without being in love. You aren't alone because you are jinxed or are doing things wrong. It's just that it takes time for relationships to take off.

Love is a big deal. If everybody were in love all the time, it would lose its lustre. You know that girl in your class who has a different boyfriend every week? Do you really envy her? Do you really think guys take her seriously?

It's hard to be patient, but if you keep yourself busy and happy and if you keep your life full of friends and activities, love will come your way. If instead, you feel sorry for yourself, other people may feel sorry for you too. Beware. Pity rarely turns into love.

> *I'm desperate!!!! I want a boyfriend very, very badly! I'm 14 and have never had a boyfriend. Right now I like this guy. He's pretty popular. I like him so much, but I know he'll never like me back. My friend Jackie invited his friend and him and me to go to Disneyland. He was fairly nice to me there, but don't say that's a start because he'll never like me. I just know it. Never, never, never!!! Is it because I'm ugly? Not popular? Or just plain undesirable?!?!*
>
> *In* Girltalk, *you said to reach out for a guy that's possible to get, but for me, everyone's impossible to get. It's not that I'm bitchy towards people – I'm not. I try so hard to be nice. SO HARD!*
>
> *I think I'm going to go nuts from being unloved. Am I wacko? Why am I so undesirable? Help!*

She's not wacko and she won't go nuts, but I wish her letter had been a little more optimistic and that she hadn't signed it Ima Reject. What Ima needs is an attitude makeover. She has to stop thinking of herself as undesirable and has to start boosting her self-esteem. Instead of dwelling on what's lacking in her life and instead of being down on herself, she needs to focus on what's going right and on her best qualities. Is she loyal? Energetic? Responsible? Does she make good grades? Does she bake scrumptious pies? Does she have a way with words? Or an adorable pet? Or pretty nails? Anything – so long as it's positive. If she thinks more highly of herself, others will too.

She should also work on her friendships as well as her love life. Could it be that she is trying too hard to be nice? Most kids can smell phoniness a mile away, and if she relaxes and is friendly without pushing it, her social life may take a turn for the better.

At 14, many girls have not yet been in love (or even in a mutual crush). And many are not the picture of self-confidence. But nothing is worse than playing the part of a loser or moaning, 'I'll never get a guy'. A defeatist attitude gets you nowhere. A winning attitude wins you friends.

This next sad letter was signed Lonely Lady.

I want to tell you about those of us who go through junior and senior high without love or friendship. Many people say that years after some embarrassing incident, you will look back and laugh. I am only 15, so all I can do is cry. I belong to the group of people who have some defect that makes teenage society reject them as outcasts. It may be crossed eyes, thick glasses or buck teeth.

For me, it's buck teeth. I now wear braces. They don't make me feel better. Many people judge on appearance, and the problems of a pretty girl in no way compare to the problems of an ugly one.

It hurts to sit in music class for an hour when I know that two boys are staring at me and laughing. It's painful to see two best friends sharing their deepest secrets when I know I have no best friend. It's scary for me to walk down the halls when I know someone might make a crude remark loud enough for everyone to hear. It's heartbreaking to see a guy holding hands with a girl when I know I will never experience that joy.

You may wonder if I have a life at all. I do. Thank God for giving me the talent of writing and imagination. I have written

*a play and am working on a novel. It is
my only escape from the harsh realities of
life outside sleeping, reading and listening
to music.*

I feel for this girl. Teenagers can be cruel (not
you, I hope), and it's awful to feel ostracized. At
one time or another, many teenagers find that a
crowded cafeteria can seem bleak and lonely. But
it doesn't have to be that way. This girl can have
friends despite her imperfect smile. And while the
orthodontist works on her teeth, she can work on
her attitude.

In my high school, a buck-toothed boy (who
was in a perpetual good mood) was one of the
best-liked guys – whereas a blonde bombshell
(who excelled at complaining) seemed hard up
for friends. The members of Byram Hills' most
popular clique were easygoing, vivacious, bright
. . . but they weren't all movie-star types. For
that matter, many stars aren't knockouts either:
Danny de Vito, Woody Allen, Linda Hunt, Bette
Midler. Oprah Winfrey is overweight, but is she
unpopular? Barbra Streisand has a big nose, but
is she without fans? Some of these people may
have felt out of it in high school, but fortunately
their less-than-striking looks did not hold them
back.

I'm not saying that attractive people don't

have an edge out there. They do. But so do smart people. And friendly ones. And natural-born comedians. And musical prodigies. And. And. And. It's good that Lonely Lady recognizes that she has literary talent and an appreciation of music and reading, but I hope she'll strive to become less self-conscious. She doesn't like everybody and everybody won't like her, yet I'm sure there are other sensitive students in her school who would welcome the chance to be her friend. Perhaps she'll meet a soulmate at the literary magazine or school newspaper. Or maybe she'll find a friend at a poetry reading or guest artist lecture.

When her braces come off, L.L. is bound to feel more attractive and less insecure, but why wait until then? Why feel deprived of friendship and doomed to solitude for one more minute? It won't be easy to change her high school image or reputation, but she can do it. She probably looks beyond looks when she gets to know people. She must begin trusting that many others do too. (And things will be easier in college.)

This next letter is more optimistic – but its writer may not know when to give up.

I've been trying to get a date with this guy for over two years. I've been chasing him everywhere and I even changed my style to be his perfect girl friend. Should I keep chasing him or should I write a letter signed by his secret admirer? Is he shy or am I crazy?

He may be shy. Or he may simply not want to be captured right now. My hunch is that she's made it clear that she's interested, so she probably shouldn't write him a letter. Is she crazy? No, but it's crazy to change yourself to fit someone else's mould. How can she know who his perfect girl friend would be, anyway? Opposites often attract, and he might have liked her just the way she was, yet want to keep his distance from the person she is straining to become.

Since she's been chasing him for two years, I'd say it's time to call off the hounds. If he approaches her, great. If not, why not start noticing other guys?

An overeager I'll-do-anything-for-him attitude is no better than a desperate I-want-a-boyfriend-any-boyfriend attitude or a plaintive I'll-never-get-a-guy attitude. Girls should be proud of who they are and what they have to offer and then try to stretch to become even more well-rounded – for their own sakes, not their crushes'.

IT'S NATURAL TO BE NERVOUS AROUND GUYS YOU LIKE

My files are full of letters from shy girls. Here are five.

> I'm 15. My problem is that I choke up with guys and I'm afraid to let the real me shine through unless I'm positive the people I'm with like me.

> There's this guy I like so much that whenever he goes by or whenever I even think of him I get goosebumps. But I can't say hi or even smile because he knows I like him and it's embarrassing.

> I'm in the tenth grade and am not ugly or fat or a geek. I think I'm nice. But I'm quiet. One boy I like is popular. I'm afraid to go up to him. He's constantly with his friends and I'm afraid they'll laugh. Should I come out of my shell? Should I call him or get a friend to call him? Should I just be patient? – but that's impossible!

I'm a shy person. If there's a guy I like, I talk to him. But I think I come away looking like a stuck-up JERK. They don't know I'm not a jerk until they get to know me better. But they don't want to get to know me better if I make a bad first impression. What can I say when my mind goes blank?

I'm scared to talk to guys. I am 19 and when it comes to talking to someone I like, I can't. When I do, I get all defensive. Let's face it, there's something wrong with me.

Even the bravest, brashest, most brazen girls can become knock-kneed and tongue-tied in front of an attractive guy. Even social butterflies can get stomach butterflies when their crush looks their way.

Guys get shy too. Some hands-down handsome types are the life of the party, but others are more comfortable in the corner. Boys aren't born knowing how to talk with the opposite sex. They're learning just as you are.

It's natural to be somewhat shy with people you aren't sure like you. But how will you make new friends that way? And how am I going to help you get a boyfriend if you won't do your part? Since you're a likeable person, try assuming that people will like you if you just relax and be spontaneous. Being shy just means that time goes by and you get nowhere.

Everyone worries about rejection. So don't be hard on yourself. But do say hi to guys you like. Will anyone laugh? Of course not. What is the worst that could happen? You might say hi so quietly that the guy will barely hear you and could be halfway down the hall before he realizes he didn't say hi back. Or if he's a real snob (but why would you be hung up on a snob?), he might ignore your greeting and not say hi. Which is what he's not saying now, right? So why not take the gamble?

And what's the best thing that could happen? Your crush could say hi back and smile (does the mere thought make you dizzy?) and pretty soon 'hi' could turn into 'How's it going?' and 'Did you finish that English composition?' and 'How was your track meet?' and 'See you at the class picnic,' and – dare you imagine it? – 'The prom? I'd love to.'

If you can talk to girls (and you can!), you can talk to guys. At first, what you say may not even be as important as your saying it clearly, cheerfully and confidently. Does cheerful and confident sound like a tall order? Try it. People will respond to your positive attitude and you may be surprised at how quickly you'll actually start feeling more positive.

How can you start a conversation? Easy! Here are a dozen ways to break the ice:

1. By the water fountain, say, 'I wish the water were a little colder,' or 'I wish the water would come up a little higher,' or 'Can you believe how many kids spit their gum out here? It's gross, don't you think?'

2. At the baseball game, ask, 'Who just caught that high fly?' or 'I don't recognize that short-stop, do you?'

3. If a radio is playing, ask what groups he likes, or say, 'I listen to this station all the time. Do you like this song?'

4. If it's Friday, say that you and a girl friend are going to the movies this weekend – has he seen any good ones?

5. On Monday, ask him how his weekend was or tell him what you thought of his movie recommendation.

6. Compliment his sweater, oral report, hand-writing, football interception, kitten, new hair-cut, whatever. (I once complimented a guy's Spanish accent after class and he told me that he used to live in Madrid. I asked him about it and before I knew it, we were a couple – for six months!)

7. Ask if he heard about the earthquake,

plane crash, flood, medical breakthrough, political event or rock star's death. Then say, 'Wasn't it amazing?'

8. In maths, ask, 'Can you show me how to do square roots?'

9. In English, ask what he thought of the short story.

10. If there's a map hanging in your history class, ask what country he'd most like to visit. If you're studying the presidents, ask which ones he would have voted for or which one he would have liked to have been. Ask what decade or century he would visit if he could travel in time.

11. In study hall or the library, ask what courses or teachers he most likes and dislikes.

12. In the lunchroom, comment on the mystery meat or ask if there is any one food he would never ever even taste.

You can't overcome shyness overnight. But you can creep out of your shell bit by bit. Read news magazines or newspapers to help expand your horizons and help you 'collect' interesting things to talk about. Practise making small talk with fast-food clerks and department store salespeople and any other 'safe' people you may never see again. Say, 'Busy day?' or 'Nice necklace!' or 'You're lucky you're indoors. It's pouring out.'

Listen carefully to the conversations of people you admire. Instead of envying the popular kids, try to learn from them by tuning in to what they say. You may find that their words aren't remarkable, but that their delivery is good – that they express themselves with enthusiasm.

Becoming a good conversationalist is more than talking without trembling. It's learning how to listen. When Fred says he broke his arm playing hockey, do you immediately tell how you once broke your leg, or do you first ask how it happened and if it hurts?

Ask boys questions about themselves (their families, their classes, their pets, their weekends, their vacations) and show them you're interested by nodding, making eye contact and saying things like 'Really?' and 'You're kidding' when they talk. If Craig is talking about witnessing a crime, and your friend Liz interrupts, don't immediately ask how her maths test went. Say, 'Liz, do you know Craig? He was having dinner in a restaurant with his family when this couple walked in – then walked out two minutes later with his mother's purse. So, Craig, what *did* you tell the police?'

Listen to yourself too. Is your voice pleasant? Or do you sound shrill or whiny? Are you relatively articulate? Or do you punctuate your speech with 'like', 'you know', and curse words?

Conquering shyness can be as simple as mastering certain social skills. Remember that if you don't have the nerve to say hi to a guy, he's never going to find out what an A1 person you are. Tell your friends to introduce you to their friends. And introduce yourself to guys too. You won't lose points for being friendly. Friendliness is what first draws most guys to a girl – because guys get nervous too, especially with girls they like.

QUIZ: HOW SHY ARE YOU?

Everybody feels timid at times. But are you so shy that people scarcely know you are there? Or are you so confident that you sometimes forget to give others a chance to talk? This quiz tests your shyness in general, not just with boys.

1. You're trying on bikinis in a department store. The saleswoman says, 'Does that one fit, dear?' and walks towards the dressing room. You
(a) Say, 'I'm still trying it on, thanks.'
(b) Murmur, 'It's not bad,' and hope she doesn't barge in.

48

(c) Stammer, 'Just a second,' clutch your sweater to your chest and hold the curtain closed.

(d) Open the curtain and ask, 'I'm not sure, what do you think?'

2. Your best friend's mother asks you to stay for dinner. You do and during the meal you

(a) Don't say a word.

(b) Compliment the food twice but can't think of anything else to say.

(c) Are the last to finish eating because you do all the talking.

(d) Talk about as much as everybody else does.

3. A guy you have a crush on (but have never spoken to) accidentally bumps into you in the hall. He says 'Excuse me,' and you

(a) Mumble, 'It's okay.'

(b) Say, 'No problem,' and give him a warm smile.

(c) Turn purple and get out of there as fast as you can.

(d) Purposely spill your books, then look into his eyes and say, 'That's all right, but would you mind helping me with these?'

4. Your sex ed. teacher asks a question about AIDS and you know the correct answer. She looks at you and you

   (a) Look down – though you wouldn't mind getting called on.
   (b) Look up and raise your hand.
   (c) Raise your hand, wave it wildly and start grunting.
   (d) Notice your throat has gone dry and your heart is beating a mile a minute.

5. You and two friends are taking a walk one Saturday and there's a silence. You

   (a) Seize the opportunity to tell about your sister's new boyfriend or you mother's new job.
   (b) Scarcely notice. Short silences are normal.
   (c) Feel very uncomfortable and pray someone says something.
   (d) Make yourself ask, 'What time is it?' just to break the silence.

6. While your father is getting out his wallet, the lady at the drugstore counter looks at you and says, 'What big brown eyes you have.' You

   (a) Wish you were invisible.
   (b) Smile and say 'Thank you.'
   (c) Say, 'Aren't you nice to say that? I was just noticing how pretty your ring is.'

(d) Blush and smile.

7. The new guy at school sits next to you in homeroom. He introduces himself and you say, 'Hi, Rich. I'm Stacey,' and
  (a) Notice your hands are clammy and your face feels hot.
  (b) Realize you can hardly bring yourself to meet his eyes.
  (c) Add, 'Welcome to Byram Hills. Where are you from?'
  (d) Add, 'If you like, I can give you a tour of the school during lunch period today.'

8. You're at the movies with one of your parents and who should sit down behind you but your French teacher and his wife. You
  (a) Say '*Bonsoir!*' then introduce him to your parents and say hello to his wife. You also offer him popcorn several times during the movie.
  (b) Are embarrassed to death and hope he doesn't recognize you.
  (c) Say, '*Bonsoir*, Monsieur Dumontet,' smile, and then don't really think about his being there.
  (d) Say 'Hi' and try to eat your popcorn extra quietly.

51

Scoring

Add up your points
1. a.2 b.1 c.0 d.3
2. a.0 b.1 c.3 d.2
3. a.1 b.2 c.0 d.3
4. a.1 b.2 c.3 d.0
5. a.3 b.2 c.0 d.1
6. a.0 b.2 c.3 d.1
7. a.0 b.1 c.2 d.3
8. a.3 b.0 c.2 d.1

(12)

0-5 You're painfully shy, but you are not alone. Many girls will do anything to avoid attention or confrontation. Beware, shyness can sometimes be mistaken for snobbiness. Life will be easier once you come out of hiding, and the best way to conquer shyness is to bolster your self-esteem. Instead of putting yourself down, spruce up your appearance and take pride in your best qualities. The more you talk with classmates and strangers, the less timid you'll become.

6-12 Like most girls, you're a little shy. Shyness can be endearing, and some guys have a soft spot for girls who blush. But if you wish to be bolder, start forcing yourself to be more forward. Say 'Hi, how's it going?' to the bus driver and librarian, compliment two acquaintances and speak up in class. Remember that while you're worrying about sounding stupid, your friends are probably worrying that they're the ones whose words ring foolish.

13-18 You're neither shy nor aggressive, neither a wallflower nor the centre of attention. you're at ease in most situations, you have good social skills and you're comfortable with who you are. When you want to say something, you say it. Bravo!

19-24 Bashful and intimidated, you're not. It's surprising how unself-conscious you are with adults, boys and strangers. Some may call you a chatterbox or say you're more sly than shy, but others envy your self-confidence and wish they, like you, were never at a loss for words. Give yourself credit for being outgoing, but be careful not to become a motormouth; others deserve a chance to talk too.

EIGHT WAYS TO MEET BOYS IN SCHOOL

Do you go to a coed school? If so, you're in luck. You are surrounded by hundreds of potential boyfriends every single day.

Question: Are you taking advantage of this shining opportunity?

Not if you have it in your head that there are only eight worthwhile guys in your whole school. You may complain that boys pay attention only to popular girls, but do you overlook all but the popular boys? Stop limiting yourself. There are probably a zillion (well, at least 31) less sought-after guys in your school who are neither nerds nor heart-throbs and whom it would be fun to get to know.

Have you really checked out every guy in every class? What about that new kid in town? Or the quiet type behind you in science? Or the foreign exchange student? How about the maths brain you've caught looking at you? True, they haven't gotten the 'in' clique's nod of approval. But so what? Are you so high and mighty that you can't give an uncelebrated guy a chance? Why not discover a guy on your own instead of joining the masses who are already swooning over the school quarterback?

How can you approach an unsung sweetheart? If you're outgoing, you can whisper hello in the library or politely ask a guy in the cafeteria line if you can join him for lunch. But there are less direct and equally efficient ways to get to know guys. The best way of all is to join a club, staff or sport, because people with common interests and schedules automatically have things to talk about.

Consider signing up for the:

1. Choir

Where would the tenors be without the sopranos? The basses without the altos? Do students who sing together fling together? Some do — why not you?

2. School newspaper

Interested in writing, editing, photography? Join the newspaper staff – and meet guys who are too. If you write an article on what it's like to be a graduating senior or on student reaction to the new school sculpture, you'll have a perfect excuse to interview someone you admire.

3. Student council

Class representatives and committee members meet guys of all ages. Are you br-br-brave enough to run for office and give a speech in front of the whole school? If so, everyone will learn your name.

4. Computer club

Okay, so it's not really a date every Thursday in room 56. You do get to see Simon and Glen without Lydia's looking on, don't you? In most schools, more boys than girls still sign up for this extracurricular.

5. Language clubs

Je t'aime. Te quiero. Ti amo. I always had a weakness for men with accents.

6. Drama club

Someone has to kiss Romeo. How about you? Even if you don't get to play Juliet, you could be in charge of costumes, set design, lights, props or programmes. And cast parties are part of the fun.

7. Outdoor club

I went on a getaway weekend with my school's outdoor club and our group enjoyed white water canoeing and campfires under the stars. Talk about romantic!

8. Sport of your choice

Don't just attend soccer, baseball and lacrosse games. Sign up for a coed sport: tennis? swim team? ski club? softball? Nothing like horsing around after practice and flirting on bus rides. You're partial to gymnastics? Then by all means join up – even if you're not likely to meet many boys on the parallel bars.

By getting busy after school, you'll not only up your odds of meeting nice guys (and girls), you'll also become a more interesting and fulfilled person. You'll even become a more impressive college candidate. So what are you waiting for?

> *I did what you said and joined lots of groups. Now I'm in the church choir, the theatre crew, student government, the American Field Service group, the speech club, the Beta club, volleyball, and I'm going to find out if I can volunteer at the hospital or library and also adopt a grandparent. Thanks for the advice.*

Whoa! Don't spread yourself too thin. My advice is to go to it – not overdo it!

A DOZEN WAYS TO MEET
BOYS OUTSIDE OF SCHOOL

I go to Columbus School for Girls, an all-girls school in Ohio. Our 'brother' school is an all-boys school. We have very few get-togethers with them. In teenage books and magazines about how to get a guy to notice you, most of them say stuff like 'Have a chat at his locker.' Well, I'm not exactly going to walk all the way across town to have a chat at a guy's locker! I wish just once someone would write something for those of us who go to private schools. I'm tired of being ignored!

Her wish is my command. This section is dedicated to the girls at single-sex schools – like CSG. Do they realize that the boys at their 'brother' schools — like Columbus Academy — are climbing the walls wishing they could meet them? And that nearby public schools — like Bexley High — are also chock full of boys dying to know new girls? And what about the local all-boy Catholic schools — like St. Charles? Or Wellington, the coed private school?

How can you get to know the male half of the population?

1. Organize something social

If you are in the student council, postpone the debate over the school uniforms and class car wash, and plan a picnic, dance or Walk Against Hunger fundraiser with the boys' school. Or be independent and get a friend (maybe one with a brother or boyfriend) to throw a party – or help you throw one.

2. Attend the events of another school

The public school is putting on a Thurber play? Go see it and tell the actors afterwards how great they were. The boys' school has a big track meet? Go with a friend and force yourselves to be friendly to the guys you meet. 'I'm Tina and this is my friend Sally. We're from CSG. What's Academy's record in track this year?' Nothing ventured, nothing gained.

3. Volunteer

Take part in a peer counselling hotline, entertain handicapped children or visit nursing home residents. Getting involved with community service is good for your soul, good for your résumé, and a good way to meet – and maybe get involved with – big-hearted guys.

4. Go to the library

Why study at home when you can go to the local library, scope out a table with a guy at it and plunk your books down with a smile? You've been working in silence for an hour? Ask him what time it is or where there's a water fountain or if he knows if 'garish' has one *r* or two. Or say, 'I need a study break. Can I bring you back some gum or anything?'

5. Find out what your town or city has to offer

Are there local swimming lessons, karate classes, youth groups, theatre companies or other activities in which teens get together? Is there a YMCA? Ask the guys you meet, 'Where are you from?' 'Have you taken classes here before?' 'When do you think is the best time to come swimming?' 'How long did it take you to earn a brown belt?'

6. Go to church or synagogue

It may seem sacrilegious to strike up a lusty liaison in a house of worship, but judging from my mail, it happens all the time. Churches and synagogues sponsor dances, informal gatherings and weekend retreats which aren't always characterized by purity of thought.

7. There's always the mall

No guys in the halls? Check out the malls. Go with a friend and be outgoing. In the video rental shop, ask a young salesman or customer about a movie you're curious about. In the fast-food joint, ask, 'How's the pizza?' In the pet shop, ask, 'Isn't that puppy the cutest thing you've ever seen?' (Psst, if you're really just shopping for boys, and he's the cutest thing you've ever seen, don't make it too obvious.)

8. Consider a part-time job

You won't meet many boys baby-sitting, but nice guys are scooping ice cream, serving burgers, bagging groceries, washing dishes and selling records all over town. Why not get paid as you hone your social skills?

9. Go to a coed camp

Be a camper or counsellor. Summer love doesn't always last until fall, but it sure can jazz up July and August.

10. Go to parks, beaches, pools, ski slopes and skating rinks

Traditional teenage gathering places are popular for a reason. Join a volleyball game at the park. Say, 'Heads up!' as you toss someone a Frisbee at the beach. Ask, 'How's the water?' as you lower your legs into the pool. Introduce yourself to a guy at a skating rink. If he ends up being a jerk, it doesn't matter – you'll never see him again. If he's a gem, who knows? You may see him again and again and again. Skiing is expensive and requires a snowy mountain, but male skiers (most of whom are handsome, young and physically fit) invariably outnumber female skiers. If you're alone in a lift line, you're supposed to yell 'Single!' and I kid you not – a guy will usually ride up the chairlift with you. Talk about an easy way to meet someone!

11. Go to fairs and festivals

The guys you'll run into at state fairs, auto shows and bluegrass festivals aren't just interested in cows, cars and country music – they're interested in you. Say, 'I've never seen a pumpkin that size!' 'Will you get a load of that Porsche?' 'Wasn't that a beautiful song?' Or simply, 'I'm Marcia and this is Hilary.' Start a conversation.

It could lead some place wonderful. (Do be cautious, though – there's no rush to give out your last name or phone number to someone you just met five minutes ago.)

12. Be creative

If you write for your school newspaper, for instance, why not do an article on the changing image of Columbus School for Girls? Do boys at Academy, Bexley High, St. Charles and Wellington think CSG girls are sexy – or snobby? To find out, you'll have no choice but to interview the fellows!

Don't stay home. Stay active. You'll have fun and you're bound to meet some boys in the bargain.

2

You Like Him – Now What?

You know what guys like in girls and you know what you like in guys. You're working on your attitude, you're overcoming your shyness, you've joined several after school groups . . . and presto! You've made some new friends and met some new boys. Matter of fact, there's this one particular boy that you particularly like. Like? Love? No, like. But it could be love. Maybe. If only he'd like you back.

How can you get a guy to notice you? How can you tell if he already has? Should you make the first move – or should you give up? How can you handle a runaway crush? Or a crush on a guy who is wrong for you? And how oh how can you go from being someone's secret admirer to being his girl friend?

If there's a guy you can't stop thinking about, this is the chapter for you.

DOES HE LIKE YOU?

Lots of girls want to know if their crushes like them. Sometimes I write them back with good news, sometimes bad news and sometimes I can't tell. Sean may be so sombre and reserved that a half-smile could signify heartfelt devotion. Aaron may be so flirtatious and demonstrative that a kiss may mean next to nothing.

Does your crush like you? Yes? No? Maybe so? Here are some questions from girls, complete with answers I sent in return. I hope reading these
letters helps you read your guy.

First let's hear from some of the younger girls. (For some of you this will be a quick jaunt down memory lane.)

> Dear Carol,
> I really like this guy named Russ. He is sooo cute (you know what I mean). But he is shy and so am I. Will I ever know if he likes me? How will I know?
> Valerie

> Dear Valerie,
> If Russ likes you, you'll pick up on it. He'll smile at you a lot, maybe even

blush or seem embarrassed. He'll stumble over his sentences or bubble over with conversation. You'll catch him looking at you. You'll hear through the grapevine that he likes you. He'll sit near you in class or tease you in the library. He'll call you or write you a note. He'll ride or drive by your house. His friends will say hi to you. Or he'll just plain ask you out.

Don't be so shy that you're unwilling to send him 'I like you' signals. But don't be so busy sending signals that you neglect to notice the ones he sends you!

Dear Carol,

Whenever I see this guy named Matt, my heart starts pounding. We look at each other in class, and I think he likes me, but why doesn't he ask me to go with him? One day at lunch, he sat beside me. I almost had a heart attack. He took my orange and put it in my chili. I picked up his orange and put it in his chili. We both laughed and laughed. Later in class, he was

poking this girl Flo in the side and she was laughing like it was the greatest thing that ever happened to her. I felt so jealous. But

when he did it, he was looking at me.
Wonderfully Confused

Dear Wonderfully Confused,
    What lobster and champagne can do for an older couple, chili and oranges can do for a younger couple. Matt probably likes you, but he may not be ready to declare undying love. Enjoy the relationship as it develops instead of trying to hurry it from stage to stage.

Dear Carol,
    I'm a seventh grader who likes a ninth grader. When he sees me in the halls, he smiles and stiffens up like a zombie. Do you think he likes me?
Becca

Dear Becca,
    Yup. When a guy acts like a zombie, it's usually a dead giveaway that he likes you. Start saying hi and help get the relationship
going.

Dear Carol,
    I'm 11. Everybody tells Bill I like him. I say I don't but I do. A LOT. But does

he like me? He gave me a string bracelet that if you cut it you're not friends any more. We haven't cut ours yet. I can't sleep without dreaming of him or eat without thinking of him.

In Love

P.S. Please don't tell me I'm too young to take boys seriously because that won't help at all.

Dear In Love,
   As long as your bracelets are on, I'd say your romance is too.

Dear Carol,
   How do I make boys stop calling me names like Kermit the Frog, Flea and Shrimp? They tease me because I'm so short. My mother says it's because they like me.

Joy (because I
am joyful
except for that)

Dear Joy,
   The boys will soon stop calling you names, but if it's all in fun, you could laugh good-naturedly or call them names

68

back. Are they flirting in an awkward way? 'Shrimp' may not sound like a term of endearment, but then 'Dear', 'Lamb', and 'Bear' are rather strange words of affection too.

Dear Carol,
Sometimes this guy I like acts so sweet and I think he likes me. Other times he acts like an immature show-off and as though I'm invisible. I see him only at church on Sundays. Is it normal for a guy to act like he likes you sometimes and not others? If so, is it more likely that he likes you or is just being nice?

Me

Dear Me,
Alas, boys often send out mixed signals. And guys who aren't ready to have a girl friend or 'go public' with their affection sometimes turn into clowns around their friends. Trust your instincts. If your crush is a sweetheart when you two are alone, that's a good sign. But young girls are usually more romantically inclined than boys. If after a month of Sundays, you still don't know if your relationship is to be or not to be, consider looking around

for other romantic possibilities.

Dear Carol,
   I really like this boy. But he kids around a lot with everybody and I can't tell if he's serious. He acts serious, but I can't tell. Should I confront him or hope that something will happen soon?
                    Crazy Over Chris

Dear C-O-C,
   Don't confront him. If he doesn't like you romantically, it will just make things awkward. And if he does, you'll find out soon enough. Flirt discreetly and get to know him better. Even if love is not in the air, he may be a fun friend to have.

Dear Carol,
   I like a guy named Cliff. I asked him whom he liked. He said Keri. I asked whom else he liked. He said he didn't want to say. How do I find out if he likes me more than a friend? Would it be okay if I called him about homework if I have girls to call? Wouldn't that be really weird? Calling a boy when you have girl friends to call first?
                    Wondering in Wisconsin

70

Dear Wondering,

Live dangerously: Call Cliff about homework. If he's friendly – great! If not, don't call again and don't worry about it.

Asking Cliff whom he likes, now that's kind of forward. He probably got the hint that you like him, so see if he lights up around you more or less than usual.

Dear Carol,

Last spring, a boy I really like told my friend he liked me. This fall, my friend and I visited his school. Right in front of me and my best friend, he said he likes another girl. He really hurt my feelings. But I still like him. How do I know if he likes me?

A Very Sad Girl

Dear V.S.,

Boys can be even more fickle than girls. Time went by without your relationship taking off, and now his feelings have shifted. Don't pine for him. I bet there are guys in your school ready to pick up where he left off.

Dear Carol,

The guy I like has been mean to me lately. He'll trip me in the hallway, or he'll shove me, then say, 'Don't push.' It makes me sick, and one minute, I'll hate his guts, but the next minute, I'll wish he'd ask me out. I don't even know if he likes me.

> *Ready to Pull My*
> *Hair Out in Ohio*

Dear Ready,

Some guys show affection in idiotic ways. Are you sure you want him to like you? It may be flattering that he's paying attention to you, but gentle and thoughtful, he's not.

A young girl may not always be able to tell if her crush picked her to join his water-gun team because of her aim or his affection. But guess what? Even girls who are several years older can't always tell whether the guys they like like them back.

Dear Carol,

I met this guy at a pizza parlour about three weeks ago. My friend and I go there every Sunday night and he always flirts with me. He pretends he is Elvis and

72

tries to sing to me and always talks to me. What does it mean when a guy flirts with you? Does it mean he likes you? Should I go for pizza on Fridays and Sundays or just Sundays? Should I just keep doing what I'm doing?

Phyllis

Dear Phyllis,

Does extroverted Elvis flirt with lots of customers, or does he want to be tender and true to you and you alone? He definitely likes you, but the question remains does he like *you*?

Why not go for pizza on Sundays and occasional Fridays thereby keeping him guessing? Otherwise, keep doing what you're doing. Sounds like it's working.

Dear Carol,

I fell head over heels in love with a guy recently. He is perfect. He's the type my parents would love. I can't figure out if he knows I'm alive or not. My mother says to be myself and not drool over him.

I thought he noticed me because he smiled and looked at me. I was convinced that he liked me because another guy thought we were going together. Then one of my friends saw him mowing a neighbour's lawn and asked him (without my permission) if he liked me. He said he wasn't sure who I was. She said she would show me to him on Monday.

My friend thinks I haven't a thing to worry about. I can't wait until Monday. But I was sure he knew me. Do you think he just gave my friend a line because he didn't want to say that he liked me?

Confused in South
Carolina

Dear Confused,
It's possible. Guys sometimes cover up their feelings until they know where they stand. But while it's good to be confident, don't be overconfident. Now that the fateful Monday has come and gone, you probably know what's up. If you're a couple, hats off. If not, ask yourself this: Was he really perfect . . . or was he a perfect stranger?

Dear Carol,
I like this guy named George. Once or twice he even said that we were going together (in front of other people). Yesterday, he asked what I was doing after

school. I told him I had swim team. He said, 'Well, how about coming over to my house afterwards to watch TV?' I said sure and he said he'd call.

When I got home, there was no message from him. So I called him around 7:00 and said, 'Did you call me?' He said no. I told him it must have been a crank call and we hung up. I can't tell if he likes me or not.

Flustered in
Florida

Dear Flustered in Florida,

He probably likes you but chickened out of calling because he realized that if you came over, he'd have to introduce you to everyone in his family and suddenly the invitation didn't seem so casual any more. On the phone, you could have said, 'Do you think it's gotten too late for me to come over and watch TV?' For now, keep being friendly, give him time and consider asking him over.

Dear Carol,

I've liked this guy named A.J. for about three years. I've heard rumours that he likes me. We talk and stuff but nothing ever comes of it and it seems hopeless but

I can't let go.

Looking for Love

P.S. How much does Princeton cost? How much does a Jaguar cost? I want both.

Dear Looking,
I'm not sure what Princeton or Jaguars have to do with romance, but we're talking megabucks. Four years at a fancy college might cost as much as two fancy cars, but cars rust whereas an education lasts forever. (And name me a car dealer that offers scholarships!)
As for A.J., keep talking and consider asking him to join you and some friends on a no-big-deal skating or beach excursion. You'll soon find out if there is any truth to the rumours. If two more months go by and nothing changes, you'd probably be wise to move on.

Dear Carol,
Derrick dumped me after he found out that I'm not into sex or drugs. He still comes up to me and looks deep into my eyes and puts his arm on my shoulder. He's worthless. I wish I could find

76

someone decent. You should try matching people up!

Sheila

Dear Sheila,

It's manipulative Don Juans like Derrick that give other guys a bad name and make other guys hard to read. You'll soon find a decent guy on your own and his deep gaze won't be just for show. (I have matched up a few of my friends. But when there's trouble in paradise, they turn to me for explanations, and then I sometimes wonder why I ever got involved!)

Dear Carol,

I'm a sophomore. After moving to a huge high school, I met a junior who is nice, interesting, popular and even good-looking. I have never been in a steady relationship, for I, over the past two years, have lost 58 pounds and have never considered myself attractive. This guy seems to notice me, but I can't tell if he likes me.

New at This

Dear New,

Bravo for losing all that weight. Keep

*being friendly to the junior – the only
way to tell if he likes you is to see if he is
friendly back. By the way, you're not the
only sophomore who is new at romance.
Many of your classmates are in the same
boat – and they too complain that the Love
Boat, it's not.*

HOW TO LET HIM KNOW YOU'RE INTERESTED

When your crush walks by, do you look down
and clam up? Or do you give him the eye and
say a quick hi? How can you let him know that
you'd like to know him better?

> *I live for the future – more specifically,
> my future with Clay. I think he likes me
> because he voluntarily sits down next to me
> in advanced biology. (There's no seating
> chart.) But when I catch his eye in the hall,
> it's all I can do to smile. I unintentionally
> found a way to get his attention, though.
> I almost ran him over in the parking lot
> after school yesterday.*

Girls shouldn't live for their crushes – or kill their crushes! What this girl should do is muster up her courage and force herself to do more than smile in the hall. Since he sits next to her in biology, he'd obviously welcome her advances. The more she talks to him (about anything from photosynthesis to photography), the more they'll grow to know – and like – each other.

> *When a boy named Jeremy first came to our school at the beginning of this year, I was the only one who associated with him. Then someone gave him the hint that I liked him. So about a week ago I started ignoring him and now he's chasing me. I'm afraid that if I start liking him, he'll creep back in his hollow log. I want to be boy-friend–girl friend, but I don't know how to be. I am 13. Please help!*

If a guy ignored you, would you think he liked you? Probably not. Her game playing may pique his interest for a few days, but game playing gets old. Right now he likes her and she likes him. Why not just be as friendly as ever?

> *A friend of mine who is a boy always tells me that I am very attractive. On*

*the phone he jokes, 'I love you,' and then
says he's just kidding. Sometimes he sounds
like he means it. I really like him but he
thinks of me as a friend, I think. We talk
for hours on the phone, both seriously and
silly. How can I hint to him to make the
first move?*

Sounds like a romance is in the works. If
she says, 'I've been dying to see the new movie
at the Plaza,' or 'We should be outside – it's a
perfect day for a walk,' he'll probably pick up
the cue.

*Last summer we moved from one part of
town to another. Across the street lives an
absolutely gorgeous guy I'll call Jeff. He
is in grade 10 in my school. Right after I
moved in, we had what I call a 'window
romance'. He would blink lights and I'd
blink back. But as soon as school started
things cooled off. At the first dance in
September I thought something might
happen. Something did: I found out Jeff
already had a girl friend.*

*Now, seven months later, Jeff is noticing
me again. This time, he calls, lets the phone
ring once and hangs up. I hope he's serious
this time because I would love to go out*

*with him. I would like to invite him over
some time when no one else is home but I
don't have the guts.*

*What do you suggest I do to let him
know I'm interested? I have never had
such a crush on a guy in my whole entire
life!*

Enough of the blinking lights and ringing
phones. All that is endearing for a while. But
he's in tenth grade, so unless he has the poise
of a parsnip, why doesn't he just talk? Why
doesn't she? They can chat at the bus stop or
walk or share a ride to school. Or she can drop
by to borrow books, sugar, a compass or a tape.
Sure, she could let his phone ring once after she
thinks he's called her, but isn't it more efficient
– and exciting – to go for broke and get to know
him?

*There's this boy that I really like. I'm 12
and he's 14. He's my first crush, but I can't
stop thinking about him. Only a few of my
friends have had big crushes like this. The
others see a cute boy, go wild, get him, go
with him and forget about him. But I have
my mind set on Josh. He's so cute. He's a
dream (and a dream is all he is to me). He's
not like other boys who have their mind set*

on one thing. He's not rude or gross like a brother either. In the summer, he talked to me and seemed interested, but now I see him only at parties. I don't want to make a fool out of myself, but I do want him to notice me. How should I act around him? Please send your letter before Valentine's Day (hint, hint).

If I were her, I'd rush him a handmade or store-bought Valentine's card. Merely sending it says, 'I like you,' so the message inside should be low-key, not mushy.

How should she act around him? Why act? Why not be herself? Being totally natural can be difficult for girls who are still discovering who they are. But why pretend to be blasé? Why carry on seductively? Why imitate a superpopular girl? Why attempt to be someone she's not? She should try to talk with him as she talks with her buddies – throwing in an extra smile here and there. Her nervousness may give her added sparkle, and there's nothing wrong with that. If she seems interested and interesting, friendly and flattering, he'll catch on that she's been thinking about him. The trick to flirting is to show your affection without going overboard.

FLIRT ALERT: A DOZEN DOS AND DON'TS

I don't know how to flirt. Please give me some advice.

Do you know how to flirt – without being a flirt? Some girls are so subtle that guys can barely pick up their signals. Other girls come on so strong that guys run for cover. Do you know how to let a guy know you're interested – without scaring him away? Here's the dirt on how to flirt.

DO	*DON'T*
Be selective.	Act coy and giddy with every boy in sight
Be visible.	Become your crush's shadow.
Be approachable.	Lock yourself inside a tight group of girls.
Look into his eyes.	Bat your eyelashes.

Dress femininely, at least every once in a while	Drench yourself with *femme fatale* perfume or wear V-necks slit down to your navel.
Compliment his new shirt or winning goal	Flatter him to death.
Smile a lot and laugh at his jokes jokes	Giggle uncontrollably whenever he's within 10 feet.
March right up and talk to him	Announce that you love him when your romance is still on square one.
Ask him questions.	Phone him for 50-minute chats.
Sound delighted if he calls	Cover the mouthpiece and scream 'It's him!' to your family.
Consider touching his arm gently during conversation	Attack him bodily

Communicate 'I like you.'   Communicate 'I need you.'

At some point, almost everybody does a don't, so forgive yourself if you too have been guilty of giggling or giddiness. But don't become the school flirt. I just got a letter from two (overly concerned?) sophomores who complained that their friend is 'so flirtatious, it's scary. She will do ANYTHING and EVERYTHING to get the attention of ANY and EVERY boy. We know flirting is healthy, but she is going too far!' Another letter writer expressed her disgust with a classmate who 'acts really "huggie-huggie" with older guys and when she hears something drop, she goes "eeek" and clings to the nearest boy.' One honest girl confessed that she is a 'big-time flirt' who 'doesn't know how to stop.' If your flirting has gotten out of hand, tone it down and have faith in yourself. You don't have to resort to trickery and wiles to hold a guy's interest. And you don't want to make a guy think you're eager to do things you're not.

SHOULD YOU MAKE THE FIRST MOVE?

It takes guts to approach the person you've been daydreaming about. Guts to say a simple 'Hi,' let alone, 'I was wondering if you'd like to check out that new miniature golf course this Saturday.' Asking someone out is scary because you run the risk that your crush might say no. And girls don't like being turned down any more than guys do.

But sometimes it makes more sense to take action and find out where you stand rather than spend two more years in a daze over Dave. And sometimes you can make the first move without having to venture too far out on a limb.

Just because you're feeling gutsy doesn't mean you have to ask a guy to go to a movie. Instead of suggesting such an Official Date, why not suggest a daytime outing with other friends – bowling, going to the zoo or an exhibit, visiting a nearby college campus, meeting for burgers and ice cream? Or just call him at home or start talking to him in school.

In June, a guy named Curtis Allen and I started getting to know each other. He told his best friend that he wanted to have a closer relationship with me. The problem is that school is now out and I don't know where he lives. Should I call all the Allens in the phone book, or should I just leave it be?

Depends on how many Allens are in the phone book. If this girl lives in Los Angeles or New York City, she may be out of luck. But if there are, say, half a dozen Allens, what the heck? A lost crush need not be a lost cause. (Prince Charming tracked down Cinderella, and all he had to go on was a slipper.) There's nothing wrong with doing a bit of detective work in the name of affection. She might reach Curtis by calling a sympathetic school secretary or by tracking down his best friend's name and number.

Then she and a girl friend can invite the boys to the amusement park. Or she can call Curtis and invite him to a party or to ask how his summer is going. Or she can drop him a card. He may be wondering what she's up to.

If she doesn't call him and he doesn't call her, what will that accomplish? If she calls and he's distant, fine; at least she'll know not to spend the entire summer sighing about the end of spring.

At school, this really cute and popular

guy talks to me a lot. But when we're at Skateworld, he hangs around all the popular girls and doesn't talk to me, though he does look at me. Could he be shy? But he's not shy with the other girls. Why doesn't he speak to me?

Why doesn't she speak to him? Why not break the ice on the ice? She can say, 'I love your sweater,' or 'Would you show me how to skate backwards?' or 'Aren't you afraid to skate so fast?' If she's feeling bold, she could even say, 'I'm taking a break. Want some hot chocolate? My treat.' Why skate in circles and hope he glides her way when she can take matters into her own hands and initiate a conversation? His reception is icy? Ouch. But better to find out sooner than later. He's all smiles? Hurray! Many guys can't resist girls who show interest.

Should I phone the guy I like and have an open, honest conversation with him on how he feels about me? Or should I just be miserable and not do anything and wait for his call?

Why be miserable? If I were her, I'd call him just to talk and maybe suggest going for a bike ride. But I would not quiz him on his feelings.

After all, his feelings may warm up once he gets to know her.

If you wonder what a guy thinks of you, learn to read between the lines rather than inquiring straight-out. When a guy says, 'Thanks for asking, but I have to study for Tuesday's test,' he's being cordial without being encouraging. When a guy says, 'That sounds great, but I'll be at my brother's graduation. How about next Saturday?' he is giving you the green light.

One reason why it's better to use your intuition than to put a guy on the spot is that asking point-blank questions can backfire.

> *This boy in my class and I are starting to like each other more than just as friends. He even said so. All my friends told me to write him a letter and ask him if he would go with me. I was sure he would say yes. But when he gave back the letter, it said. 'Not now, maybe later.' I felt like a jerk. Do you think he will stop liking me?*

No. But it is too bad that she, like so many girls, wanted to immediately label her relationship instead of just enjoying it. Couples can revel in each other's company even if the romance isn't official and even if both parties haven't signed any dotted lines. Taking the first friendly move is wise. Forcing the issue is not.

> *I've liked a guy for nine months and*
> *I can't get my mind off him. Now my*
> *grades are dropping in some of my classes.*
> *Please write back as soon as possible.*

Whether you're in love or out of love, that's
no reason to let your grades slip. Don't be
shortsighted. Doing well in school is your ticket
to a bright future. And at college and at work,
you'll meet plenty of intelligent guys with interests similar to yours. The smarter you become,
the better – for yourself and all your future
boyfriends.

If this girl is distracted by her nine-month
crush, she should make a move so that she
can begin to either go out with him or get
over him. At closer inspection, she may find
he's not as great as she thought. Or he may
admire her pluck and straightforwardness and
start looking at her in a new way. Whatever
happens, it beats spending nine more months
in Limbo Land liking him from afar while her
grades take a tumble.

> *I have the biggest crush on this guy in*
> *my catechism class at church. His name is*
> *Jerry and he's really cute. We never really*

talk to each other, but I've seen him look at me – although it could be that he was just looking around.

I wanted to get to know him better, so about a month ago, I decided to have a sledding and pizza party for the class. I finally got up the courage to phone Jerry (after about 20 minutes). He thanked me for the invitation but said that he'd already planned to go skiing with friends. I was devastated! I'd arranged the whole thing for him and he couldn't even come. He's usually outgoing, but on the phone he was kind of blah and didn't say much.

Today at church, he looked extra cute. But I can't tell what he thinks. Why don't guys just have ways of letting you know if they like you or not? Should I keep giving him clues that I like him? I also kinda like a guy in my neighbourhood named Rick . . .

Guys *do* have ways of letting girls know they like them, and he probably has already picked up on her clues but just isn't as smitten as she is. If a guy you like called you for the first time, you wouldn't be blah on the phone, right? His being lukewarm was a clue, a discouraging one, to be sure, but one she should register. And there's always Rick!

What do you make of her party idea? I applaud her for making the first move, but I wish she had called Jerry first and said, 'I'm thinking of having a sledding party for the catechism class either this Saturday or next. Which is better for you?' If he pleaded busy both days, she could have either thrown the party without him or thrown out the whole idea.

> *I've had a crush on a gorgeous sophomore for about a year now, and all we've been doing is looking at each other in the hallways and occasionally smiling. He's really popular, so I haven't tried talking to him because he would be embarrassed talking to a freshman girl who isn't that popular. I'm afraid that if I do something he could take it as a joke and tell it around school and then my social life will be blown away. Since I won't make the first move and he is probably too proud to, I am stuck. What should I do?*

She should make the first move, even if it's just saying, 'Hi' and 'How are you?' in the halls. Her social life is not so fragile that he could single-handedly blow it away – even if he were creepy enough to want to. If it turns

92

out that he *is* creepy or too proud to talk to a freshman, then she's wasting her time worrying about him. Unless she's content with another year of unrequited love at a distance, she should talk with him so she can figure out how he feels. He may be too flustered to be friendly the first time she says hello, so she may want to say hi a few times before drawing any conclusions.

Guys are as afraid of being rejected as girls. But if no one takes the first tentative step, a romance is doomed before it is born. Keep in mind that if the guy of your choice does not respond to your amicable overtures, it will be his loss and you'll be no worse off. If you always say hi and he never does, if you ask him about his weekend and he just grunts, if you offer to share your history book but he opts to share with Peter, at least you'll know where you stand. That knowledge may not thrill you, but it can save months (or years!) of second-guessing. And if he does seem interested in your being interested? Celebrate! You could have a new friend or boyfriend.

> *I'll be going into grade 10 in a few days. School is terrific for me. I'm captain of our basketball team and an almost straight-A student. But my problem is – what else? – guys.*
>
> *Everyone tells me I'm pretty and have*

a great personality. I'm talkative with everyone, including guys. But I've never been in a close romantic relationship with a guy. Oh sure, I've had numerous crushes, but not one guy has kissed me and I'm 15! Most of my friends have boyfriends. I don't know how they do it.

I know you're busy and get more important letters than this, but I'd really appreciate it if you could help. Now that another school year is here, I'd like to start it with someone special.

She signed her letter Never Had a Guy in Canada and I wrote to compliment her for being smart, athletic, pretty, friendly, articulate . . . and sensible enough to count her blessings. I also urged her to make the first move with her next crush – to somehow let him know that she thinks he's special. 'A guy who likes you might be daunted by your achievements and popularity,' I pointed out, 'and might think he doesn't stand a chance with you.'

Several months later, Never Had a Guy wrote me back.

I was thrilled when I received your response to my letter last September. I'd like you to know that for the past months, my life has been wonderful. Our basketball team won the Ontario championship! And there is a guy whom I've let know I think is special.

Lately he's been at my games and we talk, and I'm not the one who always has to start the conversation. He also asked me to the Christmas dance. We went and had a terrific time. So I'd like to thank you for your words of encouragement. I don't know if all of this happened because of your letter, but I know you were a major factor. Thanks again!

I'm taking no credit for the basketball victories and only the smallest smidgen for her new improved love life. On second thought, I can't even take that. She's the one who found the nerve to make the first move and let her crush know she liked him. And that's what made all the difference.

Did she wink at him? Did she say, 'Want to shoot some hoops?' Did she call about maths homework? Did she say, 'I'm starving. Have you had lunch?' I don't know – but it worked.

Inspiring, isn't it?

TELEPHONE ROMANCE AND RULES OF THE RING

Once upon a time, guys were supposed to call girls and girls were supposed to sit by the phone. Along came feminism and answering machines. Now anybody can call anybody and nobody has to sit by the phone.

Do you and the guy you like get along better on the phone than face to face? Or do you love each other to death in person – but bore each other to tears on the phone?

Here are seven tips to keep in mind before you dial your favourite number.

1. Think about why you are calling.

Are you calling because you want a study break or because you have something to tell or ask your crush? If you two often call each other when you're bored and then talk for half an hour to show you care, beware – your phone conversations could become snooze-worthy. Many guys don't like to while away hours on the phone, so don't call just because you want company while you polish your nails or put away the dishes.

2. Think about when you're calling.
Your families will appreciate it if you don't call each other at dinnertime or after bedtime.

3. Don't play guessing games.
'Hello, Mrs. Kelman, this is Carol Weston. May I speak to Matthew?' is more polite than 'Is Matthew there?' Identify yourself no matter who picks up the phone. I for one hate it when someone begins talking a mile a minute before I've even managed to place his or her voice.

4. Think about how you sound.
Spit out the gum, put down your soup spoon, and don't whine. Enough said?

5. Don't develop answering machine phobia.
If it's the first time you're calling him, it's natural not to want to leave a message. But if you call his house often, don't hang up at the tone. Say, 'Hi, this is Jennifer. Neil, could you call me before 10 if possible? Thanks.' If you're giving your phone number to someone who doesn't have it, say it twice so that he or she won't have to rewind the tape six times to

get it right.

6. Know how to give and takes hints.

If Christopher says, 'So, Jessica, thanks for calling,' that's your cue to say, 'It was fun talking to you. Take care.' And if *you're* ready to wind things up? Don't trample on his feelings by saying, 'I gotta go.' Try, 'Well, Chris, I'm glad you called and I'll see you fourth period tomorrow.'

7. Be able to pass the lie-detector test.

If you say, 'I called all weekend but got no answer,' and Blake's family has an answering machine, he'll know you are lying. In the age of technology, it's best to be honest – or keep quiet.

I got several letters about long-lasting phone romances between pairs of teenagers who'd met only once or twice. While such relationships may lend girls a sense of security, I think it's healthier – and more fun – to strike something up with someone close by.

Here are two more typical letters – with answers – about love on the line.

Dear Carol,

I have known a boy named Graham for over three years. He's 14, I'm 13. Our relationship has gone up and down a lot. At first he liked me and I liked him. Then I liked him and he didn't like me. Then we hated each other. Then we liked each other. Now we're friends – really good friends according to him, God knows what according to me.

The problem is that one night he's talkative and deep on the phone and the next night he's rude and immature. Also he says he'll call me, yet I always end up calling him. It's gotten to be a habit I can't break. Tonight I called him and he said, 'Hi, dear, hurry up, I gotta go.' That made me upset since we were talking great last night. It's like he's rude to me every other phone call. I know I should bug off, but I like him too much.

Rebecca

Dear Rebecca,

He probably likes you, but he is entitled not to want to chat every night. Instead of 'bugging' him, give him a chance to call you. You say you can't break the habit, but you can: you are in control of your behaviour. Next time you get an urge to call, take a walk or call a friend – or dial weather or time! If you skip a day or two between calls, I bet he'll be less rude and more eager to talk with you. If you keep calling, however, he may keep resisting and may feel that you are demanding too much of his time. So stop being predictable. Put down the phone. Things may pick up.

Dear Carol,

I liked this boy, Lee, but he didn't know me. I got his phone number and on a Friday two weeks ago, I got up the nerve to call him from a friend's house. We talked for over 30 minutes and then he called me five times during the weekend! On Monday he was going to see me for the very first time. I went with a friend to meet him and she pushed me right into him. Neither he nor I knew what to say so I said 'hi' and left. The next day at lunch, Lee said, 'not to worry about it, we were just embarrassed.' (He said 'we'!) Since then he has not called and we just say 'hi' in the hall. Does he not like me because of what I look like? I am not ugly though. (I've enclosed a photo.)

                                    Heather

Dear Heather,

Thanks for the photo – you're downright cute. Alas, a telephone flirtation doesn't guarantee an instant relationship. What you need now is some person-to-person conversation. If things don't click with Lee, hang up on that romance and give other guys a chance.

QUIZ: HOW WELL DO YOU KNOW YOUR CRUSH ANYWAY?

You know he has a great smile, sparkling eyes, and that he's always on your mind. But what else do you know about the would-be Love of Your Life? Answer these questions, guessing only when you're fairly sure of your response.

1. If he won $20,000 (over £10,000), he'd
   (a) Save it, probably for his education.
   (b) Pack his bags and travel.
   (c) Buy a fancy stereo and designer clothes and start leafing through car magazines.
   (d) You have no idea.

2. Is he a novice or a Casanova? How many girls has he kissed in his life?
(a) 0 to 2.
(b) 3 to 7.
(c) 8 or more.
(d) You have no idea.

3. Has he ever shoplifted?
(a) Of course. Hasn't everybody?
(b) Maybe once or twice, with other guys.
(c) He would never shoplift.
(d) You have no idea.

4. How are his grades?
(a) He's a mostly A student.
(b) he has a B average.
(c) He makes C's – and worse.
(d) You have no idea.

5. Of the following, where would he most like to go this weekend?
(a) A sports event.
(b) A rock concert.
(c) A play or museum.
(d) You have no idea.

6. What religion is he?
(a) Jewish
(b) Catholic.

(c) Protestant.
(d) Other.
(e) You have no idea.

7. How does he feel about abortion?
(a) He's mostly pro-choice.
(b) He's mostly anti-abortion.
(c) He hasn't thought about it.
(d) You have no idea.

8. Will he be a college graduate some day?
(a) Yes.
(b) Probably. He'll definitely enroll in one anyway.
(c) Doubtful, but you never know.
(d) You have no idea.

9. Does he smoke cigarettes?
(a) Constantly.
(b) Every once in a while.
(c) Never – no ifs, ands or butts.
(d) You have no idea.

10. Does he do any drugs?
(a) Often. You name it, he's done it.
(b) He smokes marijuana occasionally and may have tried some other drugs at some point.
(c) Never.

(d) You have no idea.

11. If someone invited him out to dinner tonight, which of the following meals would he prefer?
   (a) Duck, swordfish or rack of lamb in an elegant restaurant.
   (b) Spaghetti or veal parmigiana in a homely Italian trattoria.
   (c) Hamburgers, pizza or fried chicken in a fast-food chain.
   (d) You have no idea.

12. About how many hours does he work out a week, including any practice for a sport?
   (a) Up to 3.
   (b) 3 to 7.
   (c) Over 7.
   (d) You have no idea.

13. How many not-for-school books has he read in the last year?
   (a) Fewer than 5.
   (b) 5 to 10.
   (c) Over 10.
   (d) You have no idea.

14. Is he prejudiced against white, blacks, Asians, gays or any other group of people?

(a) Yes, very.
(b) No, although he's not quite as open-minded as he'd like to imagine.
(c) No, not at all.
(d) You have no idea.

15. Does he keep up with the news?
(a) Yes, he reads newspapers and news magazines and he discusses local and international events with friends.
(b) He sometimes skims headlines or catches the news on TV.
(c) No, he's pretty oblivious to what's going on in the world.
(d) You have no idea.

Scoring

The purpose of this quiz isn't just to determine whether your crush is a sporty type, brain or druggie. The point is to find out how much you've already found out about him. Count the number of times you checked: (d) You have no idea.

0-3 You know your crush well – at least you think you do. Why not take the quiz again, this time answering for yourself? Do you and he have similar values, interests, habits? If not, ask yourself why you're so drawn to him. If your responses are similar, here's hoping your perseverance pays off and your one-way crush becomes a two-way relationship.

4-7 You may know your crush fairly well without knowing whether he prefers duck to chicken or has kissed two girls or ten. Part of the fun of going out with someone is getting to know him better. If you think your values mesh <u>and</u> you can't shake your crush, then go for it – make that frightening (and often rewarding) first move.

8-11 Granted, you might not score 100 even if the quiz were about your brother or boyfriend. But if you really have no idea if the guy of your dreams is a scholar athlete or a racist kleptomaniac, what makes you think you'd be a perfect pair? If you know little about him because you just met him, fine. But if you are just now realizing that he's a virtual stranger or that you two are not cut from the same cloth, then don't be in such a hurry to surrender your heart.

12-15 It's one thing not to know your crush inside out. It's another to hardly know him at all. It's one thing not to know his favourite colour or his mum's maiden name. It's another to have no idea about his stance on education, religion, drugs or abortion. You and he don't need to agree on everything, but you should be able to respect his beliefs and interests. Before you clock another year in love from afar, learn more about him so you can determine how compatible you would be as a couple.

ARE YOU IN LOVE – OR ARE YOU OBSESSED?

I went camping for two weeks at a nearby lake and I met a guy, sort of. I saw him near the phones. He was about my height, he had red and black Nike sneakers on, jeans and a T-shirt. His hair is jet-black and shoulder-length. After that, every time I saw him at camp, I got all hot, sweaty and nervous. I was in LOVE!

A couple of nights later, I saw him at an arcade. We talked for a minute and I found out he was 15 – a great age for me. (I'm 14.) I only saw him once more after that, but I can't stop thinking about him. It is getting so I can't concentrate on anything and I am not interested in anyone else.

What am I going to do? School starts soon and I won't be able to concentrate. Help me, Carol!

If she took the 'How Well Do You Know Your Crush?' quiz with him in mind, I'm afraid she'd fail miserably. She likes his age and his looks, but what else does she know about him? Getting zapped by an attraction is not uncommon (and can be fun), but letting the attraction take over all your waking moments is crazy. Next time her mind drifts to the raven-haired camper, she'll have to make herself 'change the channel'. It may take effort, but she can concentrate on the here and now. She's in control and she can break the spell he inadvertently cast. Who knows? If she had been brave enough to actually get to know him, she may have found that he wasn't the person she thought he was anyway.

If she has his address and wants to drop him a card (a card, not a care package of chocolates, flowers and poetry books), well, okay. But if she has no way of even contacting him, then it's especially pointless to spend another minute thinking about him. She is not in love. Love usually makes life feel bigger and better. She's infatuated. And being infatuated with a faraway almost-stranger can be an exercise in frustration.

*Two years, five months and 21 days ago
I was lining up for lunch recess, staring
down at my old tennis shoes, when I felt
this presence looming over me. I looked up
and found myself staring into these eyes,
eyes that were so deep I felt I was intruding
upon his soul. Eyes that penetrated my own
soul – I felt half-naked, I tell you – eyes
that drew me like a magnet. Anyway, I
stared at this face for about 25 seconds.
Then he turned and left and I was jerked
back into reality.*

*I don't believe in love at first sight
because I believe that love is something
two people work for as they develop,
change and grow. I do, however, believe
in chemistry at first sight.*

*I never saw him again. But I think
about him 25 hours a day. I daydream,
I cry, I get this dull throbbing inside me.
I saw him at the end of sixth grade and
now I'm in ninth grade. We go to different schools, and I stare at his photo
in friends' yearbooks and treasure every
piece of gossip I hear about him.*

*I haven't touched another guy since –
literally. Once a boy said, 'Gimme five,'*

and I put my hand out and then something inside jerked it away so I wouldn't touch him. I never flirt. I've become a snob.

Probably one of the reasons I've stayed in 'love' so long is that I've never met him, so I'm free to fantasize all sorts of wonderful things about him. These probably make him seem better than he really is. Part of me says to try to forget him. I probably could shove him to the back of my mind temporarily, but I know I'll never truly forget him and I don't want to. What would be my hope, what would be my reason for life?

I have his address and phone number and I know all sorts of things about him by way of informed sources. But I can't just call him up and say, 'Hi, I saw you once three years ago, will you love me?' This is truly a case of a crush that has been fanned into a forest fire. Is there anything I can do? Do I even have a problem?

Yes, she does have a problem. She has brought her life to a stand-still and become a snob all because of a long-ago lunchtime look. What can she do? Assuming she's not going to call the mystery man, she can listen to the part of her that says to forget him. Rather than spend another two years, five months and 21 days in a glazed state, rather than continue to stunt her growth, she can get busier, study harder, give guys five, and focus on the flesh-and-blood people in her school.

Like it or not, she must free herself of this fixation. She must take her love life off hold. He should not be her raison d'être. He may have been the first boy to awaken in her romantic and sexual stirrings, and that's fine, but she'll feel chemistry with other guys if she gives herself a chance. And when she does fall in love, she'll find that it bears little resemblance to the quicksand she's been sinking in.

Here's one last letter from a girl who has let a crush get out of hand – and who may also have read one too many romance novels.

> *About seven months ago, I started going to a skating rink. I thought I was going just to have fun, not to start a pain in my heart that I can't live with. One Saturday, I was putting on my skates and all of a sudden, a strange feeling washed over me. I looked up and my eyes met the eyes of the cutest guy I had ever seen. We stared at each other for a minute, but in the end, he broke off the stare. That feeling changed me. I knew from that moment on that I*

111

could never be the same.

I avoided the rink for two months, but when I went back, he was there. I guess he felt me staring at his lean, athletic body moving gracefully, ever so gracefully, over the floor, because he looked up. To my surprise, he smiled at me.

A friend told me that his name is Chad and he goes skating every Friday. I immediately started going every Friday too. Friday seemed like heaven. I am 13, but I look and act 15 or 16. He is 16, but he looks about 18.

I looked up his address and started to write him. I signed all the letters, 'Please write back. Love always, Your Secret Admirer.' Once I included my initials.

My friend asked him why he didn't write me back. He said he didn't write to people he didn't know. Chad and I still didn't even say hi and I stopped writing to him.

Last week I motioned him over and asked him to sit down. He had a look on his face that said, 'This sounds serious.' He was gazing intently at me and a smile played on his lips. Oh that smile! It takes my breath away. My eyes were brimming with tears as I apologized for bothering him with the letters. He said, 'Don't worry about it. Now I'm embarrassed. Forget about it, okay?' then shot off like lightning.

Carol, I'm afraid. I cry every night for Chad. I'm in love with him. Do you think I should ask him to couples skate when there's a lady's choice? Do you think there's a chance for us?

Maybe a very slim chance. Sure, she can ask him to couples skate. But if he says no, or acquiesces without enthusiasm, she should take the hint. He knows she likes him (which is fine), but she should accept the fact that he hasn't jumped at the chance to become her Friday skating partner. Three years can be a big age difference, no matter how old she thinks they each look.

Enough of the nightly tears. She needs to distract herself with girl friends, afterschool activities and more promising male prospects. Why be a loser with Chad when she can be a winner with someone else? Sometimes giving up is the first step to cheering up.

SHOULD YOU GIVE UP
ON HIM?

Way back in second grade, when your mum told you that only quitters give up, she was referring to school problems and work problems, not boy problems.

If you've been depressed for months over a guy who still stumbles over your name, you're better off moving on than hanging on.

'But but but,' you ask, 'doesn't persistence pay off?'

Sometimes yes, sometimes no. This section can help you figure out when to abandon ship and when to hold tight and hope the tides turn.

> *I'm 14 and I'm having big problems with Bryan, who is 15. About six weeks ago, I went on an all-night party with a fellowship group from my church. We met, we talked, we flirted, and soon we were holding hands, cuddling, kissing and then French-kissing. I think it's tacky to do this in public, and I told him to stop. I said I did not want people to get the wrong idea about me. He said they wouldn't because they were all doing the same thing. Later he said that he didn't have time for a*

relationship, but he wanted to be really good friends. After that he didn't seem as anxious to hang around with me.

I decided to call him and tell him I wanted to be more than friends. The next day I called three times. First he was on the other line. Then he wasn't home. Then he was eating dinner and said, 'Just call back in three minutes.' Of course I didn't!

Since then he's spoken to me once. He's also driven his bike past my house a few times (if that counts for anything).

Carol, I really like him, and I think he may be interested too. I've tried to give him up, but I can't. Please don't tell me that's what I should do.

That's what she should do. How come she likes him so much anyway? He's more into kissing than kindness. He's willing to fool around with her but not to hang around with her. And sorry, but if he were interested, he would have called her back instead of asking her to call a fourth time. I think she should chase him away from her thoughts and recognize that he's not Mr. Marvellous anyway.

I am 15. Whenever I see this boy, Hal, in the hallway, I could just melt.

A friend of mine, Dirk, asked me if I wanted him to ask Hal if he likes me. I hesitated, then decided, 'Why not?' The next day, Dirk asked Hal three times and each time Hal said, 'I don't know yet.' Then one day, Dirk asked him again and Hal said, 'To tell you the truth, there's another girl.' Boy, did that make me feel stupid.

Weeks went by and Dirk asked Hal how he was making out with his girl. Hal said, 'I'm not.' Dirk and I thought that finally meant there might be hope. But Hal doesn't really talk to me. He's probably shy.

Sometimes I think, 'It's no use. He doesn't like me.' But I know I can't just give up.

Why not? If she gives up, her social life may pick up. And since Hal knows she likes him but has done nothing to indicate that feelings are mutual, she'd be smart to stop spinning her wheels. There's a difference between being patient and being too patient.

It's time to get over Hal, zero in on someone new and pull Dirk off the case – better to do her own flirting in the future.

I'm 13 and very very shy when it comes to boys I like. There's this one boy I really really like. I've liked him for four years. But he barely knows I exist.

I'm so shy that I only get up the courage to call him once in a great while and when I do, I run out of things to say. He never really joins in or asks me anything. He says we are friends, but if we are, why doesn't he talk to me?

On the last day of school, I gave him a letter. It told him how much I like him. I also wrote my phone number and told him to call me if he had the chance. Well, the summer is almost over and not one call. (It's not like I sit by the phone waiting.)

My mum and all my friends are sick of hearing about him. They tell me I should give up on him, but I just can't. He seems like my whole life.

Let's hear it for friends and mums with good advice. I join the chorus of those who say she should give up. If he 'barely knows' she exists yet he seems like her 'whole life,' she has let her life get much too small.

And what's this about her being shy? She's called him. She's written. She's told him she likes him. Shy? She's shy as a fox. What she's doing is shying away from recognizing that he's not smitten back.

Why did he say that they are friends? Because that goes over better than saying, 'Buzz off' or 'I don't want to be more than friends.' Just because he's being polite doesn't mean she should refuse to read the writing on the wall.

Are You in the Throes of an Unrequited Crush?

• Giving up can be a sign of strength, not weakness.

If a five-star general realizes he can't win a battle, he should surrender, not send in more troops. If an investor's stock keeps heading south, she should sell and cut her losses, not wait for it to hit bottom. If you've spent forever liking the same guy and he can't even recognize a good thing when he sees it, then enough! Bow out with dignity.

• Give up on your crush; don't give up on love.

Just because you stop mooning over what's-his-face doesn't mean you can't start noticing someone else – someone who might notice you back. Love may be around the corner, but if you're stuck in your tracks, you'll never find it.

- Expand your horizons.

Do something with the time and energy you used to devote to daydreaming. Join field hockey or join the Y. Start reading the paper. Make yourself so interesting that you'll never be one-track-minded again.

- Recognize that your crush wasn't perfect after all.

Don't dedicate yourself to trashing his personality, but do realize that he gets pimples with the best of 'em. Is he really a gentleman, intellectual, athlete and comedian rolled in to one? Or now that the fog has cleared, do you see that he's just another, yawn, nice guy? The mere fact that he didn't snap you up shows that his vision isn't 20/20, right?

One of my 'pen pals' reluctantly gave up on her crush, then wrote me months afterwards:

> *Thanks for the letter. If he doesn't like me, he doesn't know what he's missing. By the way, he wasn't worth all the fuss I made. I found out he's pretty conceited. I'm now going out with this other guy who is so nice . . .*

'With time and patience, the mulberry leaf becomes a silk gown,' says a Chinese proverb. And far be it for me to say that every girl with a one-way crush should abandon hope. In some cases, time and patience really can work wonders. If the future seems promising, don't give up too soon.

Here are two letters from a girl who decided to be persistent.

> *In* Girltalk *you suggested going for the less widely acclaimed guys. Well, I did just that. Fell head over heels for a junior. (I'm a freshman.) He doesn't date and we have a lot in common. He writes poetry, he's really interested in theatre and the list goes on.*
>
> *My best friend told me 'Go for it!' so I wrote him a note and he wrote back and said to just talk to him. The next day, we tried to talk but I got really nervous. I guess I was too much in awe of him. Anyway, I blew it.*
>
> *We finally got back to saying hi every morning and I took your advice and did the sound effects for the junior/senior play. We started talking more and more.*
>
> *His younger brother says I have a great chance with him and my best friend*

thinks he probably likes me but is too shy and inexperienced to do anything. I sent him a rose for Valentine's Day and since we called each other Mr. X and Miss X in our notes, I signed it 'Love, Miss X.' (Do you think writing 'love' was too forward?) He said thank you.

What I want to know is this: should I give it up? I've liked him for four months.

Give it up? Absolutely not – not yet, anyway. I warned her against harbouring sky-high hopes but encouraged her to continue 'going for it' and keeping up her end of the conversation with Mr. X. Was she out of line to write 'love' on her note? No. Signing 'love' at the end of a letter or note is nowhere ne r as heavy-duty as saying 'I love you.'

Here's what happened:

Hi. It's me again, writing to share some great news. Remember the guy I was so crazy about? Well, Monday he stopped me after school and asked me how I'd feel about going to the PROM! I seriously about died on the spot. But I told him I'd love to. Can you imagine? An invitation to the prom was the last thing I expected.

121

Sometimes knowing a girl likes him is all the welcome mat a guy needs. And I for one am a sucker for happy endings.

HAVE YOU FALLEN FOR A FANTASY CRUSH?

I don't know about his effect on you, but Mel Gibson just about undoes me. If I hear that he'll be on the *Today* show, I'll videotape the whole thing just so that I can later search for and savour his six minutes in the spotlight. If I hear his latest movie is mediocre, but the publicity poster shows him shirtless, I'll stand in line to buy a ticket. If I'm grocery shopping and spy his face on a magazine cover, I'll push my cart to the back of the longest line and then leaf through the pages, pausing on every picture.

Never mind that Mel lives in faraway Australia, is years older than me, is married and has kids. I'm married too. And I still think he's sexy.

Celebrity crushes are common. Your mum may have giggled with her classmates about which Beatle was cutest: Paul, John, George or Ringo. Even your grandmum probably had her favourite actor, singer, athlete or idol.

How about you? Are you in love with the Lowes? Could you find harmony with Mark Harmon? Have you been stung by Sting? Individual stars come and go, but fantasy crushes are here to stay.

Not only is hero worship common, it can be healthy. Sighing over someone unattainable can be the first step to learning about love. You can safely swoon from afar, knowing that the object of your affection isn't going to hurt or reject you. You may never meet him, but at least he won't turn you down for a date.

Stargazing can be a bridge to two-way love. A young girl who first idolizes her brother or father may later develop a runaway crush on a TV doctor or policeman. Next she may flip over a camp counsellor, teacher or the most popular (and out-of-reach) senior in her school. And finally she may be ready to flirt with a same-age classmate. Such a flirtation is trickier: it comes with the risk of his betraying her feelings, but also with the possibility of his returning them full force.

Of course, not everybody sticks to this sort of romantic timetable. And for some girls, fantasy crushes aren't just good clean escapist fun but become too all-consuming. If you are so in love with a rock star that you consider boys your own age too immature to take seriously, you're not doing yourself any favours. If you can't transfer your unrequited crush on a hockey player to anybody under 200 pounds, he's limiting your life instead of enriching it. If you're more involved with 'reel' life than real life, it's time to ask yourself if you're ready to test your luck with guys within range.

> *I'm 12 years old. I have a huge problem. I have a crush on Michael J. Fox but he has no idea I exist. I'm dying to meet him. I'd do practically anything to meet him. Please write me back. I'm miserable!*

Lots of girls think Michael J. Fox is a fox – and I don't know any surefire ways to meet him. But I know this: silver screen crushes are supposed to add zest to your life, not be 'huge problems' that make you 'miserable.' If your celebrity crush is dragging you down instead of lifting you up, you might be taking it too seriously.

Besides, the private Michael may be very different from the public one. I read in a *People* magazine story about the 5'4" clean-cut cutie (I confess: I like him too) and was surprised to learn that he was a chain-smoker and fast driver. Michael J. Fox isn't Alex in *Family Ties* or any of the characters he's played in *Back to the Future*, *The Secret of My Success*, or *Bright Lights, Big*

City. He's someone else whom we don't know nearly as well.

> *I'm happily attached to my boyfriend, but at 16, I'm hopelessly infatuated with the German tennis star Boris Becker. Instead of talking with my boyfriend (who is often busy working), I'm found rummaging through German and tennis magazines to find out more about Boris and his status as an eligible bachelor. At night instead of fantasizing about my boyfriend, I think about how it would be if Boris and I knew each other well. What makes this worse is that I speak German and am going to Germany over spring break. I love my boyfriend and I know the odds of getting to know Boris are slim, but I can't help hoping for a miracle.*

It probably would take a miracle to meet Boris and have him willingly take time away from his tennis game to get to know her. Nothing wrong with dreaming about him, though – unless fantasy gets in the way of reality. The fact that she has a boyfriend but is obsessing about Boris makes me wonder if she isn't restless in her current relationship. She shouldn't dump her boyfriend for a stranger-idol, but she should ask herself if her relationship has run its course – or if she wants to try and liven it up. The ball's in her court.

> *I have a problem: my social studies teacher. I like him more than a teacher. I think he likes me more than a student. Today we were taking a quiz and I asked a question. He came over to answer me and he put his arms around me and put his face to mine. I thought he was going to kiss me. I really wanted to. After school that day he was walking down the hall and I was playing with two other girls. He picked me up and looked down my shirt. I had a tube top on and you could see my breasts. I really want him. I'm only 13 and he is 27 and not married. I really want him.*

Like celebrity crushes, teacher crushes are common; I've survived several. They are usually harmless and pass quickly. But this is not always the case. Unfortunately, instead of maintaining their professional distance, a few teachers try to take advantage of student crushes and of their own power position.

What about this social studies teacher? It could be that the student is misinterpreting his gestures. But if he ever really kisses her, he'd be

WAY OUT OF LINE and she'd be in over her head. It's understandable that she's attracted to her teacher: not only is he an older man and an authority figure, but he's interested in her ideas. But this 27-year-old should be fooling around with women nearer his age, not vulnerable students.

If a teacher (or counsellor or music instructor) ever harasses you or asks for a kiss, he is breaking an accepted code of ethics – and possibly the law. Report him to your parent, another teacher or the principal. Your teacher crush probably likes you back, but if he ever acts on it, he is being exploitative. Teachers and students are not on equal footing and romances between them are rarely healthy.

On a brighter note, I know one woman who fell for her French teacher when she was a senior in high school. When she was in college, she married him! She was young to be making such an important decision, but they've been husband and wife now for 10 happy years.

> I am 16½ and fairly attractive. I meet lots of guys, but when they ask me out, I usually turn them down – even if I really like them. I would rather spend time with my cats or girl friends. Am I scared or just a jerk? I can't be scared of all men because

I work in a men's store and I find myself falling for older men. Am I in my own little fantasy world? Do I need help?

She's not a jerk. She *is* a little scared. And since she signed off 'Sad and Alone in the Suburbs,' I encouraged her to say yes next time a boy she likes asks her out. She can make it a movie date (no need to talk much or kiss) or a double date (less pressure to keep conversation going or become intimate). She's probably been falling for older men because they seem safer – she doesn't think they'll really call. But as you're about to see, while older men may have mystique, falling for one can be a mistake.

YOUNGER GUYS, OLDER GUYS

I am 15 and I want to meet older guys.

Is a guy's age the first thing that draws you to him? Age shouldn't be as important as maturity but age does affect what teenagers think of each other. When you start liking a guy, are you automatically impressed if he's older, depressed if he's younger?

My high school boyfriend and most of my college boyfriends were slightly older than I, but my husband Rob is two years my junior. Age differences alone shouldn't make or break a relationship, especially if the difference is just a year or two.

Younger Guys

Since teenage girls often mature faster than boys – a fact which we love to keep telling them – many girls prefer to go out with guys their age or older. Is the guy you like a few years younger than you? Some classmates may snicker and your romance might have to withstand a little ribbing.

Yet dating down has big advantages. Girls who are tongue-tied among peers may open up among younger boys. And younger boys are less apt to pressure girls into drinking, doing drugs, having sex or rushing into marriage.

Many mature younger guys are drawn to older girls. If you truly care about a younger guy and your relationship works, more power to you. But if your boyfriend's idea of a good time is blowing up mailboxes whereas yours is discussing Schubert and Shakespeare, you may find his company less than stimulating. A boyfriend should challenge you socially and intellectually so that you're learning, blossoming and becoming more confident – not retreating back into childhood.

Older Guys

It is flattering and exciting to be singled out by someone older and to be included in parties with older couples. If you like an older guy, and he respects you, treats you as an equal, and isn't trying to make you grow up too fast, terrific. If he treats you like a child and acts embarrassed to be seen with you, that's not so terrific and you should ask yourself if the budding romance is making you feel better – or worse – about yourself. If what most appeals to you about him is the number of years he has lived, that's also not fair to either of you.

A 16-year-old who said that she and her mother bought *Girltalk* one day as 'a joke' but that (surprise!) she liked it wrote, 'I think teenage guys are so shallow and boring. To me, older guys are much more sensitive, deep, creative and interesting.' To each her own, but sweeping generalizations don't always hold water. Some grown-ups are fools and some young boys are finds. Besides, what good is dating up if it makes you look down on your contemporaries?

> *I am 12. I have a problem (obviously). I like a lot of my older brother's friends (they're about 16), but they probably don't like me. On the other hand, one of them once made what you could call a 'pass' at me. But maybe it wasn't a pass. How do I get my brother's friends to know me as more than Will's little sister?*

It won't be easy. The 16-year-olds may hardly think of her as her own person, let alone as girl friend material. I know. My brother Mark is over three years older than I, and his friends didn't really take me seriously until I was in college. There's no harm in flirting with a brother's friends, but if your heart is set on more than a flirtation, be very patient – or snuff the crush. If one of the 16-year-olds did take this girl to the drive-in, she might find that they are each looking for different things in the relationship. When you think about it, it would be pretty sleazy if one of the older boys came on to the 12-year-old.

> *I met a guy named Wayne at a country fair. He's 17 and I'm 13. We talked a lot. He's nice, gorgeous and fun to be around.*

He's on vacation now but when he returns,
should I try to get him or leave him alone?

Leave him alone. Why? Because like 12 to 16, 13 to 17 is a big age jump. If she were 23 and he were 27, the four years might not matter, but 13-year-olds and 17-year-olds are usually worlds apart in terms of experience and maturity. Her chances of striking up a good relationship are much better with younger teens. A crush is one thing, but if she really wants to 'get' Wayne, she may be setting herself up for a fall or walking into a situation that could quickly become too hot to handle. (What if he drove her to a lover's lane and tried to take advantage of her innocence, fear and naiveté?)

> *Six months ago, in June, I met a guy who was 20. I'm 15. Sometimes he acted so nice and other times he would say he was too old for me and would act really turned off. He said we should have sex, and we did. (It was my first time.) I thought maybe he was trying to use me but I just couldn't say no. He really confused me. He would come over every couple of days and then not call for weeks. I'm still – I don't know if I should say it – in love with him.*

The trouble with age-gap romances is that they often mean more to the younger, more vulnerable person. While this girl is still losing sleep over their brief affair, the man may be sleeping with someone else. It sounds as though he too felt ambivalent in June. His high-minded side was coaching, 'Leave her alone. She's underage and impressionable. Don't get involved.' But his baser side was screaming, 'Go for it. She's willing, isn't she? What are you waiting for, wimp?' Alas, his baser side won out.

One *Girltalk* reader wrote to say 'The only disappointment in your whole book is that you didn't have anything on getting hooked on a married man.' My advice in a nutshell: unmarried men are complicated enough; stay away from married ones.

I am 16. Last week my dad took me and my three sisters to a surprise birthday party for one of his friends whom he hasn't seen since high school. The friend, whom I'll call Alex, is 40. His wife, who is pregnant, invited us. When Alex arrived, he was driving a really cool expensive sports car. His wife said he likes to take people for a ride in it and if we wanted to, he would take us too.

So after the party, Alex took us for a

ride. I sat in the front and my sisters sat in the back. He turned up the music and after a while, he asked if I liked backrubs. I said, 'I guess so,' so he began massaging my back and down my side. He started running his fingers down my arm to my hand which was on my leg. When he put his hand on my leg, I removed it. But then he began tapping his fingers on my knee to the music, and then rubbing my knee.

The whole thing made me nervous. I felt like it couldn't be happening to me. My sisters didn't notice because they were having a fun time listening to the music and looking out the open back of the car. Finally we arrived back at Alex's house over an hour later.

Now I don't know how to feel. At first, I was shocked. Now I can't seem to stop thinking of Alex. My dad said we might go over there again this weekend, and to my surprise, I can't wait. What is wrong with me? He is married and is much too old for me. I know I can't be in love with him, but I can't stop thinking about that night.

Boy, this makes me mad. I hate to sound like a prissy old lady, but shame on Alex for acting like a dirty old man. If he is going to have a midlife crisis, I wish he'd do it on his own time, or with his buddies and pregnant wife, rather than hitting on a 16-year-old girl and leaving her in a muddle of conflicting emotions.

Unfortunately, there will always be Alexes out there on the lookout for easy prey. It's heady stuff to win the attentions of an older man in a flashy car. But if you find yourself in this sort of situation, keep your wits about you. Older guys are more likely to rush girls into sex than younger guys, though a simple strong direct 'No' stops almost all guys cold.

This girl isn't guilty of starting things, but I hope she manages to stop things. She shouldn't go anywhere alone with Alex and she should try to protect her sisters from him too. If her dad keeps wanting to schedule family outings at Alex's, she might consider telling him about the would-be-seduction. Sunday drives with Alex can lead only to a dead end.

> *For eight months I have been seeing a guy who is 23. I'm 18. I asked my mother if I could invite him over. She asked whether he was in school or had a job and where he lived. Like a jackass, I told the truth. She had a fit. He and I still see each other, but behind my mother's back.*

It's not that 18 to 23 is an impossible age difference, and I doubt anything exploitative is going on between these adults. But what women should look for in a man is not the same as what they may look for in a boy. A 12-year-old girl may just want a popular boy to like her. A 15-year-old may long to love a thoughtful guy who will try to understand her. At 18 and beyond, a woman may seek a man who is not just sweet and loving but who, ideally, shares her values, is as well-educated as she is and has a paying job he enjoys. If the woman is thinking about kids, she should also ask herself if he would be a good father: a good rôle model for their children as well as a good provider in case, for instance, she can't or chooses not to work while their kids are young.

Unless this 18-year-old considers her romance a short-term fling and is in it just for the kicks, she shouldn't scoff at her mother's questions. Her mother wants the best for her and has a right to be concerned. Flirtations are one thing, but coupledom comes with its own complications and challenges. And that's what the next chapter is all about.

3
You're a Couple!

You've been crushed by crushes. You've pined for your teacher. You've given up on the guy next door. And you're on the verge of abandoning hope altogether when, miracle of miracles, you and a wonderful boy fall in love (or at least in like).

Happy day! You laugh with your boyfriend but also feel safe enough to cry – and occasionally argue. You're part of a pair and love is not a letdown. This chapter takes you from your first awkward date to your first major fight. It includes information on everything from how to recharge your romance – to how to ruin it. There's a quiz on what to expect from a boyfriend and there are letters on long distance love and parent problems.

Remember Chapter 2's quiz 'How Well Do You Know Your Crush Anyway?' Do it again, this time with your boyfriend in mind. You probably know him well, and you can use any questions you don't know as a springboard for conversation.

Are you getting your romance off to a good start? Do you two want to be together not for status or security but because you revel in each other's company? Do you idolize your boyfriend, or do you recognize that he is imperfect, but respect and care about him just the same? Is your relationship going anywhere? Have you two done any, as the song about the couple sitting in a tree puts it, K-I-S-S-I-N-G?

Love. Let's get to the heart of the matter.

QUIZ: WHAT DO YOU EXPECT FROM A BOYFRIEND?

I'd like to know if it's okay to dream about a boyfriend who doesn't exist. I do sometimes but I'm worried that it is ruining my chances of really having a boyfriend because I want a perfect one even though I know there is no such thing.

There's nothing wrong with occasionally

dreaming about a made-in-heaven sweetheart so long as you remain relatively realistic about what to expect from a down-to-earth one. Are your expectations so high that a real boyfriend could never measure up? Or are they so low that you'd be willing to put up with rudeness and misery in the name of love?

Roses are red, violets are blue, take this quiz, and see how you do!

1. True love
   (a) Usually hits like a thunderbolt.
   (b) Grows stronger as two individuals get to know each other.
   (c) Is rare as the whooping crane. Most people fall for a pretty face or a fat wallet.

2. If your boyfriend came over with flowers, you'd
   (a) Go into shock – did you forget your own birthday?
   (b) Thank him and think up something thoughtful to do for him.
   (c) Hardly be surprised – you'd expect frequent bouquets for no reason.

3. Valentine's Day is
   (a) A good excuse for your boyfriend and you to do something fun together.

(b) An institution invented by card companies and florists eager to make an extra
buck.

(c) The most romantic day of the year –
you hope your guy sends you a singing
telegram or invites you to a candlelit dinner.

4. Will you and your boyfriend ever fight?

(a) No. Your parents may but you never will.

>(b) Sure, but you won't stay mad at each
other long – you'd rather make up than
break up.

(c) Constantly – that's what guys do best,
right?

5. You expect your boyfriend to

>(a) Be an all-round good guy.

(b) Remember your name most of the time.

(c) Be gorgeous, popular, smart, rich, talented
and devoted.

6. Will your boyfriend like all your friends?

(a) Yes, and he'll fit right in.

>(b) He'll like some of them, and you'll like
some of his.

(c) He'll either flip over your best friend
or not like any of them.

7. Your boyfriend will
>(a) Try to understand you most of the time.
 (b) Probably excel in insensitivity – boys usually do.
 (c) Read your every thought and empathize with your every mood.

8. When you first kiss, it will be
 (a) Bliss.
>(b) Exciting and maybe a bit awkward.
 (c) Awful – you'll worry you're doing it all wrong.

9. Once you're a couple, you'll
 (a) Smile at each other in school but rarely talk.
 (b) Spend all your time together or on the phone.
>(c) See each other a lot but still keep up with family, friends and schoolwork.

10. If you and your boyfriend were watching the Miss America pageant and he commented on Miss South Dakota's legs, you'd
 (a) Throw your popcorn at him but figure all guys are fickle.
>(b) Laugh and say, 'Mine aren't half bad either, bucko.'
 (c) Know you were dreaming – he'd never

look at another woman.

11. When you think about honeymooning, you imagine

(a) Newlyweds walking hand in hand and gazing into each other's eyes at sunset on a faraway tropical island.

(b) Ralph Kramden and Ed Norton scrapping with Alice and Trixie.

(c) A couple toasting with champagne in a fancy restaurant.

12. In Homer's *Odyssey*, Penelope wove and unravelled a cloth day in and day out as she waited for her husband Odysseus' return. You think

(a) He would have waited just as patiently for her if she'd been at sea.

(b) She was out of her mind to waste all those years.

(c) You can't judge ancient heroines by today's standards.

13. If you were in love, you would

(a) Be torn between getting out the megaphone (the news might make you more popular) and keeping it under wraps (he might drop you tomorrow).

(b) Tell all your close friends.

✗(c) Not need to tell anyone – you'd look so radiant, people could guess.

14. Will your boyfriend send you candy on your 10-week anniversary?
(a) He'd better.
✗(b) Highly doubtful. Who keeps track of that stuff?
(c) No, and he'd probably let a 10-year anniversary slip by too.

15. Being in love means you
(a) Can't eat, sleep, study, and nothing matters except him.
✗(b) Feel happier and more energetic than usual, but your life and routines don't change much.
(c) Feel jealous, possessive, upset and paranoid: today could be the day he'll come to his senses and bid you farewell.

Scoring

Give yourself points as follows:

1. a.3	b.2	c.1	5. a.2	b.1	c.3
2. a.1	b.2	c.3	6. a.3	b.2	c.1
3. a.2	b.1	c.3	7. a.2	b.1	c.3
4. a.3	b.2	c.1	8. a.3	b.2	c.1

9. a.1   b.3   c.2   13. a.1   b.2   c.3
10. a.1   b.2   c.3   14. a.3   b.2   c.1
11. a.3   b.1   c.2   15. a.3   b.2   c.1
12. a.3   b.1   c.2

36-45 You have high expectations about love. You envision a fairy-tale romance with a picture-perfect guy. You look forward to letting your world revolve around your boyfriend – and having him worship your words, cater to your whims and understand your every sigh.

Uh oh. Have you been watching too many soaps? Are you setting yourself up for disappointment? Even if your boyfriend is one in a million, you two will sometimes argue and he won't be above noticing a beauty queen's legs. Don't get so carried away by how magical you think love should be that you wait forever for Superman and miss the chance to go out with the nice Tom, Rick and Larry's in your school.

25-35 You are realistic about love. Though the first few weeks of courtship may make you dizzy, you wouldn't expect a two-year relationship to continue at such a feverish pitch. You know that you and your boyfriend won't be able to read each other's minds and that you'll sometimes have to work at understanding each other. But that's okay, you look forward to long discussions and to taking the time to let love grow and blossom. Cloud Nine in Seventh Heaven is not your style. You'd rather find real love right here on earth.

15-25 You have low expectations about love. It's good that you aren't lost in a happily-ever-after world of make-believe dreams – but don't become a cynic. It's good that you aren't expecting constant flowers, candy and dinners out – but don't let your standards dip too low either. Your boyfriend should be attentive, thoughtful and caring.

Okay, okay, so love won't solve all your problems or fulfil all your needs, but it is fun to adore and be adored. Even if some guy once broke your heart or even if your parents went through a bitter divorce, don't reconcile yourself to a life alone. Pick up the pieces, use what you've learned (e.g., that relationships require compromise and aren't as easy as a-b-c) and give love a chance to surprise and delight you and to make you feel both confident and special.

YOUR FIRST DATE

How many times have you imagined your first

date? Does it go something like this?

You've been dancing with your pillow, smothering your cat with kisses and singing to yourself since noon. But now it's 6:45 – time to get ready for the evening you've been waiting for. You've already tried on three blouses and you're still not satisfied with the way you look. Nervous? Of course you're nervous. Who wouldn't be?

By the time you decide on a blouse, brush out your hair, and apply makeup and cologne, it's almost 7:30.

So where is he?

Did he change his mind? Did he forget? Did he have an accident? Did his old girlfriend kidnap him? Just when you're fearing the worst, the doorbell rings.

You count to four (no point in seeming over-eager), then open the door and say, 'Hi. Come on in.' You hope he doesn't hear the quiver in your voice.

Your parents suddenly loom behind you. They introduce themselves and extend their hands.

Everybody sits down. Your date, perched on the edge of the sofa, says how nice your living room is and your parents ask what movie you're going to see. He tells them, looks at you, and adds, 'We should probably get going if we want to get tickets.'

Everybody stands up. Your father says, 'Have

146

a good time.' Your mother says, 'Ditto – but get home before 11.'

And you're off. Just the two of you.

He opens the passenger door for you. You get in and lean over to open his door for him. You both buckle up.

'Your parents seem nice,' he says as he starts the car.

'They're okay. We get along pretty well.'

There's a moment of silence, and then you both speak at once. Then you say 'Go ahead,' at once. Then 'No, you,' at once. And then you laugh. The ice is broken.

At the movie ticket counter, he takes out a $20 bill. You say, 'I can pay for myself,' but he says, 'No, I've got it. Thanks anyway.' While you get on the popcorn line, you look around to see if you know anybody. You can't help wishing that Lindsay, the boy-chaser in your maths class, could see you now.

The movie isn't bad. Your arms are about two inches apart and at one point he puts his arm over the back of your chair – but not exactly around you. During a scary scene, you grab his shoulder – but let go right away. Your fingers meet in the popcorn.

After the movie, he says, 'Let's get a soda.'

'Okay,' you say, and in the car, you sit a teeny bit nearer to him than you did on the way over.

At a diner, you each order the same kind of soda and you talk about the movie. Then you talk about some mutual friends at school. Then you talk about his violin recital and your track meet next week. Then you realize it's twenty to 11.

As you head towards the car, you say, 'Aren't the stars beautiful?'

He says, 'Yes. I wish we had time to go for a long walk.'

You think you might melt into his arms.

But you don't. You both get in the car, and this time you sit as near to him as you can, considering you have your seat belt on. You casually rest your hand in the middle of the seat in case he wants to hold it, but he keeps both of his hands on the steering wheel.

There's another silence, but somehow it feels sort of peaceful, and as he pulls into your driveway, you say, 'This was really fun. I had a great time.'

He leans over (is he going to kiss you right here? Are you going to faint straight away?) and says, 'Me too.'

He gets out, goes around, opens your door, takes your hand for a second to help you out and walks you to the front door.

'Thanks again,' you say.

'Thank you,' he says. 'I'll give you a call.'

You know guys always say that. You hope he means it.

THE DATING GAME

When your mum was your age, girls could go out with one guy on Friday and another guy on Saturday and no one looked askance. Unfortunately, by the time I was a teenager, dating was already less casual. Today many teenagers don't date at all unless they're officially going with someone. And many assume that if you and a guy show up at one measly party together, the case is closed: you're boyfriend and girl friend.

Whether dating in your hometown is considered a major big deal or a normal weekend activity, here's how you can make sure things go as smoothly as possible with you and, sigh, Jared.

What to Wear?

Dress comfortably. This is no time for wobbly shoes you can hardly stand in or too-tight pants you can hardly sit in. If you're not sure whether you're going bowling or dancing, ask – or wear a versatile outfit that can look both festive and casual. Wear your hair however you like, but make sure it's squeaky clean. Makeup and cologne? Easy does it. You don't want to look like you're dressed for an ordinary school day, nor do you want to knock him over with a whole new you. Jared may be nervously deciding what to wear too – and odds are good that he'll nick himself shaving.

Meeting Your Parents

You needn't feel embarrassed even if your mum comments on how pretty you look right in front of Jared and even if your dad sounds gruff as he announces your curfew. Jared's parents are probably caring and concerned too.

Give everyone something to talk about by briefing your parents on Jared and vice versa. Tell your parents that he is a junior on the tennis team, that he lives on Hardscrabble Road and that his mother writes the Around Town column in the local paper. Tell Jared that your dad teaches history at Greenbriar and that your mum is in real estate and collects autographed books. That way, they'll all have something to talk about with each other.

If Jared said he'd pick you up at 7:30, be ready at 7:30. Even if you're sure everybody will hit it off, you don't want to make them chitchat forever.

What's the Plan?

Most guys take full responsibility for the first dates. But if Jared says, 'What do you feel like doing tonight?' don't just shrug and say, 'Whatever.' Help him out. Suggest going to a movie or bowling alley or club or ice cream parlour. If it's daytime, suggest walking around a park or visiting a museum or playing cards or baking brownies. If you have a VCR, consider renting a tape that you both pick out and watching it at home – unless you're sure your little sister would be joining you.

If Jared has planned the ideal date, terrific. But if there's a hitch, be ready to offer ideas of your own.

Have Fun!

Don't worry about each five-second silence or how he's reacting to your every word. And don't be quick to judge him. If you're deeply disappointed because his shirt isn't hip or because he eats spaghetti noisily, you're not giving him a chance. On the other hand, if you can't get over your dream boyfriend's being a mere twelve inches away, you may become too dizzy to be good company. Relax and get to know each other, and don't be in a hurry to decide if you want this date to be your last – or the first of forever.

Do You Pay Your Way?

A first date is one thing, but if you and Jared have been going out for months, why should he pick up all the tabs? Unless he has pockets full of money, it may mean you two won't be able to go out as often as you'd like. And if you always get a free ride, how can you each be sure that you love each other and not just the trappings of romance? Besides, some guys think that if they spend big money on you during the date, they're entitled to squeeze it out of you afterwards!

You may be thinking, 'Yes, but I don't want to go Dutch everywhere.' Fine. Don't split every bill. But do make occasional contributions. Spring for the hot dogs at the stadium and splurge on the tickets now and then. Buy the popcorn at the movie or the ice cream cone in the park.

Be considerate: when he is buying dinner, don't order the most (or least) expensive item on the menu. And always say thank you when he covers your expenses.

When you plan to invite, be cool about it. Just say, 'This one's on me,' or 'My treat.' Don't insist if it makes him terribly uncomfortable and don't explain that since he shelled out last week, it's only fair that you fork out this week.

No matter how generous your boyfriend usually is, never leave home empty-handed. Always have a little 'mad money' on you so that if you want to (or have to) get home in a hurry, you could afford a cab or at least a phone call.

ALL ABOUT KISSING

In third grade, my friend Debbie and I heard about French-kissing so we stuck out our tongues and touched them for about a millisecond. 'Gross,' we concluded.

In sixth grade, I played Spin the Bottle at a Halloween party, and Michael, a goofy guy who liked me, puckered up and pressed his lips squarely on mine. 'Yecchh,' I thought.

In seventh grade, my neighbour Tom and I were watching a Beatles movie with his younger sister and my older brother. Tom yawned and stretched his right arm up above his head, then down around my shoulders, and next thing I knew, he was kissing me. Not only was I caught by surprise, but I was worried that my brother would see. When I looked over, however, Eric had his arm around Patty, and they were smooching too. After that, the four of us sometimes timed our kisses with a stopwatch to see who could kiss the longest. (I think Tom and I won, but Eric and Patty might have told you otherwise.)

In tenth grade, a few years and kisses later, I was at a New Year's Eve party. At midnight, everybody toasted with champagne and ceremoniously started kissing everybody else. A cute junior whom I'd scarcely met approached me and within a minute we were making out! It was exciting, but it was out of character for both of us to be so forward, and afterwards we felt awkward and barely managed to make small talk in school.

It took about three months before I conned Eric into arranging a double date in which the junior and I would go bowling with Eric and my best friend. At the bowling alley, I proceeded to roll three gutterballs in a row. A bad omen? No. The date was a success. We didn't kiss, but on the way back, our knees touched in the backseat of the car.

Patience was in order, because it took several one-on-one dates before he finally got up the nerve to really kiss me again. When he did, he said, 'May I kiss you?' and scarcely waited for me to whisper, 'Yes.' It was paradise, but I wished he'd picked a more private moment – we were in the middle of the dance floor of the Byram Hills High School's cafeteria on Golden Oldies Night.

> *I'm 14, and all I know about kissing could be put on the point of a straight pin. I have no older sisters or brothers and I'd feel like a total fool asking my friends. Please write back and explain in detail how to kiss.*

> *I'm 15 and have lots of friends, but I've only had two sorta boyfriends. The problem is that I get along fine until they go to kiss me. Then I crumble. What can I do to get through my first real kiss? (A peck doesn't count.) My best friend is in the same boat. As soon as one of us kisses, I'm sure it'll be a lot easier. We talk and describe everything.*

> *I've never had a 'real boyfriend'. I've*

flirted a little and I give a close male friend a kiss on the cheek after school each day. I'm starting to have a relationship with this one kid, and before it gets too serious, I want to make sure I can kiss him correctly. I kinda tell my friends I'm not as innocent as they think, so I can't say anything to them. I'm just so self-conscious that I'll mess up terribly!! I saw an ad for a book called Secrets of Kissing. *Will it help me? Can you help?*

Girls across the nation are panicking about puckering. Yet the real secret of kissing is that it's not all that complicated, and practice makes perfect. There's a first time for everybody, and if the chemistry is right and you and your guy really like and respect each other, you have nothing to worry about. Guys are shy too and yours may be less experienced than you think. Who knows? He may not be the World's Greatest Kisser in the beginning either.

Kisses come in all varieties – soft and delicate and intense and passionate. There are no right and wrong techniques because people's preferences are different. Ready? Then take off your glasses, nuzzle close to him, shut your eyes, and touch your lips to his. Instead of trying to pretend to be a pro to your boyfriend, you could consider admitting to him that it's your first time – he may find your innocence endearing. If you like, you can even ask your guy how he likes his kisses and give him a few to choose from. Chances are he won't go for the ones that are too dry and tight-lipped or too wet and slobbery.

Other dos and don'ts?

• Don't apply fresh lipstick or unwrap a new piece of gum seconds before you suspect he may make his move.
• Do be warm and sensual; Sleeping Beauty might still be asleep if the Prince's lips had been stiff as a statue's.
• Do feel free to kiss him if you think he's shy but would like to kiss you.
• Don't jam your tongue in his mouth; start kissing gently and let feelings build.
• Don't chomp on his earlobe, brand him with love bites, or make loud, smacking *mmmwwaaa* sounds; you're kissing him, not conquering him.
• Do relax. Lots of girls and guys are jittery about their first, second, even fiftieth kiss.

By the way, it doesn't help to fib to your friends about your innocence or lack thereof. It's easier to be honest and true friends will like you more if you are. And not-so-true friends? Be discreet. Don't tell all in the hall as Nervous in New Orleans did.

> *I went on a date with a guy and he kissed me and I kissed him back. Now we never talk or anything because we're too embarrassed and don't know what to say. And to top it off, I had to go and tell our school's big mouth and now she is probably going to tell the whole school. Help!*

A kiss that's shared too soon could be the first among many – or could be the finale of a fleeting romance. If I were Nervous, I'd try to start talking to my former date and I'd steer clear of class gossips.

> *One of my friends told me that if you don't get kissed in junior high, you get a bad reputation. Is that true?*

You won't get a bad rep if you don't kiss any guys in junior high. You could get a bad rep if you kiss too many!

The next letter was signed Mixed-Up Scaredy Cat.

> *I am pretty popular in school but not with the boys. Anyway, a boy just asked*

me out. He's 16½, I'm 15. So he's more grown-up and knows more about foolin' around. I am a real flirt and lead him on all the time but when he makes his move, I chicken out. I want to do more with him, but I am afraid if I do something wrong, he'll tell everyone or he won't think of me in the same way. I don't even really know how to kiss. Please could you help me before I get myself into trouble? I want to go on to do stuff but I don't know how!

If you really think a guy would think less of you or spread tales about you just because you haven't yet fine-tuned your kissing, he doesn't sound like good kissing material to me. Truth is, many guys are actually relieved to find that their girl friends aren't superexperts and won't judge their puckering performance. Guys don't want girls who've been practising their kisses on everybody on the soccer team. Although they may enjoy it when you flirt with them, they want to think that it's because you think they're special, not because you'd corner anybody under the mistletoe. If you lead guys on, they'll expect more from you than you may be ready to give. Which means you could end up with a reputation as a tease – or with sexual pressure you would rather not have to deal with.

In the section called 'Kissing, Etc.' of Girl-talk, you said to be 'soft, sensual and creative.' I was recently with a boy I really liked and I experienced my first real 'make-out.' I wasn't sure exactly how I would do, but I wanted to please him. And you know what? I remembered your three words and it helped me enjoy myself all the more. The best thing was that afterwards he said, 'You know, you're the best kisser I've ever kissed.'

Well, how about that?

And how about French-kissing? One girl asked about the 'proper procedure' for tongue-kissing and added, 'I know how – I'm just curious.' Another wrote,

I am 13 and I have just one question. How do you French-kiss? My boyfriend and I have kissed but we haven't Frenched yet. I have the feeling he knows how, but the problem is, I don't. So if you would write down the details of how French-kissing starts and ends and how to hold him during the process, it would be helpful. But I need the information very soon so please HURRY!!! Thanks.

When you're French-kissing, you could let the guy take the lead. If he explores your mouth with his tongue, you can gently squeeze his tongue with your mouth or let your tongues do a slow dance together. Kissing and Frenching should feel good and come naturally. They shouldn't start and end abruptly. As for how to hold the guy, you could curl your fingers around the nape of his neck or around his back or hold his hand or do whatever feels comfortable.

If you don't immediately warm up to kissing, it doesn't mean you're frigid. If you prefer regular kissing to French-kissing, that's A-O.K. too. Some girls expect stars and rainbows and can't help but feel let down when 'a kiss is just a kiss' – as Sam the piano player sings in *Casablanca*. Kissing is most wonderful when you're in love.

The next two letters are from the same girl.

> *Dear Carol,*
>
> *I really like this boy, James, and if he asks me to go with him I want to say yes, but I might end up saying no just because I can't kiss well. I really have tried but I just can't get it right. I'm 15. Could you give me a few helpful tips on how to be a better kisser? I know this all sounds funny but it is very important to me.*
>
> *Can't Kiss*

Dear Carol,

I recently wrote you about this same problem, but here goes. I've been going out with this guy named Gene but there's one thing missing: We haven't kissed yet. Every time he tries to kiss me, I turn my head. He asked me what I have against kissing him and I said 'Nothing,' but I still refuse to kiss him because I don't know how to kiss. I think you're about the only person who could understand my problem. Write me soon.

Still Can't Kiss

Dear Can't Kiss,

Please forgive me for not writing back immediately. I was away over Christmas and just got both your letters. Before I give you kissing pointers, let me ask you this: Did you realize that your late-December letter was about James and your early-January letter was about Gene? Slow down! You have to decide whom to kiss before you polish your style.

Anyway, your 'problem' sounds more emotional than physical. Physically, kissing isn't hard. You just meet his lips gently and apply a little or a lot of pressure depending on how steamy the situation is. You've seen a million TV and movie stars kiss, right? If you want to practise on your pillow or in the mirror, you won't be the first girl to do so. Or why not ask Gene to give you a kissing lesson? I'm sure you'll find kissing a lot easier and more fun than you imagined.

How about you? Are you still nervous?

• If you're worried about bad breath, brush your teeth with toothpaste before you go out, and bring mints or gum. Avoid onions, anchovies and garlic on the day of your date.

• If you're worried about P.D.A.(public display of affection), tell your boyfriend you prefer kissing in private.

• If you're worried about beard burn (stubble trouble!), kiss gently or suggest that next time he shave before going out.

• If you're worried about sexual pressure, remember that you always have the right to say no and that you can enjoy kissing for all it's worth before letting heavy-duty intimacy even become an issue.

• If you're worried about AIDS, you should know that in 1987, the World Health Organization stated that there is no evidence that the HIV virus spreads through French-kissing. To play it extra safe, don't French-kiss someone you think may be or may have been an intravenous drug user or a bisexual (someone who is sexually attracted to men and women). Be especially careful if you have a cut or open sore in your mouth.

- If you're worried about your braces locking together and having to make an emergency appointment at the orthodontist's ... you're worrying too much!

LONG-DISTANCE LOVE

Some couples don't spend their time together in school, at parties, at dances or on dates. Some hardly see each other at all. Have you ever gone with a guy in another city? Or fallen for someone when you were away on vacation? Or moved but left your heart back home?

I spent my senior year of high school not at home but in France, on a programme called School Year Abroad. It was *magnifique* – except that my high school boyfriend of several years was back in America and we had to depend on the international postal service to keep our passion alive.

The advantage of that arrangement was that

I felt secure and loved (though sometimes lonely) and could immerse myself in French and French culture instead of being distracted by the debonair French *garçons* and the dashing American students. The disadvantage was that to be faithful, I declined several invitations from debonair *garçons* and dashing students. I might have enjoyed a new romance and learned from it, but instead I remained true to my hometown honey – whom I ended up breaking up with soon after my return.

How do guys feel about long-distance love? Does absence make the heart grow fonder? Or does absence make the heart go find her? It's not easy to sustain a relationship through letters and phone calls. And it's not always worth it to pledge allegiance to someone far away. But if you have a faraway crush or boyfriend, give long-distance loyalty a whirl and see what happens.

> *Dear Carol,*
> *I am 13½ years old. I live in Maine but I used to live in Vermont. There's this boy in Vermont that I had started liking. When I visited a friend there, his mother invited us over for pizza. I would like very much to write to him but I don't know what to write. Do you think 13½*

*is too young to think of long-distance boy-
friends?*

> *Chelsea*

Dear Chelsea,
    *No, and I bet the boy in Vermont
would love to hear from you. If you didn't
thank his family for the pizza dinner, it's
not too late – and that's a good excuse to
write. You could also wish him a happy
holiday (if one is around the corner) or
send a postcard (if you go on vacation or
visit a local museum or attraction).*
    *Don't be sappy; just tell him about your
new neighbourhood and school. What do
you write your girl friends about – besides
boys? Well, there you go! If you want to,
you can also tell him that you miss
(ah-hem) Vermont.*
    *I hope he writes back, but don't take
it hard if he doesn't. Some good guys are
lousy pen pals.*

Dear Carol,
    *My boyfriend, Shane, is moving away.
I said we could keep in touch by writing
each other, but he said no. He said we
could call each other – but he hardly calls
me now. We've been going together for*

*two months. I really like him but I don't
think he likes me.*

Lindsay

Dear Lindsay,
   *I hate to be a pessimist, but if you and
Shane don't talk much now, I doubt matters will improve when he moves. Write
him at least once before writing him off,
but don't dedicate your life to him or
idolize him once he's gone. If you keep
being friendly to the guys (and girls) in
your school, you'll find living in the here
and now more interesting than hanging
on to a long-distance romance that isn't
charging full speed ahead.*

Dear Carol,
   *I met Joel at a lake my family was at
this summer. He is 14. I have been writing
him and he wrote me once. I want him to
write me again! Every day I hope to get a
letter from him. He lives pretty far away.
Do you have any advice on how to get him
to write me?*

Peggy

Dear Peggy,
   It's hard enough to get a guy to notice

you when you're in town; it's even harder when you're miles and miles away. If you write Joel a short sweet letter and ask him a few questions (How's school going? Has he seen any good movies? Will his family be going to the lake?), he may respond. If not, don't lose heart but do be realistic. A one-way long-distance romance can't last, but this summer you may see him again — or meet someone else.

Dear Carol,

There's this guy I'm really in love with, but he's in college and I don't get to see him that much. He's 18; I'm 15. He's everything a girl could want and everything a girl dreams of. He's romantic, caring, loving, sweet, understanding, gorgeous, kindhearted, muscular and has a great body. He said he would never hurt me and that we would keep in touch all the time.

I met him four months ago during his Christmas vacation. I was waitressing and he asked me for my phone number. He called and I saw him every day for the next two weeks. He would pick me up at school and take me out to lunch and then pick me up after school and take me to expensive restaurants for dinner.

He is a real gentleman and once gave me a flower with a note that said,

'With eyes as blue as diamonds
And hair as blonde as snow
Your beauty surely resembles
A rainbow whose true colours show.'

Nobody had ever written me a poem before.

I tracked him down at the airport on his last day here and he said he was going to miss me so much. I was crying and he almost started crying too.

I know he has his work and school and his friends and stuff, but he has only called me a few times and I've called him at least 50 times and written him 10. I know guys seem to have a hard time writing letters but couldn't he at least call me? He didn't even send me anything for Valentine's Day and I sent him a bouquet of flowers, a card and balloons. He didn't even call to thank me for them. I had to call to see if he got them.

He's coming back in a few weeks, but I don't know what to do because I don't want to call and bug him. I'll be crushed if he has forgotten about me. He said he

never would.
                    Very Very in Love and
                            Very Confused

Dear Very Very,
    *If you've called Mr. Kindhearted 50
times, yet you've barely heard from him,
you don't need me to tell you that things
look grim. Yes, he might call you in a
few weeks. But he might not, so prepare
yourself. If he does call, I'm not even sure
you should welcome him back with open
arms – he hasn't exactly been romantic,
caring, loving and sweet (or even polite!)
during the past few months. Ask yourself
this: since you two said good-bye, has the
relationship brought you more joy or sorrow?*
    *You say he is a gentleman, but he
didn't even acknowledge your generous
(too generous?) Valentine gift. Nor has
he responded to your many (too many?)
letters. It's too bad that he's of the out-of-
sight-out-of-mind school, but your best bet
now is to be glad for your merry Christmas
and move on. Don't smother him with any
more undeserved affection.*
    *Long-distance relationships have a bet-
ter chance of survival when a couple have*

been together for many months or even years before separation. You two had only two weeks. His being in college also isn't helping matters because he's surrounded by other young women. (Sorry, but it's true.) So stop romanticizing him – always a danger with long-distance love – and get on with your life. He was the first among many boyfriends. And if you don't sigh away the summer, another romance (with or without expensive dinners) is sure to come your way.

Pssst, I didn't have the heart to break it to her, but diamond eyes? Rainbow beauty? The guy may have money and muscles, but Shakespeare he's not. I hope she'll soon meet a guy who is less showy, more sincere. And while the college boy got her love life launched, if she's lucky, she'll find someone closer by and closer in age to keep it going.

Dear Carol,
  My mum gave me Girltalk for my seventeenth birthday and I really loved it. Two years ago, I moved from my old town and was absolutely miserable. But I ended up making lots of friends, finding lots to do and even falling in love. I was

mostly happy, but then I started getting sick of my friends. I decided to visit my best friend in my old town. I figured a week away would restore my perspective. Not so!

While in my old town, I met one of the nicest guys I've ever known. His name is Patrick and we hit it off instantly. We fooled around a couple of times, but we never really had a chance to talk. When he came to my friend's house to say good-bye, we couldn't think of anything to say. It was the worst good-bye I've ever had, but I think that's because he didn't want to say good-bye at all.

I miss him, I miss my best friend, I miss the whole town, and now I hate it here even more.

All I want to do is sit in my room and listen to records. I don't know how to get myself out of this slump and what to do about Patrick. I really like him and want to know him better so I can keep liking him.

Kristin

Dear Kristin,

To get out of a slump, get busy. Look for a part-time summer job or get involved *in some volunteer work. You may soon be in college or on your own, but in the meantime, it does you no good to hate your home, so try to make the best of it and try to make some new friends. If you lived elsewhere and visited your town for a week, would it really seem like such a bad place?*

What about Patrick? You two had a great time together, but you didn't really do enough talking to get a real relationship under way. your letters will help you get to know each other better. Will you like what · he says and how he says it? Or will you be disappointed by his boring news and poor spelling? Breathless flings don't always have staying power. Give yourselves a few weeks to see if yours is different. If you find that Patrick isn't writing or calling or that he's not as interesting on paper and the phone as he was in person, do yourself a favour: don't stay faithful to a happy memory.

Sometimes long-distance relationships can, well, go the distance. I've had long-distance relationships that fizzled fast, but during the summer of my freshman year in college, I lived in Madrid and fell in love with Juan, a graduate student whom I then went out with for nearly four years. The Atlantic ocean came between us much of that time, but after our first summer as sweethearts, he spent a summer and a long Christmas vacation in America, and I enjoyed two nine-month stays near his family in Madrid.

When Juan and I were apart, we wrote letters and postcards, and eventually came to an agreement: it was okay to go out with other people. Sure, it made us both a little jealous when the other was seeing somebody, but it also kept us from getting too frustrated with the whole situation. And in the long run, it made our relationship stronger because we kept putting it to the test and finding that we didn't like anyone else more than we liked each other.

Juan and I finally broke up when I met Robert, who is now my husband. Looking back, do I regret having spent my college years in love with a guy who lived on another continent? Not a bit. Perhaps I would regret it had I let myself become a hermit at college or had I let my happiness depend solely on whether a new love letter greeted me each time I opened my P.O. box. But since Juan and I enjoyed a long-distance love that didn't limit us, I often felt I had the best of both worlds.

PARENT PROBLEMS

Which is harder? Being a teenager or being the parent of a teenager? It may be a toss-up. While teenagers can't believe their parents won't treat them like adults, parents can't believe their children are turning into adults. According to your mum and dad, just yesterday you would burst into tears whenever they left you to go out for dinner, and you wanted a Cabbage Patch doll in the worst way. Now you wish they'd go away every weekend, and what you want is a boy-friend. Of course they find it difficult to adjust to your growing up, up, and away.

Please understand that if your parents embarrass you, they aren't doing it on purpose. If they're overprotective, it's not because they're mean, but because they mean well. You want to be adventurous; they want you to be careful. You want to test your wings; they want you to ace your tests. You can't break up with your family, but you will be on your own (in college or at work) before you know it. In the meantime, try to get along with your parent or parents. They love you, and believe it or not, they want, and need, your love in return.

Their Romances

Kids complain about meddling parents, but if you live with a single parent – and approximately one in every five teenagers does – you may wish you were invited to meddle in your mum or dad's love life.

> *My mum is going out with this guy who has just separated. I really like him and I don't want her to see anyone else. Mum says they're just friends but I can't stop thinking I wish they were together. I'm driving my mum crazy with my match-making, but what can I do? I like this guy.*

> *My mum is still going out with that gross boyfriend I told you about. What if they get married? I don't think I could handle that! I know Mum should be happy, but it still hurts me so much. I just have trouble dealing with another guy trying to take Dad's place. How come Mum got over Dad's death so fast and I can't?*

It's natural for you to root for or against a particular parental romance. And it's okay to tell your parent your opinion. But his or her feelings (and those of the sweetheart) count first, and in the long run, you and your parent will be lucky if he or she can find a loving partner.

If one of your parents has died, it can be especially hard to accept a romance or remarriage. When I first met my mother's fiancé, several years after my father died, I tried to make conversation with him, but my eyes kept filling with tears. And I was in my late twenties! My mother and father had had a wonderful marriage, but when Dad died, it ended. I'm glad my mother's love life didn't end along with it. Lewis, my stepfather, is terrific and he and my mother are very happy together. Did Lewis try to take my father's place? No. I still think of my father every day. Did my mother get over my father in a hurry? No. But isn't it better that she be a newlywed instead of a widow?

If your parents are divorced and your mother, far from dating, keeps telling you how rotten men are, you may sympathize with her, but try not to share her hostility. Your romances may be more successful than hers.

Your Romances

When it comes to boys, no matter what your parents say or do, it's bound to annoy you.

May I recommend that you *not* engage in door-slamming fights about dating privileges and curfews if your first date may still be two years away? And may I ask that you *not* get all bent out of shape if your parents, who know you are impatient to fall in love, invite some guy friend of yours in for cake or cola? And may I suggest that you *not* indulge in a primal scream if they describe, once again, how boys will soon be lining up around the block and how you'll have to beat them off with a stick? If dating is not yet an issue, don't fight about it, and if your parents are just trying to be encouraging, don't discourage them.

What if your parents think you are too young to be going out – but you disagree?

> *My boyfriend and I kissed for the very first time in front of a few friends at the roller rink. My mother found out and she flew off the handle. Sometimes she can be very understanding but sometimes she can be so overprotective I can hardly breathe. I am almost 12. Do you think I'm too young to kiss a boy?*

Although many girls' first kisses don't come until much later, I don't think 11-going-on-12 is too young to kiss a boy. (I do think it's too young to go beyond kissing.) Is the mother being unreasonable? Not really. Give Mum a break. A conscientious mother knows about teenage pregnancy statistics and sexually transmitted diseases and is naturally concerned that her daughter could stumble into potentially dangerous situations.

What if you're 12, 13 or 14 and your parents forbid you to go on evening dates? Don't start sneaking around and lying. If you get caught, your parents will pull in the reins that much tighter. Talk to your parents about the possibility of your boyfriend's coming over for dinner or to play a board game or watch TV and ask if you can go out with him (or with him and another couple) during the day.

> I'm 13 and my boyfriend Dave is 15. We have been going out for 10½ months. We recently had a very large fight but we got through it – though not without pain and tears. (Oh Lord, were there tears!) Now we find ourselves getting closer and closer.
>
> I feel deeply in love. I want to do so many things with Dave and I want to make him feel good about himself and I want to share so much. He feels the same way – we've discussed it. We're so happy

together. (My eyes are beginning to water up!)

> *My dad really believes that Dave and I are a great couple and that with time and patience we will get married. He already treats Dave as if he were a son-in-law. I just know it will happen. But then there's The Big Green Mother From Outerspace. She insists that her little 13-year-old isn't old enough to have sexual feelings or be in love. She says it's puppy love. And she gets all upset when Dave and I even give each other a good-bye hug (yum) and kiss (yum, yum, yummy). I don't know how to tell her that I really am in love.*

It's lucky that this girl's dad likes Dave, and I understand her frustration with her mother, but I also feel for Mum. Thirteen is young to get so serious. Would her mother object to any boyfriend right now? Or does she have reason to disapprove of Dave? She probably has her daughter's best interest in mind.

How to tell parents that you are in love? Don't go on and on about your feelings. You may be tempted to share all your experiences, but as you get older, it sometimes gets harder to go into every detail of your life – yummy or yukky. Just tell them you are happy and reassure them that you are being responsible so they don't worry that you're playing sexual roulette.

Here's another letter.

> *Let me tell you about myself.*
> *Age: 13*
> *School: I am in seventh grade in a private Catholic school.*
> *Church: I go once a week.*
> *Parents: My father is a sheriff and is very protective.*
> *My mother goes along with him.*
> *Boys I like: Greasers.*
>
> *My problem is Julio. Julio is a greaser, exactly what my parents don't like. Let me tell you about him.*
> *Age: 16.*
> *School: He is in eighth grade in a public high school that is considered 'rough'. He is not smart, but I don't think people should reject him.*
> *Church: The last time he went was 'about ten years ago' (direct quote).*
> *Parents: His dad is a pusher and his mother doesn't care about him. They had him when they were 17.*
> *Girls he likes: Wear a medium amount of makeup, have lenient parents and love to party.*

In general, he likes parties, smokes, hates school, hates parents, and usually wears ripped faded jeans with scraggly tennis shoes. He is a nice kid with a lot of problems.

My problem is that my parents disapprove of Julio. My sister and brother were real troublemakers so my parents are extra strict with me. But I like Julio.

Oh boy. I hate to side with the grown-ups, but sometimes Father knows best, and I'm not sure Julio is an ideal boyfriend. I'm sorry Julio wasn't blessed with more caring responsible parents himself, but alas, he doesn't seem to have set himself on a better path. At 16, he is only in eighth grade. And he goes for party girls with permissive parents. With that kind of attitude, he may end up following in his father's footsteps and could have a child of his own by age 17 – before he is even halfway through high school. That would be a shame for him, for the child and for the mother.

The sheriff probably hopes his daughter will get involved with a more ambitious boy and will some day marry a man whose background has nothing to do with drugs that poison other people's lives. This girl knows why her parents aren't wild about Julio. She should try to figure out why she is. (If it's simply because he's cute or because she wants to rebel, I hope she'll rethink her priorities.)

> *I have a parent problem. I am 13 and very responsible. My parents have the wrong idea about my boyfriend Toby because he and my dad were at a red light and Toby floored his 4-trax (a large racing four-wheeler) and sprayed rocks all over Dad's car. Toby called to apologize, but my dad is still peeved and won't let me go out with him. It didn't even put marks on his car! Help!*

This girl may be responsible, but is Toby? Her parents don't care about the rocks; they care about their daughter's safety. And they're worried about trusting her life to a speed demon in a racing car. Accidents happen and male teenage drivers pay high car insurance premiums for a reason.

> *My mum doesn't like my boyfriend Rollin. She says I'm better than him, I look rich compared to him and our house is a mansion compared to his. But I figure, what does that have to do with it? I feel as long as you love someone, that's the point. I'm*

183

*15. He's 17. We'd like to be together for-
ever. His parents argue about money all
the time like I'm supposed to do something
about it. My life is the pits and I feel like
running away.*

Does love conquer all? Not always. The depth
of your affection is more important than the size
of your bank account, but money problems can
take a toll on love. Of course, financial situations
can change. Many millionaires hail from poor
families and there's nothing wrong with a wife
making more money than her husband.

If Rollin's parents are expecting money from
her, however, they aren't playing fair. At 15,
this girl doesn't need to decide about forever.
She should enjoy the day and be realistic about
the future. And she should make sure she's not
seeing her boyfriend to spite her mum.

Running away would not be a happy situation. Many teenage prostitutes were innocent,
confused runaways and wish now that they'd
tried harder to make things work at home. If
your home life ever feels unbearable, look into
family counselling. (See the *Information* section
at the back of this book.)

*I am 18 and have been seeing a guy who
is 19 for about a month. I'm white and he*

*is black. When we are together, we forget
that our skin colour is different. My parents are prejudiced and would have a fit if
they knew. Do you think we should forget
our feelings just because people frown on
black-white relationships? Does it matter
what race you are if you love each other?*

They've gone out just one month – is it
definitely love? An inter-racial couple can live
happily ever after even without all of society's
blessings if they are devoted and determined
enough to ignore certain pressures and prejudices.
But this girl should be realistic about the added
obstacles her romance may need to overcome.

What's important isn't just love but whether
you and your boyfriend have similar values, feel
that you are equals, feel that neither of you is
settling for the other and like yourselves as well
as each other.

If your parents are worried about your choice
of boyfriend, remind them that you aren't engaged, you're just dating. Minimize the relationship in their eyes, no matter how important it is
to you. If the romance lasts a lifetime, good luck!
If not, let it go. Don't hold on to a challenging
rocky relationship just to irk your parents or
prove how noble you are.

His Parents

What about his parents? Have you met them yet? If possible, keep the first meeting brief and informal. If you meet them in a crowd or are one among several girls being introduced, that will ease the pressure too.

What if they invite you to dinner? How can you be sure to make a good impression?

• Dress neatly and not too outrageously. (I was wearing pale blue nail polish the first time I had dinner at my boyfriend's house. I was lucky they invited me back!)

• Ask your boyfriend to brief you on his family. (Is his father a practical joker? Is his mum as gung ho about mystery novels as you are?)

• Eat the mushrooms and try the squash. (You don't have to clean your plate, but if you look like you're going to gag, you'll lose points. Compliment the meal even if you wish there were a hungry puppy under the table.)

• Speak up. (If you're quiet all through dinner, they won't dislike you, but nor will they be bowled over by your charm.) Tell them about your school activities and summer plans and ask them questions: did they grow up around here? Who made the delicious carrot cake? The flowers outside are so beautiful – who's the gardener in the family? Try to sound interested, not nosy.

Chances are, you'll be a hit with his family. If not, talk it over with your boyfriend. If they're upset because his grades have gone down, vow to study harder and see each other less often during the week. If their complaint is that he's never home any more, plan an occasional evening at his house, studying, making popcorn, watching TV or whatever. If they think your family isn't as la-dee-dah as theirs, show by your good grooming, good manners and good grades that you can measure up to their standards (even if you think they're superficial).

Siblings will also judge you, for better and worse. Get your boyfriend to tell you about them before you meet, and pay attention to them so they don't feel that they are losing their brother and gaining nothing in return.

Just how involved should you be with his family? It depends. They're his family, not your in-laws, and it's not the end of the world if you don't like them or vice versa. If you and his mum get along famously, but you and her son are on the brink of a breakup, that can complicate matters too.

Sometimes it's smart to keep a little distance.

I have an unusual problem. I found out that my boyfriend's mother is a prostitute. It's really tough on my boyfriend because his sister and brother hate her and want nothing to do with her. My boyfriend is trying to help her all by himself and he's being torn apart inside. Is there any way I could possibly help him? He's been to a psychologist. It is ruining my relationship.

This girl's problem is a tough one. But it isn't her problem. She and her boyfriend both need to realize that it is the mother's problem. Her boyfriend may want to ask a trusted teacher, clergy member or doctor for advice or he may want to make an anonymous call to an agency that specializes in families in trouble. (See the *Information* section at the back of this book.) And the girl? I hope she'll stand by her friend as long as she wants to, but I also hope that if her feelings change, she won't feel too guilty to break up with him. It's good to want to help, but if the mother doesn't want to change, the kids shouldn't ruin their lives in a futile attempt to save hers.

(And you thought you had it bad because your boyfriend's mother can act a little moody!)

ROMANCE RECHARGERS
(BECAUSE HE'S WORTH IT)

Just because you have a good thing going is no reason to start taking him for granted. Showing your boyfriend that you care can be as easy as one, two, three . . . four, five.

1. Surprise him.
Wink at him when he least expects it. Catch him off guard with an impulsive kiss. Pass him a note in the hall, slip a message in his maths book, leave a letter in his locker or mail a card to his home. Give him a flower. Give him a backrub. Tell him to save a particular Saturday, and then (shhh) splurge on tickets to a concert or sports event.

2. Learn to share some of his interests.
Is he a football fanatic or an astronomy enthusiast? If so, brush up on field goals, interceptions, Giants and Cowboys, or rockets, black holes, Pluto and Mars. Whether he is an expert on cars, coins or cats, if you learn the basics, you'll have that much more to talk about. Or take up a new hobby or sport together – anything from backgammon or birding to biking.

3. Go on a Saturday night – or Sunday morning – picnic.

Instead of meeting for pizza or brunch, be creative, romantic and economical. For an evening repast, bring a blanket, a thermos full of hot chocolate or lemonade, seedless grapes, homemade chicken or sandwiches and your own chocolate chip cookies. Don't forget the insect repellent. Now lean back and look for shooting stars. For a morning date, bring muffins or croissants with jam and orange juice. Choose a pastoral setting if possible, and if you're early risers, get up before the sun (just this once) and watch it make the scene.

4. Go to his recitals, rehearsals, meets, practices, games.

If you attend his piano recital or play rehearsals, and praise him afterwards, he's bound to appreciate it. If you're on the sidelines cheering, he may swim that much faster, jump that much higher or score that many more goals. Why not take your camera along and take photos of him in action? Then give him copies. Better still, start a scrapbook for him complete with cut-out magazine headlines proclaiming his talents.

5. Give him a gift he'll love.

Lots of girls ask: 'What should I get him for his birthday?' Answer: it depends. Don't just dash out and buy him a tie – unless it's particularly fun or fashionable. And don't buy him heart-speckled socks that melt your heart unless you're pretty sure they'll melt his too. You know him well. Think about what he'd like (a new football? a mobile of the planets?) and try to get him something his mother wouldn't. Will you regale him on his birthday, Christmas and Valentine's? Lucky guy. Of course, you can show your affection by giving him a present out of the blue too.

Consider a homemade gift. Besides a scrapbook, your boyfriend might love a batch of brownies, knitted scarf, portrait you've drawn of him, or custom-made tape of his favourite music. Instead of spending big money on a last-minute Christmas gift, you can give him a stocking full of little presents (a model car, key chain, heart-shaped balloon, deck of cards, tiny stuffed animal, toy for his dog) that you can start collecting and wrapping in early November. Or how about giving him an album, book, belt, cufflinks, framed photo of you two, game, giant chocolate kiss, knick-knack from an antique store, magazine subscription, poster, roll of quarters for video games, T-shirt, or wallet (with your photo tucked inside)? If you want to go all out, you could stage a surprise birthday party, but check with his parents first.

A word of caution to the excessively generous: don't feel compelled to spend a bundle, and don't give away your grandfather's pocket watch or anything else you might one day want back.

ROMANCE WRECKERS (A WHAT-NOT-TO-DO GUIDE)

Barbie and Ken's love is perfect – but make-believe. True love runs deeper – and runs into snags. Will you and your boyfriend succeed in avoiding the common pitfalls? Or will you unwittingly trip up your romance by analyzing it into the ground, struggling to endlessly improve each other, playing games or becoming dependent? Here are some guidelines on what NOT to do.

1. Become green-eyed monsters.
Jealousy can ruin a relationship. If you become so possessive and insecure that you worry each time your boyfriend talks to another girl, you'll

stop enjoying each other's company and he'll start resenting your private eye attitude. Having a boyfriend who sees green is no fun either.

> My boyfriend (16) and I (15) have been together for almost six months. He says he loves me and I really love him. But whenever I do things with my friends without telling him first, he gets mad and jealous and won't call me for a while. He puts himself down a lot; do you think he thinks I am putting him down in the same way? I'm not! When he does things with his friends without telling me, I never mind at all.

Jealous people are usually insecure. Instead of trusting the strength of their relationship (and working to make it stronger), they fear that their loved ones will be lured away by the first temptation.

If you suffer from jealousy, try to get busier and work on your self-esteem. If other girls find your boyfriend cute, try to feel pleased instead of panicky. Many girls flirt with guys who are taken because it's fun but less scary than approaching more eligible guys.

If your boyfriend is jealous, reassure him that you care and boost his ego with compliments.

The better you each feel about yourselves, the less vulnerable you'll be to jealousy. Love shouldn't be a watchdog.

2. Declare love too soon.

Just because you'd love to be in love doesn't mean you've found the right guy yet. And just because your romance is jogging along doesn't mean you should force it to sprint. Don't rush your romance; let it develop naturally. If you say 'I love you,' before you've really grown to know and cherish each other, you may scare your guy away or feel worse if the relationship does a nose dive.

> *My boyfriend is almost 21 and I am only 16. We spend a lot of time together. But whenever I am with him I tense up and can't let out my feelings. He's the same way. When we go out I get so speechless. I don't know what to say to him. I mean, if I tell him, 'I love you,' I don't know if he'll dump me or if he'll say the same thing back. Help!*

If she doesn't know how he'd react to her words of love, she should hold off saying them. Is she really in love? Or is she in awe of her older man? She can say, 'I really care about you,' but more important, she should try to improve their communication in general. She should relax instead of turning each date into a pressure cooker situation. If weeks go by and they still are barely talking, this match may not be ideal, and all the more reason not to label it love.

Another girl recently wrote me to complain that guys 'think they will look weak or wimpy if they cry or say "I love you," to their girl friend in front of their friends.' Granted, some guys have trouble expressing emotions, but why should a guy say 'I love you,' in public? Love isn't a status symbol; it's private and personal and if a guy loves you quietly, that's enough. Don't despair if he is devoted but unable to say the three little words. Some people say, 'I love you' as easily as others say 'Pass the salt.' What counts is how you each really feel.

3. Bore each other to death.

While some girls get speechless with their boyfriends, others don't know when to stop talking. You and your boyfriend can have a top-notch relationship even if you don't talk on the phone each night, whisper during every scene of a movie or fill each other in on every detail of your day (what you learned in maths class, had for dinner, thought of a TV commercial).

When you're with guys (or girls), try not to sound like a run-on sentence. Don't complain nonstop about your schoolwork, mother or gym coach. Don't get stuck on one subject (a rock star, your family, your bad habits). Do your best not to make a short story long. And when you talk, notice whether he looks interested – or looks around.

If you're worried your boyfriend may start yawning not because of your yammering but because you are so silent, look over the shyness sections in Chapter 1. And talk! Will one foolish word mark the beginning of the end? No way! Pretend you are interviewing him. Ask how he felt when he made the save in hockey, what he remembers of his first day in school or whether he ever finds it hard to talk to his father or older brother. If you are planning to phone him, but are afraid you may clam up as soon as he says hello, why not prepare a list of subjects you may want to bring up? That's what I did when I was first getting to know my high school honey!

4. Never see each other

While some couples stifle each other, others never get together in the first place.

I'm 15 and very frustrated! I am going with this guy who goes to a boarding school 15 miles away. He's always going away to wrestling meets or to his parents on weekends. During the week we never get to see each other any more. My parents don't let me date and he has a 10:00 curfew. I don't know how much longer I can take this!

It is frustrating to feel like you're conducting a long-distance relationship with someone nearby. Calls and letters are nice, but so is getting together. Maybe these two can see each other on Saturday mornings before he leaves or maybe her parents will loosen their grip on weekday evenings. Having an invisible boyfriend or girl friend gets old. Time together is an indispensable ingredient in most successful romances.

5. Worry so much about yesterday and tomorrow that you forget to enjoy today.

Don't tell your boyfriend all about your exes (and how well each one kissed) and don't worry about his exes (his past helped shape him into the great guy he is now).

I've had a crush on a boy named Jacob for about a year and we are now going out. He's everything to me. But I'm afraid we won't last long. When he calls, I can't think of anything to say. When he was going with his ex-girlfriend, they talked and did everything together. They were great together. I know he's thinking of how things used to be with her and I am so scared of losing him. I can't imagine life without him.

It's hard to make small talk to someone who is larger than life and perched way up on a pedestal. Instead of sabotaging her relationship, she should think of Jacob as a normal guy – rather than a God descended from heaven. She should concentrate on making the most of today – rather than getting hung up on his past and their future. She can even tell him that she sometimes gets nervous because she cares so much. She can collect interesting things to talk to him about. And she can tell herself that life *would* roll along without him. There are millions of good guys out there; Jacob just happens to be lucky enough to have met her.

I'm 14 and Troy is 16. This summer he's opened up to me and we get along great.

But the only thing I's scared of is: what happens September third? Will he 'love me and leave me'? Or can I trust him?

Everybody wants to look into the crystal ball, but there are no guarantees. Some sizzling summer loves do cool off with the demands and distractions of school. Others last a lifetime. Instead of fearing the worst now, why not make every effort to have a great summer and build such a caring friendship and sparkling romance that neither she nor he will want it to end?

YOUR FIRST SERIOUS SPAT: A DOZEN POINTERS ON FIGHTING FAIRLY

Some couples constantly bicker; others rarely quarrel. I used to have a mile-long fuse, but when I got mad, I got livid. One of the loudest fights I ever had with my high school boyfriend was on a lazy July day when I caught him cheating at Monopoly. I yelled even more then than I did when I found out that he and my friend Rosemary had shared a drunken kiss when I was on vacation.

When the going gets tough, do you immediately start crying, swearing, hitting or apologizing? People have different fighting styles, but it's important to know how to end a fight before it ends your relationship.

● Don't displace anger.

If you're mad at your mother or your maths teacher, don't take it out on your boyfriend.

● Don't pick fights.

If you taunt 'Why was your phone busy? Been talking to Jillian?' you're asking for trouble.

● Don't argue late at night or before a big test.

If you're tired or stressed, beware. You run the risk of heating up over trivial things that ordinarily wouldn't bother you.

● Don't fight in public.

Keep your kissing and kicking private. Your friends don't want to take sides.

● Don't criticize his mum, his dog or his nose.

If you fight dirty, he'll fight dirty back.

● Don't drag in last month's fight.

If you're mad at him for picking you up an hour late, don't pipe in about how he curses too much, flirts with Marianne, and forgot your birthday. Choose your battles.

● Don't attack him with 'You' sentences.

Say, 'I disagree,' not 'You're full of it.' Say, 'I feel bad when you call me Duckface,' not 'You better cut it out with that nickname.'

• Don't lose your case by overstating it.

Instead of screaming, 'You don't care about anyone but yourself,' lower your voice, be specific, and say, 'I'm disappointed that you didn't come to my play.'

• Don't expect to agree on everything.

He is a Republican and you're a Democrat? Fine. You can enjoy spirited discussions – and don't need to convert each other.

• Don't insist on having the last word.

If you've each had your say, be willing to apologize or accept his apology, and then let the subject drop.

• Do be positive.

It won't kill you to say, 'I got upset because I care so much about you,' or 'You're usually so incredibly thoughtful, so I was surprised that you didn't call.'

• Do kiss when you've made up.

Unless you want to pull the plug on this relationship, it's better to make up than break up.

Think of your first fight not as the beginning of the end but as a rite of passage. If you each hurt, it's because you care and because you want a relationship that is not based on lies and lust, but is built on solid ground. You want to be friends as well as sweethearts.

4

Friends and Boyfriends

In your pursuit of the Perfect Boyfriend, do you sometimes take your friends for granted? Do you get so caught up in being in love – or lovelorn – that you forget to enjoy the rest of your life, even if it is more platonic than romantic, more pals than passion? Have you ever let a romance muck up a friendship by leaving girl friends high and dry the moment a boyfriend enters the picture?

Girl friends often last longer than boyfriends – but not if the friends neglect each other or let romances split them apart. Some girls compete with treasured friends over guys who are scarcely worth squabbling over. Other girls ask a friend to find out if a boy likes them – then despair when the boy falls for the friend. Still others get so hung up on analyzing their relationship with a boy (is the romance budding or are they just buddies?) that they forget to simply savour his company.

Juggling friends and crushes, boyfriends and boy friends can be tricky. This chapter lends a hand.

WHEN YOUR FRIEND LIKES YOUR CRUSH

You've been telling your friend all about David David David and what a nice smile he has and how hunky he looks in his green sweater and how he's so sensitive that he plans to be a psychologist and how he's got such an incredible backhand that if the psychology doesn't pan out, he could be a tennis pro and how he's basically just an all-round perfect catch and that's why everybody is after him. You go on and on and on about David David David. And then it hits you: she's after him too.

> I've liked this guy Justin for about four months. He is starting to notice me because I recently got contact lenses, a new hairstyle and different clothes. I think he likes me. My best friend Kay thinks he likes her.

203

Last Friday, I wore a denim miniskirt to school and I received many compliments from guys, especially Justin. That afternoon, Justin, Kay and I were sitting on the school steps and talking. I was sitting with my legs up and my knees against my chest. Justin was lying down and Kay said, 'You better stop sitting like that because you can see right up your skirt.' Justin sat up really fast like he wanted to see up my skirt. Somehow every conversation we get on ends up being about sex.

Kay is a lot shorter than I am. I'm 5'5" and she is 5'0" and is really really skinny (we're talking bony here). I guess you could say I'm the right height for my weight. I have blond hair and green eyes.

Justin and I always talk during first period. But Kay usually has to say something first to start a conversation with him. What do you think about all this?

Having been bony myself in junior high, I think she shouldn't put so much, ah-hem, weight on appearances. I also think she shouldn't rest her chin on her knees when wearing a mini. If Justin asks her out, it shouldn't be just for her shapely thighs and green eyes.

Her competition with Kay? It's a shame, but

friends often find themselves competing for the same guy. Why? Because friends often have similar tastes and some girls feel more secure liking a guy their pals consider a good choice rather than picking one out on their own. These two are in a bind and until one of them opts out or until Justin chooses between them (does he deserve such power?), their friendship will be strained.

Instead of becoming arch-rivals, they should bring the subject out in the open. She could confess to Kay that she likes Justin or say, 'It's kind of awkward that we both like the same guy, isn't it?' She could also make a point of talking to Kay about other cute guys. And she should recognize that, like it or not, Kay has every right to like Justin. You can't call dibs on a crush. All's fair in love and war – especially when the love isn't even in full bloom.

I remember a party at which a college roommate and I were both flirting with the same dimpled sophomore. For him, it was probably an ego trip. For me, it was awful. I don't know if I finally tossed in the towel because I was being mature or because I thought I'd lost the contest. I do know it hurt later when he called our room to ask her out.

But guess what? She and Dimples broke up ages ago; she and I are still friends. I'm glad we didn't let our common crush come between us.

My friend Donna is trying to take my boyfriend Gary away from me. (Well, he's not my boyfriend yet, but we do like each other a lot.) I think she's just jealous of me because I have better things than she does and I make better grades. She's been hanging around Gary and hugging him.

Donna got sort of upset when I asked her if she'd be my bridesmaid for my wedding with Gary, but she tried to hide it. I think she really wants to be the bride! We're like sisters and I've helped her a lot and this is the thanks I get.

A lot of girls want Gary and I'm sure others will try to take him away too. Everybody tells me not to worry about Donna since she's fat, ugly, four-eyed, doesn't believe in deodorant and doesn't even wash the back of her neck. I love Gary with all my heart and I just can't understand why Donna – my closest friend – is doing this.

Fat? Ugly? Four-eyed? And I thought calling a friend bony was bad! This girl signed her letter Angry in Oregon. She claims she's helped Donna a lot, but I wonder why she has not helped her even more. You'd think she might offer Donna a washcloth and some grooming tips.

206

Angry may not want to accept this, but other girls are entitled to drool over Gary. (Get a mop someone, quick!) You don't become a girl friend just by claiming a guy is yours. And you don't become a bride just by lining up bridesmaids.

> *My friend recently told me that she might ask this guy Ted to a dance, but I had planned on asking him (before I even knew she was interested in him)! I also know that Ted likes her only as a friend. What should I do? Should I wait and see if she does ask him?*

If she waits and Ted says yes to her friend, it will hurt. If she waits, and Ted says no to her friend, it will be clumsy to turn around and try her luck with him. And if she waits and her friend never gets up the nerve to invite Ted, she may kick herself for having sat on the sidelines. What to do? She could tell her friend as good-naturedly as possible that she has a crush on him too. Then they can decide who should ask him when, or they can simply hope he shows up at the dance – where they can each dance with him.

If you ever find yourself falling for your friend's guy, ask yourself whose affection means more to you, his or hers. And ask yourself if you're really attracted to him and him alone or if you're actually trying to prove something to yourself and your friend about your own attractiveness.

> *Last week this guy and I went to the movies and I kissed him good night. I found out a couple of days ago that my friend likes him and would do anything to get me out of the picture. When I talk to Phil on the phone and he tells me to do something for him and I say no, he says, 'Fine. I'll go out with Tiffany.' And then I do what he tells me. I know he likes me, but he won't tell anyone because he's in twelfth grade and I'm in ninth grade and he says people would say he's robbing the cradle. What do I do? I don't want to lose him to Tiffany and I don't want him to rule over me.*

Personally, I'd give him to Tiffany in a no-return box. Better yet, I'd warn her that Phil is a demanding, manipulative jerk. The more I think about him, the less I like him, and I bet this girl and Tiffany can both do better. Remember what I said about older guys sometimes trying to take advantage of younger girls? Why put up with a guy (even if he is a senior) who resorts to telephone threats and won't own up to their having gone out?

> *My friend Charlotte said all these things
> to get me to call Cory, so I thought, 'What
> the heck,' and called him. We liked each
> other and started going out. But then Char
> started flirting with him. I blew up! I told
> her if she wanted him that badly, she could
> have him. But I don't want to give up on
> him just like that. Or should I?*

I wouldn't. She can have Char as a friend
and Cory as a boyfriend and if they flirt a little
– 'what the heck'.

My own best friend and boyfriend flirted,
and though it didn't thrill me, I was glad they
got along so well. (When boyfriends and friends
don't take to each other, that's not ideal either.)
So long as Char and Cory aren't sneaking off
into the bushes together, there's no problem. If
Char were my friend, though, I might try to get
her interested in some unattached guy.

Are you in Char's shoes? Are you in a love
triangle – or like triangle – in which the guy you
like likes your friend?

WHEN YOUR CRUSH LIKES
YOUR FRIEND

It's bad when someone you like likes someone else, but it's worse when that someone else is your friend.

If your crush likes your friend, you'll feel crushed. No getting around it.

Nancy is my best friend and all the guys in school want to go out with her. We were at a dance and this guy I like, Peter, asked me to dance. All the time we danced, all he did was ask questions about Nancy. I thought he had some nerve asking me to dance, then giving me a list of questions.

Some nerve indeed. That's a bummer and if there is any justice in the world (and I'm not saying there is), someone some day will be asking Nancy questions about her.

I like this guy I'll call Miles. He acted like he liked me. I guess he led me on because suddenly he stopped calling me. Then my 'close' friend Heather told me

*Miles called her. I'd been telling her lately
how nice and sweet he is! I like him a lot
but he likes her and she likes him. What
should I do?*

Scream? Cry? Break a vase? She has little
choice but to try to be as happy as possible for
Miles and Heather (not easy!) and set her sights
on someone else. I doubt Miles was purposely
trying to lead her on. But I'm not surprised that
she feels hurt and betrayed. Did Heather break
the rules? Kind of. Not really. There are no set
rules. For now, it does no good to hate the pair,
and her best bet is to continue being friendly to
them and to other girls and guys.

*I have loved, not liked, this guy for
four months and I just found out that
he is going with one of my good friends.
The one good thing is that my friend said
she would fix me up when they break up,
but they will probably stay together for a
very long time. What should I do?*

What can she do? Look on the bright side.
Their romance will make it easy for her to get
to know him. And she may find that he's not
her type after all. Even though she says she is in
'love', infatuation might be a more accurate term

since they scarcely know each other. With luck, she'll soon home in on another guy. Her friend's break-up-fix-up scheme is a real long shot – and a recipe for disappointment.

> *I've liked a guy named Dean for about two months. My shy best friend Tricia decided to talk to him for me to find out what he thought of me. Well, now he likes Tricia! It would break my heart if they went out, and she insists that she doesn't like Dean as a boyfriend, but what if they were 'meant for each other'? I really like Dean a lot, but Tricia has been my best friend for four years.*

She's liked Dean for two months. She's liked Tricia for four years. Which is the more important bond? I don't believe Dean and Tricia were 'meant for each other' (sounds a bit Hollywood). Tricia may be hoping her friend will say, 'Go out with him. I'll enjoy it vicariously,' or Tricia may honestly not be interested in Dean. Time will tell and the girls should talk now to avoid a fight later.

Sometimes talking with a guy's spy or enlisting one of your own can muddy a romance. But sometimes helpful friends are just that – helpful. How do you feel about go-betweens?

GO-BETWEENS: FOR BETTER AND WORSE

Sometimes friends can help launch your love life.

> My friend Tracy told me that she and
> Susan had come up with the conclusion
> that Keith (a boy who sits across from
> me in home-room) liked me. At the time
> I had a crush on someone else and I
> couldn't believe it. But she convinced me
> it was true and somewhere in the back
> of my mind, I knew I had liked Keith
> all along. The next weekend there was a
> school dance and he and I danced. I was
> floating on Cloud 9!

Sometimes friends can make a mess of everything.

> I fell in love with Frank the first second
> I saw him. He knew I liked him but Joan
> had to tell him for the one hundredth time.
> This time he said he'd have to prove to
> me that he hated me. He still likes me
> as a friend, but he makes rude comments
> to me. I've tried to reason with him but

213

nothing works. What should I do? Please write back before I die of embarrassment.

There's not much the second girl can do besides go about her business until the crisis passes. She can ask Joan to keep her well-intentioned trap shut. She can stop defending herself to Frank. She can tell herself that this too will pass. And she can make a mental note not to tell Joan about future crushes.

When you enlist – or listen to – a go-between, you run a risk. Is it worth it?

I like this boy named Brad and I want to invite him to a party at my friend Carey's house, but I don't know how to ask him. I was thinking of having my friends ask him for me. Should I?

Depends. Would her friends be good match-makers – or meddlesome middlemen? Are they trustworthy? Discreet? Or are they busybodies who don't know when to quit?

Having friends phone Brad may seem like the easy way out, but why miss a chance to talk with Brad herself? And why give that chance to other girls? If I liked Brad, I'd call him and say, 'Carey is having a party and you're invited. I hope you can make it,' and try to judge his reaction.

True, he might be a monosyllabic blob on the phone. Worse, he might say, 'Your voice sounds familiar. What did you say your name was?' But he'll probably be warm and friendly as soon as she says hello. And at least she'll know where she stands rather than having to accept someone else's report.

> *I am 13 and my boyfriend is 11. We have been going together for four months and he has never held my hand or kissed me. I made the mistake of telling my four girl friends, and three of them immediately started making plans to get him to kiss me or hold my hand. I liked their eagerness to help, but they're doing it behind my back and telling my boyfriend what he should do. I don't think he minds. Rather, he welcomes the advice. But for my sake, do you know any ways to keep my friends out of my love life?*

Next time she can keep her love life private by revealing less about it. (Not easy, I know. Boys are fun to talk about.) In this case, she can tell her friends something like, 'I appreciate what you are trying to do, but I've decided I'd just as soon let things go at their own pace – even if that means slow motion. So please don't give him any more pointers, okay? Thanks!' She's lucky her boyfriend didn't mind the tips. Many guys would bristle if a pack of girls started suggesting how far and how fast they should go. And many younger guys aren't ready to show physical affection – so why rush them?

Girls aren't the only ones who are reluctant to put their egos on the line without first checking out the situation. Guys have spies too. In sixth grade when I had just moved to a new school district, a guy named Robby handed me a guy named Alan's ID bracelet and said Alan wanted to go steady with me. But even as Robby held it out on the school bus, he advised, 'If he can't give it to you himself, I wouldn't take it.' Some love messenger! He had a point, though. I barely knew who Alan was. Maybe if he'd called me or talked to me in the halls or walked me home from school or something (anything!) before suddenly sending his bracelet my way, we'd have gotten to know – and like – each other.

> I like this boy Ron. I went out with him for two weeks, then he dumped me, though I like to say we broke up. Today his friend Judd asked me if I'd go out with Ron again. I felt like saying YES!! But I didn't want to sound desperate, so I said, 'If he asked me, I might possibly say yes,

if he asked me.' Then I said 'Why?' He said, 'Forget it.' I asked 'Why?' again. He didn't say anything. I'm so confused!

Relationships are confusing. When you add a third party, they can get even cloudier. Ron probably asked Judd to gauge this girl's feelings. But wait. Could it be that Judd likes her and is asking where she stands for reasons of his own? Either way, I don't blame her for being a bit cagey. If someone asks you if you like a certain guy, and you do, you too may want to protect yourself by saying 'A little' or something wishy-washy, instead of panting and saying 'Yes', or lying and saying 'No'. Why should you put all your cards on the table if your crush won't even confront you directly?

It's too bad people are always asking their friends' crushes 'Do you like him?' or 'Do you like her?' instead of talking with their own crushes and gradually growing to like each other. If you're not going to be straight-ahead (though subtle) about your affection, at least pick your messengers carefully.

Have you ever been the messenger for someone else? In Greek tragedies, kings sometimes kill messengers who bring bad news. These days, messengers may not have to take their life in their hands, but bearing ill tidings is still a thankless job.

> *I am in a jam. This guy I like, Tucker, told me he likes Megan, my best friend. That's not a problem. Actually, he talks to me a lot now. But every day in maths, he tells me to ask Megan if she likes him. (She doesn't.) He also asks, 'Does she still like Tony?'(She does.) And 'Would she go with me?' (She wouldn't.) Could you tell me what to say to him? I don't want to hurt his feelings.*

Tucker is going to have to face the music sooner or later. To spare his feelings, she can emphasize that Megan likes Tony rather than emphasizing that she doesn't like Tucker. Why not ask Megan for her advice? And why not seize the opportunity to talk to Tucker about other things too? She can ask how his weekend was and how he did on the maths test. She can compliment his haircut. Maybe he'll slowly but surely switch his interest to her.

P.S. Even grown women sometimes get friends to find out what their crushes think of them. Some things never change!

QUIZ: HOW WELL DO YOU JUGGLE YOUR FRIENDS AND YOUR BOYFRIEND?

Is there room in your life for new love and old pals? Or do you think friendship and love are mutually exclusive? Take this quiz about a developing romance – and try your hand at juggling.

1. You and your best friend Allison are supposed to go skating Saturday afternoon. On Friday, Todd (the hunk of the class, the star of your dreams, the love of your life) calls and asks if you want to go to a Saturday movie matinee. (Want to? You'd pay for the privilege. You'd do Jane Fonda for 20 hours straight. You'd wash all the cars on your block.) You

(a) Accept without hesitation. Allison will understand why you have to cancel.

(b) Say you'd love to but you might have a conflict so you'd like to call him right back before saying yes. You'll ask Allison if she minds, reschedule your date and tell her you owe her one.

(c) Say, 'I'm sorry, but I have plans. I'd love to another time.' You hope you won't secretly despise Allison for ruining your life.

2. You and Todd have now gone out three times and tonight you're at a big party where you both know lots of people. You
   (a) Mostly hang out in a corner with Todd.
   (b) Make a point of introducing him to your friends but also talk with them alone and meet some of Todd's friends.
   (c) Mostly hang out with your friends. You hope you and Todd will leave together, though.

3. For seven weeks you've been in seventh heaven. You and Todd have an open trusting relationship and you often go out both Friday and Saturday nights. This Friday, Joy is having a slumber party, and you're invited. Six of your favourite friends will be there. You say,
   (a) 'I think Todd and I are going out. Thanks for asking, though.' Todd might be mad if you aren't available.
   (b) 'Sounds fun! Let me call you back and get the details.' You call Todd right away, tell him you'd like to go to Joy's and suggest that he might want to plan a night with his family or out with the boys.
   (c) 'Count me in.' You're afraid that if you

220

don't go, your friends might say you're becoming stuck-up.

4. Todd and your close friend Holly often joke around together. You trust them both, but sometimes you can't help but feel a little jealous. You
  (a) Are beginning to resent Holly and are moving farther away from her – and towards Todd.
  (b) Feel lucky that two of your favourite people get along so well.
  (c) Hate what your romance is doing to your friendship, so you start pulling away from Todd.

5. Todd doesn't particularly like your friend Ariel, but you and she have been close since third grade. You
  (a) Stop seeing Ariel.
  (b) Get together with Ariel at lunchtime or when Todd is not around.
  (c) Keep going out of your way to get them to like each other.

6. Whenever a guy kissed you in the past, you told Allison all about it – what he said, where it happened, whether you Frenched, the whole bit. You and Todd have occasionally gone a bit

221

beyond kissing, and you

- (a) No longer talk about such personal things with Allison.
- (b) Tell Allison that you've done more than kiss but are vague about how much more.
- (c) Give Allison the play by play, detail by detail.

7. When you talk with your friends on the phone, you usually

- (a) Go on and on about Todd.
- (b) Chat about your romance, your school-work, a new hit song, and say, 'What have you been up to?'
- (c) Don't mention Todd unless a friend asks about him.

8. If Allison found out she flunked history and swore you to secrecy, and Todd told you that his mother got fired, but begged you not to tell, you would

- (a) Tell Todd about Allison's grade. She knows you can't keep anything from him.
- (b) Almost spill the beans to both Todd and Allison – but succeed in keeping your lips sealed.
- (c) Tell Allison about Todd's mother. You two share all your secrets.

9. It's been four blissful months since your first date. You and Allison are supposed to spend Saturday afternoon getting your hair cut and shopping. Todd calls to invite you to a movie. You say

(a) 'What time?' then call Allison to apologize and rearrange your plans.

(b) 'Allison and I are going out today. How about Sunday?'

(c) 'I can't. Allison and I have plans.'

Scoring

Mostly **a**'s: Your boyfriend is your number one priority. You're constantly with him (or thinking about him) and he has become your closest confidante. Nothing really wrong with that – except that it can be hard on your old friends to always have to take a backseat to your new guy. It's good to be an attentive girl friend, but don't let it be at the expense of being an attentive friend of the girls.

Mostly **b**'s: You're a judicious juggler. You put a lot of effort into your relationships (romantic and otherwise) and you get a lot in return. You know that there's nothing either/or about romance and friendship, and you are able

223

to strike a good balance between them. Your social life is rich and rewarding.

Mostly **c**'s: You are a faithful friend. You're not the type to become totally wrapped up in a boyfriend, stick to him like Superglue, neglect lifelong pals – and then wonder why friends are scarce when the romance ends. It's commendable that you don't go all to pieces when a guy strides into your life. But don't be such a conscientious chum that you end up being insensitive to your boyfriend or resenting the girls because of the 'romantic sacrifices' you're making for them.

YOUR BOYFRIEND AND YOUR BEST FRIEND

When my best friend and next-door neighbour Judy started going out with her first serious boyfriend, I stopped running over to her house at all hours of the day or night. It's not that Judy made me less welcome. It's just that I didn't want to interrupt anything. I suppose I imagined that they were always in some sort of profound conversation or Do Not Disturb tangle.

Later when Judy and that boyfriend broke up,

and I fell in love, it was Judy who hesitated to call or drop by when she thought my boyfriend might be over. Her sudden aloofness baffled and hurt me – even though I, with the best of intentions, had backed off from her in the very same way.

There's room in your life for friends and boyfriends. If your best friend has a new boyfriend, you don't have to do a disappearing act. If you're the one with the new romance, you can (and should) go the extra mile to make sure your friends know you still have a place in your heart for them. Even if you two aren't spending quite as much time together as you used to, you can make the time count.

Granted, some flimsy friendships may bite the dust when a boyfriend enters the picture. If the main thing you and your best friend have in common was your so-called desperation, and if your conversations centred on which cute guy you liked and how he'd never ever in a million trillion years like you back, and then, abracadabra, one of you gets a guy, yes, that friendship could crumble.

But most friendships run deeper than that. Romance is heady stuff, but sometimes it's like fireworks – thrilling and short lived. It's not worth it to ruin a friendship that could last a lifetime for a courtship that lasts five days or even five weeks. Enjoy romance for all it's worth. But take care of your friendships, too, okay?

Here are some questions and answers about common conflicts.

Dear Carol,

Whenever I have a boyfriend, my best friend stops spending time with me. She says she doesn't want to interfere. I can see that. But she stops talking to me completely. I don't think this is fair. It's not like I'm ignoring her. I still try to be there for her. Once before when this happened, I broke up with my boyfriend for her and everything was back to normal. But now that I have a new boyfriend, I'm not going to give him up. How can I keep my best friend without losing my boyfriend?

Doesn't Want to Choose

Dear Doesn't,

Your friend isn't playing fair – you shouldn't have to choose. Reassure her that you care about her as much as ever and invite her to do things with you alone. If she asks for more, she's asking too much. If you drop your new guy for her, you'll resent her, and what good will that do?

226

Dear Carol,

My best friend and I are in a big misunderstanding. Four weeks ago, she started dating this guy named Roger, and ever since we haven't talked or anything. She tried calling me at first, but I didn't know she called. I call her and leave her notes, but – nothing! It's like we were never best friends. I'm not asking her to leave her boyfriend but to be my friend too.

Minus a Friend

Dear Minus,

It's a shame your friend doesn't realize she can be close to you and Roger. You might want to write her another note saying that you miss her and are really happy that things are going well for her and would love to get together with her. Don't be vague; be specific. Ask her to go shopping Saturday afternoon at 3:00. If she doesn't respond at all, she's not only being silly, she's being rude. Meantime, spend time with other girls. I hope you and your friend will some day be close again. If not, it's her loss. She will be minus a mature and sensitive friend.

Dear Carol,

I like this boy Guy. We were going together but we broke up because he is my best friend Michelle's boyfriend and I knew it was wrong. Michelle and I had promised each other that we'd tell each other everything. I don't know how to tell her this – but if I don't, he will. It might ruin our friendship.

Toni the Troubled Teen

Dear TTT,

Yes, it might. You shouldn't have seen Guy on the sly. In winning his attention, you may have lost a friend. Now what? You could write Michelle a note that says something like, 'Our friendship is really important to me. I did something wrong and I ended it and I hope you can forgive me. I was jealous of you and Guy, and I went out with him for a short while, but it's over. We both care more about you than we do about each other and I'm really really sorry I betrayed you.' Forgiveness is not guaranteed, but it's worth a try. If she yells or cries? Apologize again rather than lamely defending yourself or screaming, 'It was Guy's fault too.'

Dear Carol,

A boy named Gerard and I dated for 10½ months and broke up 13 months ago. When we were going out, we got real close, became best friends and were together every day. We never went out with our friends. We didn't want to. We were both overprotective and jealous of each other. We got along real well, but had our fights as all couples do. One day, we got in a fight and broke up. He told me he loved me a lot but wanted to date around and that some day we might get · back together. He cried very hard while saying this. It was awful. I cried; he cried.

We talked for about a week after we broke up, and then he started dating my best friend. She is no longer my best friend. How could she have done that to me? She knew how much I loved him! I wrote him a personal letter and he read it to her. Why would he do that? She told him not to talk to me or she would break up with him, so we haven't talked in 11 months! How can you not talk to a person who was a part of your life for so long?

Gerard and his new girl friend have been going out for 13 months. They argue and fight and she's cheated on him twice, but he doesn't know. I think she won't break up with him because she's scared he and I will get back together.

He was my first love and I do want him back. Every day I look at pictures of him and me. And I read his letters. I'm doing terribly in school because I sit in class daydreaming about him. I see him in the hall and get depressed. I cry at nights. Next year, we're going to the same college. (We're seniors. His girl friend is a junior.) I've tried to forget him but I can't. Can you really love someone forever?

Lost in Love

Dear Lost,

You can love someone forever, but if he doesn't love you back, it's a dumb way to spend your life. In college, you and your ex may pick up your old friendship, but more important, you will meet many wonderful new guys. For now, STOP daydreaming in class, STOP looking at his photos, STOP crying at night, and START getting on with your life. It doesn't make sense to spend more time pining over a guy than you did going out with him.

I'm sorry your friend moved in on Gerard and that she's now being possessive and unreasonable. That stinks. But I'm

*also sorry you and he let your friendships
slide when you were seeing each other.
That was a mistake.*

*I don't mean to be hard on you. Falling
out of love is difficult and it takes a long
time to get over a first love. But you can
do it. If you find you just aren't getting
over him, consider talking to a counsellor.*

This last letter is from a mother whose daughter lost her best friend and boyfriend in one fell swoop.

Dear Carol,

*I am a 51-year-old mother who has
had four decades of teenage girls and
their problems. Myself in the 50s, a foster
daughter in the 60s, my oldest daughter
in the 70s and my youngest, Cassie, in the
80s.*

I read Cassie's copy of Girltalk *and I
wanted to ask you whether it is ethically
or socially acceptable for your best friend
to immediately begin to go with your ex-
boyfriend.*

*Cassie was 16 when she started going
with Grant. It became a very close and
loving relationship that lasted about seven
months. When problems started, they both*

wanted to stay together but after off-again, on-again attempts, they broke up.

Cassie's best friend, Anne, was supportive and helpful to her and to Grant (who was supposedly taking it very hard). Cassie dated other guys (not enthusiastically), made new boy 'friends', and continued to trust and confide in Anne.

Need I spell out what happened? Anne and Grant fell for each other and were dating secretly for a long time before Cassie figured it out. Then the girls had a tearful scene: Cassie called Anne a sneaky backstabbing bitch; Anne called Cassie immature and selfish.

Anne and Grant are still together and Cassie is devastated, humiliated, and very depressed. Her friends are not on her side. They seem to feel she has no right to be angry. Since they had broken up, they think Grant was 'fair game' for any girl, even her best friend.

Do you feel there should be loyalty between girl friends and that a friend should resist temptation? Even after all these years I still wonder about right and wrong. Thanks for listening – it was good to get it off my chest!

Erica

Cassie is lucky to have such a caring mother – and unlucky that Anne was simultaneously being confidante and creep, friend and fiend. I believe there are unwritten rules about loyalty among best friends. But many say rules are made to be broken and it's a dirty world out there.

If you feel tempted by your best friend's new ex, try to resist it. At the very least, wait a while before pouncing. In a few cases, dating your best friend's ex works out well. More often, it means jeopardizing your friendship and self-respect and ultimately losing more than you gain.

BOYS AS BUDDIES

Do you have any male friends who really are just friends? Having boy buddies can make you more comfortable with guys in general and can help you better understand the male mind. If you have boy friends (or brothers), you already know, for instance that:

- Boys, like girls, get embarrassed around their crushes.
- Boys, unlike girls, think burping contests are amusing.
- Boys, like girls, think everyone else is more

experienced than they are.

- Boys, unlike girls, think they're supposed to be born knowing how to take apart – and reassemble – cars and toilets.
- Boys, like girls, worry about pimples.
- Boys, unlike girls, aren't sure whether they're supposed to be macho or sensitive.
- Boys, like girls, are only human.

Platonic relationships can be more relaxing than romantic ones. If you and your pal Norm are out on a bike ride, you probably aren't worrying about how you look when you sweat, what to do if there's a two-minute silence, whether he'll think you're unfeminine if you race him and win. There's no reason to be so overly self-conscious with a crush either, but hey, who are we kidding? If you've flipped over someone, at first you may be as concerned about making a good impression as you are about just having fun.

Are You One of the Boys?

If you like being one of the guys, no problem. Any girl who kids you about being a tomboy is probably envious of your easygoing relationship with members of the opposite sex. While she may be sitting home hoping Arthur will call, you can just give Artie a buzz and make plans without thinking twice. Male friendships are fun in their own right and they teach you what makes boys tick and what boys like to talk about: sports, cars, sports, movies, sports, music, sports. . . .

Have you ever felt like a freak because you're not boy-crazy? Romance is not on a timetable, and you may be in college or at work when you first meet a fellow who takes your breath away.

Are You Falling for a Friend?

Suppose you and Norm always have a great time biking, watching late-night movies, making tuna sandwiches and joking at the bus stop. Now suppose you suddenly catch yourself looking at him dreamily and hoping for flowers and sweet nothings. You may be setting yourself up for disappointment. If your friendship doesn't change, you could feel foolish and frustrated. And if instead of turning into a romance, it just turns sour, that's even worse.

What can you do if you can't squelch your crush? You can ignore it and hope it fades away. (It probably will.) You can flirt discreetly and dress more femininely. (He may or may not notice.) You can throw caution to the wind and flirt openly or even admit that you like him.

(Might he have a hush-hush crush on you?) Or, if you think the romance doesn't stand a chance, you can order yourself to "Stop this nonsense," and if necessary, avoid one-on-one get-togethers for a week or two.

Time for true confessions. I really did have a neighbour, Norm, and sometimes when we were together, I did feel more affectionate than friendly. Anyway, I'm glad I never forced the issue because today Norm (a father and businessman) is still a good friend. If we'd had a quick fling, he might not be. After all, he doesn't keep up with his prom date, and I haven't seen my high school boyfriend in years.

You can't make a friendship get mushy. You can consider yourself very lucky if you have a caring circle of true-blue friends – male and female.

Is He Falling for You?

The situation is equally delicate if tables turn. What if you are sketching, fishing or playing cards with your pal Tyler and all of a sudden you notice Ty giving you the eye? If you've always hoped this would happen, three cheers. If not, tread lightly.

Assuming you don't want to be tender with

Ty, you can either ignore or acknowledge his change of heart. If you pretend not to notice his new feelings and offer no encouragement, he may return to his old self in no time. Do you two ever discuss your love lives? You could mention how your crush on Fritz is going – Ty, sigh, may get the message.

You favour the direct approach? Fine, but be gentle. Saying, 'You know how much I care about you, but I don't want our friendship to change' will go over better than 'Look, I'm not interested.' Don't schedule long talks to discuss the predicament. And don't round up your friends and wail, 'Tyler is madly in love with me and I don't know what to do!' If you can let Ty know where you stand without unnecessarily hurting his feelings, your friendship can survive – and thrive.

When Friends Become Sweethearts

Once in a while, two close friends will be simultaneously struck by Cupid's arrow. Romances that begin as friendship are wonderful because the couple hasn't been merely worshipping each other from afar but has already discovered how much they have in common and how much they enjoy each other's company. Don't look at all your close boy buddies as potential dates, but do be aware that warm friendships can sometimes wax romantic.

When Exes Become Friends

It's difficult to salvage a friendship with someone who once made your pulse race. If you gave him his walking papers, he may not want to be your chum. And if you're still half in love with him, you may not want to hear him talk about superficial subjects or, worse, another girl.

·If you both want to remain close and if you are both able to weather the painful transition period, maybe you can beat the odds and become good friends. I hope so. I hope you can go your separate ways but still be a part of each other's lives. It's a challenge.

I'm no longer close to my high school boyfriend or my Spanish beau Juan – both of whom I went out with for over three years. But I'm glad that at least a few of my other boyfriends are still my boy friends.

BOYFRIEND, BOY FRIEND:
THE BOUNDARIES
SOMETIMES BLUR

A couple of months ago, a boy seemed to like me. He would shout hi to me and walk down the hall with me. He tried to start conversations, but I didn't know what to say. A few weeks later, he found out I liked him. He said he liked me as a friend. I also found out that he was going steady with someone the whole time. I felt like he just led me on to hurt my feelings. I felt he treated me like a nothing.

He didn't treat you like a nothing. He treated you like a friend. He wasn't being nasty. He was being nice. There's no crime in saying hi to someone whom you don't have a crush on. There's no harm in starting a conversation with someone you'd simply like to know better. The boy was offering his friendship, not his love, but friendship is also a valuable gift, and she needn't feel so cheated.

Last summer I asked a boy to go to the movies with a group of girls (I didn't want him to think it was a date) and we had fun. But during this entire school year, he has treated me like an acquaintance, nothing more. I feel hurt. Sometimes he talks to me outside of school, so I can't tell if he wants to be friends. That's all I want to be, friends. I know it sounds like I like him more than a friend, but I don't. It's weird, I want his friendship so bad, I think about it all the time. I wish I could stop wanting to be friends. One thing is for sure, though. I don't like him more than a friend (I like someone else that way). I know I keep saying that, but I want to make it clear.

It's clear, all right. So how come I don't believe it? And how come she won't recognize that she'd love to go out with the guy? Maybe she'll have the chance. Maybe she won't. But it doesn't really help to deny your own feelings.

Here's another letter from a girl who is kidding herself about the fine line between friendship and romance.

I'm a sophomore in college. Two months ago I got a computerized list of my Top Ten Compatible Mates on campus. Cameron was No.1 on my list; I was No.5 on his. I found out he has a girlfriend at home.

Cam started asking me to come to intramural ball games and to watch late-night TV with him. We started getting together almost every night, and although I wanted to keep it like brother and sister (because of his girl friend), he started being more physical – tickling me and having me sit on his lap and stuff.

Three nights ago, he started tickling me and we were rolling all over the floor. Then he kissed me for about fifteen minutes. I didn't stop him.

All of a sudden he stopped. He was really upset, but we talked about it for about an hour. I thought that showed what good friends we are. He said he loved his girl friend and was using me as a replacement for her. I didn't mind because he was replacing my brother for me (at least I was trying to convince myself of that). We assured each other that we'd still be friends.

But last night he asked me over to play cards and started tickling me again. I had vowed I wouldn't let anything happen, so I left.

I don't want to lose him as a friend

or to break up him and his girl friend.
Do you have any suggestions?

Cam isn't a stand-in brother. He's a sit-on crush. She doesn't like him as a friend. She likes him as a boyfriend. And I suspect she'd do cartwheels if he and his hometown honey were to split up. So enough game playing! Cam and she should talk about how they feel about each other. If it's okay with everybody, he can go out with her when he's at college and with his girlfriend when he's at home. If that's not okay – if he wants to be faithful or she doesn't want to share him – then he should stop staging midnight tickle fests, they should cool down their friendship and she should look elsewhere for romance.

> *I'm in a bind. I'm 15; Eddy is 17. We've developed a good friendship where we can talk about everything: sex, parents, religion, fantasies. But lately we'll be talking and a silence will pop up and swallow us. We both find each other attractive, but I know his girl friend and I don't want to hurt her.*
> *When Eddy visited me at work yesterday, the awful silence came over us, and he bent over and kissed me. It was like I was waiting for it to happen.*

> *I think about him, but in my heart,*
> *I only want him as a buddy. I just hope*
> *this whole thing doesn't ruin our friend-*
> *ship. Help!*

This girl has to ask herself what she really wants from Eddy. A platonic friendship? A flirtatious friendship? (Would that be fair to him?) A love affair? Since they talk so openly, it's time they talk about their relationship. Even if she's guilty of having led him on a little, she is not obliged to follow up with a romance she doesn't want. If she truly wants to cool things, she should cut down on the conversations or conduct them over the phone for a while.

> *I slept over at my friend's house in a*
> *tent in her backyard. Our friends Kirk*
> *and Bernie came over around 1:00 a.m*
> *and slept in a tent too. Kirk was trying*
> *to make out with me. How do I find out*
> *if I like him that much?*

Does she like him as a friend or a boyfriend? If you resist a guy's kiss, it could mean either that kissing makes you nervous (which is perfectly natural) or that you don't really feel drawn to the kisser (which is perfectly legitimate). It's better to take your time than to try to talk yourself into an instant romance. Besides, many guys do just want to fool around and aren't prepared to follow up with a relationship.

> *I have a friend in my bio class named Scott. He's 16 and enjoys drinking, etc. He's been going to a drug counsellor. He's just the type of person I shouldn't be around because I don't do any of that.*
> *I just about convinced myself that I could do better, but this week I find I'm letting him hold my hand, etc., and I know he's got a lot more on his mind. He tells me he's very attracted to me. I'm attracted to him and want to have a relationship with him, but at the same time, I don't want to be seen with him. He keeps trying to kiss me in the halls and I hate backing away – I can see the disappointment in his face – but I don't want anyone to know we're sort of together. I don't want to call him because I don't want to push anything that I might not want later. My brother says I shouldn't hang around with people with drug problems because people will think I'm a druggie too.*

Never mind what people think, she should be careful for her own sake. I hope she knows

244

that she can always say no to alcohol and drugs – without apologies or sermons.

Having a guy gaze at you is flattering and playing with fire can seem exciting, but if a girl is embarrassed to be seen with a boy, that should tell her something. She should delicately tell him – and herself – that she wants to be his friend, not his girl friend. (Girls should be especially cautious about getting sexually involved with intravenous drug users since they are at risk of contracting AIDS. See chapter 7 where I'll talk about AIDS.)

> *There's this nerd, Terry, who keeps following me around and telling me how pretty I am. He comes up to me in the hall and puts his arm around me. He's so ugly and so gross. I don't want to hurt his feelings but I don't know how to get him to leave me alone.*

If the King of the Nerds ever comes after you, give him a chance, he may be a prince of a guy. If not, let him down gently. Thank him for the compliment but let him know you're not interested in flirting with him.

Never be cruel. You'd hate it if a guy you liked were mean to you, so go easy on the male ego. What if your pursuer doesn't catch on that you never smile at him, look at him or talk to him? If you say you have plans on Saturday, and he asks you out for the next five weekends, say, 'I'm sorry, and I hope you understand, but I really don't want our friendship to change.' Say this even if your friendship hardly merits the name.

> *What is wrong with me? I liked this boy in summer school, and we started looking at each other a lot. Whenever the teacher told him to take something to the office, he would always ask me to come with him. I figured he must like me too. So I wrote him a note and told him that I liked him. He wrote back saying that he liked me too but hadn't wanted to say anything in case I didn't like him back. So now we like each other. But the minute I found out he liked me, I didn't like him as much. Is it because I'm confused or scared or what? We are now going together but I don't know what to do.*

Hmmm. It could be that she really wasn't ready to have a boyfriend and was content with just having a crush. (That's fine.) It could be that she's getting to know him, she realizes she'd rather be his friend than his girl friend. (That's fine too.)

Or it could be that she likes liking a guy more than getting him – chasing him more than catching him. If this is the case, or if she stopped liking him because she concluded, 'If he likes me, he must not be so great after all,' then she needs to work on bolstering her self-esteem. Groucho Marx once said, 'I don't want to belong to any club that will accept me as a member' – but he was kidding!

When two people declare that they like each other, it doesn't make them automatically under- stand each other that much better or find each other's jokes that much funnier or empathize with each other's troubles that much more deep- ly. There's no rush to be a guy's girl friend if you are happy being his friend, because while love is wonderful, it takes work and doesn't always last. And when love ends, it hurts an awful lot. Matter of fact, breaking up is so hard to do that I wrote an entire chapter about it.

5

Breaking up

Last night Rob went out to buy some asparagus and wild rice for a dinner party. He came back in a·daze. 'I ran into Maggie,' he said, then checked himself in the mirror. 'Did I look okay?'

'Very handsome,' I assured him, glad that he always wears his wedding ring.

'She's engaged.'

'Well, that's good news.'

'I can't believe I ran into Maggie. The last time I saw her was seven years ago. I really liked her. She played the piano. She wrote great letters. I even liked her parents.' Rob stared into space. 'You know, we never really officially broke up.'

'I'm sure she caught on when you got married.'

'She looked great.'

'And engaged, right?'

'I'm really happy for her.'

'Me too. Did you get the vegetables?'

'Yeah,' said Rob. 'And some lilies. Bringing flowers to my wife suddenly seemed like the thing to do.'

'What a guy.' I laughed. 'Where are they?'

'They're not here?' Rob checked the shopping bags. 'They're really not here? Could I have left them at the grocer's?'

'I wouldn't put it past you. Listen, why don't you go back and get them? They need water and you need air.'

'I can't believe I ran into Maggie,' Rob said and headed for the door.

When it comes to caring about someone you once loved, Rob and I are the same. When it comes to breaking up, we are as different as can be.

Rob and his high school girl friend split without a word some time during his freshman year of college. And Rob and his college girl friend Maggie parted ways quietly some time during his junior year abroad – when he met me. Both breakups were silent and subtle.

My breakups have always been loud and clear, painful and drawn-out, maudlin and messy. My high school boyfriend and I broke up and got back together and broke up and got back together a number of times before the curtain finally fell. And Juan? We met when I was 18 and said adios when I was 22. Those last months were a killer:

we talked endlessly about our relationship, and I went through boxes and boxes of Kleenex.

If you were to do a scientific breakdown of breakups, you would probably find that they come in as many varieties as snowflakes – though they certainly aren't as pretty. There are invisible breakups, over-and-over breakups, long-winded breakups, shortsighted breakups, no-big-deal breakups, end-of-the-world breakups. . . .

'The magic of first love is our ignorance that it can ever end,' said Benjamin Disraeli.

But not every relationship is supposed to last a lifetime. And you may enjoy many romances – and survive many breakups – before you settle down for keeps.

They say misery loves company. If you and your boyfriend are about to set each other free, or if you're having a hard time bouncing back after a breakup, this chapter has your name on it.

SHOULD YOU BREAK UP WITH HIM?

Has your relationship gone down the tubes? Are you growing in different directions? Have you met another guy? Don't throw away a satisfying romance that happens to be going through a stormy period, but don't hang on if it's time to move on.

> *I have a semi-problem. I've been going out with this guy for almost three months. Now I don't know. I'm not trying to be mean, but I'm kind of getting tired of him. I haven't felt like talking to him in a few days. Most of the time I've been busy (really!) but I may be busy all summer. Help! I'm afraid if I tell him, he'll hate me forever. Maybe I'm too young to go with anyone – that's what my mum would say!*

If you spend ten months chasing Chester and finally snag him, it will come as a rude surprise if he turns out to be a snooze. Are you stuck with him in joy and in sorrow, for richer and for poorer, in sickness and in health, as long as you both shall live?

No.

If Chester's parents just announced that they are getting a divorce or if Chester's doctor just informed him that he's seriously ill, you might want to hold off a little before pulling the carpet from under him. It's also not sporting to end the relationship right before his big game/test/interview or when he picks you up on prom night. But don't stay trapped in an unhappy situation. It does no good to prolong a dead-end romance.

> My problem is that I want to break up with the guy I'm going with because he is very boring at times. But I'm not sure how to do it. Got any suggestions?

Who, me? The Suggestion Queen? You better believe it.

If you want to break the news about breaking up, and you're chicken, you can stop taking his phone calls and avoid him in school. He'll get the message that the honeymoon is over, and in a few cases, the easy way out actually beats confrontation. If your romance had barely gotten off the ground, for instance, it might be presumptuous of you to assassinate his character or rattle on about the impossibility of your future together.

But in most cases, you'll owe it to, say, John to be direct and gentle. And I don't mean you should directly and gently tell his best friend to pass the word that as a couple, you two are kaput.

Should you tell John he is a crashing bore? No. Tell him you think you are too young to be serious about anybody right now. Or tell him you'll always remember the good times, but you think you should each be free to see other people.

Or tell him you feel you are growing apart, but that you'd like to stay friends.

John may be none too pleased about all this. And it may be easier on you both if you write him a note instead of having it out face to face. Your Dear John letter might read something like: 'I've really enjoyed going out with you, but I think we should stop seeing each other right now. I'm just not ready yet to be so serious about anybody. I hope you understand and I hope we can still be friends.' Be kind but don't give him false expectations. Don't say you need time alone if what you need is a lifetime without him. If you want to try a temporary breakup, make that clear. (Watch out, though. Temporary breakups often end up permanent but leave everybody with false hopes.)

Breakups hurt even when handled with care. But if you proceed with tact and sensitivity, you needn't feel guilty for the rest of your days. You are entitled to change your mind about a guy after you've gotten to know him (even if he is your parents' dream son-in-law). And you are allowed to pursue other interests (even if they are of the male persuasion). Your boyfriend-turned-ex will be upset just as you'd be upset if a guy you liked told you to take a hike. But those are the breaks – and breakups. If your relationship has run its course, then let each other go. If your twosome is tiresome, don't string him along. Breaking up could be that much harder later on.

I've been going out with Larry for almost two months. He is a freshman in another school. Two weeks ago Larry and I had a misunderstanding and for a week he insulted my school and me. I was upset and talked to Don, his best friend and neighbour. Sometimes Don would call me and sometimes I'd call him. That weekend Don's girl friend broke up with him and he called me to comfort him.

I asked him if he liked any other girls, and he admitted that he liked me. He then asked me if I liked anyone else, and I told him that I liked him.

Last night Larry sounded so depressed. He said that even if we break up, he doesn't want Don to have me. I really like Don, but I feel sorry for Larry.

Feeling sorry for Larry is no reason to keep going out with him. Sure it will be tough on Larry if his best friend and his ex become an item, but it's not for Larry to choose her next boyfriend. She may want to talk to Larry before giving him the axe. She may also want to take a breather before telling Don she is available. No one says she has to have a boyfriend every second.

*I've been going steady with Allen for
about five months. Lately we've been
arguing about trivial things. Two weeks
ago, I met a really nice guy, Paul, over the
phone and we've been talking and writing.
He's from out of town. He wants to go out
with me, but I don't know if sacrificing my
relationship with Allen is worth it. Do you
think it would be low of me to tell Allen
that I want to see other guys too? I know
he'd be upset and would probably say that
I was just keeping him around because he
lives in town whereas Paul lives an hour
away. But I do care for Allen – just not
as much as I used to. I'm starting to feel
tied down and am tired of his getting disappointed at me for everything I do.*

Do I think honesty is always the best policy?
Well . . . It's often best to speak the truth, the
whole truth and nothing but the truth. But in
matters of the heart, proceed with caution. The
truth can be more than some guys want to hear.
Maybe it's low of me to suggest that she play it
safe by not speaking too soon, but if she thinks
her relationship with Allen is worth saving, she
should talk to Allen about it and perhaps have one
friendly outing with Paul (shhh) before making
any out-loud decisions.

Did I write that? Shame on me! The thing is, I'm not so sure she'll even like Paul in person. And she should realize that while a long-lived relationship can't offer the thrill of first-time flirting, Allen, not Paul, might be there for her in a crisis. Should she and Allen try patching things up instead of breaking up? Yes? No? Her decision should not depend on whether she has a replacement boyfriend waiting in the wings.

I'm going out with this guy, Randy. But this other guy, Doug, asked me out. I found I could really talk to him on the phone, so I told him I was going to break up with Randy to go out with him. He said okay, so I did. But the next day his friend called and said Doug doesn't want to go out with me after all. I nearly flipped! I'm so mad. I can't ask Randy to go back out with me because I'm afraid he'll say no.

See what can happen when you speak too soon? If I were Randy I might not take her back either. Of course, they must not have had much of a relationship if she was in such a hurry to dump him. Next time she should take 10 before rushing in and out of romance. For the moment, a little time on her own may be just what the doctor ordered.

My boyfriend is a senior in another school and is in the band there. I am a junior in the band here. My problem is that I kinda like this other guy in the band in my school. Recently our band went on an out-of-town parade and the other guy and I sat together and talked during the two-and-a-half hour bus ride back. I'm afraid to say anything to my boyfriend because he always says that if I break up with him, he'll never find anyone else. He's been telling his friends (who tell my friends) that we're engaged and that he bought me a ring. It's true about the ring, but it was a birthday present, not an engagement present.

As long as she and Guy No.2 are just talking, I wouldn't alarm Guy No.1. The question is: is their romance about to go belly up anyway? If so, I bet he will some day find someone else. (And if not, that's his problem, not hers.) Sometimes it's legitimate to have your 'eyes open' while going out with someone. But again, beware of comparing the madcap excitement of flirting with the low-key contentment of dating. The ring? If it was a big fat diamond, she probably should have said, 'I can't accept this.' But assuming it wasn't presented as an engagement ring, she did nothing wrong. Frankly, I doubt she'll end up married to either of the boys in the band.

Some girls break up (or should break up) with their boyfriends not because they are bored by them or because they're attracted to someone else, but because their boyfriends are trouble or are abusive.

> *I found out that the guy I like takes drugs (all kinds) and lies a lot. When I call him, he is either waiting for someone to call or sleeping. I lent him money because he said he needed it badly. I know he'll never pay me back and he keeps asking for more. Whenever I say no, he says, 'You don't love me,' so I do what he asks. I don't like doing it, but I don't want to lose him. One more thing – he barely ever talks to me in school. I know he likes me but what can I do?*

He takes drugs, lies, won't talk to her in school or out and borrows money with no intention of returning it. And she doesn't want to lose him. Here's my question: why not? She should stop lending him money and stop shortchanging herself. He may have somehow convinced her that she is small and powerless without him, but she must rebuild her self-esteem (with the help of friends, family and possibly counselling) so that she can begin to recognize that she deserves better, much better.

I'll talk about AIDS in Chapter 7, but having sex with a drug user (who at some point may have contracted AIDS from sharing a contaminated needle) can be dangerous, even deadly.

> *My boyfriend is 14 and drinks. We've been going out for six months. A month ago his friends had a party and most of them, including my boyfriend, got real drunk. After that he said he wouldn't drink. Last night he had a party. I went to take a sip of his Coke and it had Jack Daniel's in it. I know he drinks but won't admit it. Should I talk to him? Should I break up?*

Many teenagers experiment with drinking. That in no way excuses this boy's behaviour, but I wouldn't necessarily say he's on the road to alcoholism. He may be one more boy trying to be cool and succumbing to peer pressure. It would be a terrible shame if he did become addicted to alcohol, and habits are acquired early. If he can't cut back, he should go to Alcoholics Anonymous for strength and support. If his parents are problem drinkers (children of alcoholics are more vulnerable to the disease), he might want to go to Al-Anon. See the *Information* section at the back of this book.

The girl friend may want to encourage (not nag) him to shape up rather than immediately canning the relationship. She should also give herself a round of applause for not drinking. And she should ask herself if he has a drinking problem. Does he drink in school or on school nights? Can he drink friends under the table? Is he unable to stop before getting drunk? Is he becoming dependent on alcohol? She should also ask herself if she cares enough about him to put up with behaviour she understandably disapproves of.

> *I am eighteen. When I was younger, I dated a guy for two and a half years. I grew so tired of him but didn't know how to leave him. I don't like to hurt anyone. Eventually he started hitting me and once my parents had to rush me to the hospital. He'd pulled me into his car and rammed my head against the steering wheel.*

If she doesn't want to hurt her boyfriend, but he is willing to hurt her, her diplomacy is misplaced and it's time to make a quick exit. A physically abusive guy might slap or shove his girl friend. A verbally or emotionally abusive guy might tell her she is worthless and could never make it without him. Getting hit, put down or mistreated is not a sign of love. While there are many good reasons to consider ending a relationship, abuse tops the list. And abuse is all too common.

If your boyfriend hits or hurts you, find the nearest door and leave – without looking back. If you're afraid to leave him, talk to a parent or trusted adult or call a centre for battered women for help. See the *Information* section at the back of this book for addresses.

QUIZ: IS YOUR ROMANCE ON ITS LAST LEGS?

Do you two enjoy each other's company more than ever: Or is change in the air?

1. When the phone rings, you
(a) Hope it's not your boyfriend.
(b) Hope it is your boyfriend.
(c) Don't even wonder if it's your boyfriend – he never calls.

2. When you phone your boyfriend,

(a) He's usually too busy to talk.

(b) You chat for a while.

(c) Not applicable. You never call.

3. After the movie, he says, 'Let's get a burger.' You

(a) Would just as soon have gone straight home.

(b) Can't wait to hear what he thought of the ending.

(c) Know you're dreaming. You never go to movies together.

4. When you two kiss, you

(a) Usually think about his handsome brother, your maths homework or whether you remembered to feed the cat.

(b) Think of him him him him mmm mmm mmm mmm.

(c) Kiss? Hasn't happened yet!

5. If his father said something that upset him, you'd

(a) Try to stay awake as he told you about it.

(b) Feel terrible for your boyfriend and try to be supportive.

(c) Probably never know about it.

6. Your parents want to go skiing over spring vacation. You can't believe it! You

(a) Put off telling your boyfriend – he may be jealous or try to convince you to stick around town with him.

(b) Call him right up and let him in on the exciting news.

(c) Figure you'll send him a postcard, or one of your friends may mention it to one of his friends.

7. You and the male lead of the musical have to kiss in Act II. You

(a) Slip him your tongue.

(b) Tell your boyfriend it means nothing to you and pucker up out of duty, thinking, 'For God, for country, and for Covington High.'

(c) Kiss him, no prob – but it's the conductor you're really lusting after.

8. Have you two made any plans for this weekend?

(a) No, but he sometimes calls late Saturday evening.

(b) Yes, a party Saturday and a matinee on Sunday.

(c) No, but that's par for the course.

9. When he walks with you to school or in public, you
   (a) Feel sort of embarrassed.
   (c) Can't help smiling.
   (c) Wonder whether it was a coincidence that may never happen again.

10. If your boyfriend broke up with you, you'd
   (a) Be partly relieved and would recover fairly fast.
   (b) Be destroyed – but you hope it never happens!
   (c) Hardly notice.

Scoring

Only you can know if your relationship feels right, so take these answers with a sprinkling of salt.

Mostly *a*'s: Are you sure you *want* to go out with him?

Mostly *b*'s: Hurray! Your romance is in top shape.

Mostly *c*'s: Are you sure you *are* going out with him?

DID YOU BREAK UP –
OR DIDN'T YOU?

Girls who should break up with their boy-friends often don't. Many hang on to rotten or almost nonexistent relationships instead of declaring independence. Many let the guy make all the decisions. And many wait for a guy to announce that it's officially over when it should have been clear that the romance had long been rendered null and void. Guys get insecure too. Some boys break up verbally without actually breaking away; others break away without verbally breaking up. And some split-apart couples kiss one last time. Confusing? Almost always.

> *My boyfriend and I met in June. Now it's November and I don't know if we are still going out. I don't want to call him because I'm afraid I'll make a fool of myself. But I'm sick of waiting for him to call. Help!*

I hate being the bearer of bad news, but if they aren't talking, they aren't going out. And if she wastes one more minute of her youth waiting by the phone, *I* may call and give her an earful! This guy may have taken Invisible Breakup lessons from my husband, but that's still no reason for her to put her life on hold.

If she's determined to make contact, she could drop him a card. Nothing too mushy or tearful. Just, 'We haven't talked in a while, but I wanted to wish you a happy Thanksgiving.' (Or Halloween or St. Patrick's Day.) No response? At least she'll know it's really-and-truly beyond-the-shadow-of-a-doubt over. And if her note does rekindle the romance? Great. Maybe this time they can do a better job of keeping in touch.

> *I'm 12. There's this boy I'm really crazy about. He's 14. We've gone together for a few weeks, but he keeps breaking up with me. Actually, we've broken up nine times. What should I do?*

Read the writing on the wall. Accept the fact that they won't be pouring Grape-Nuts for each other in old age. And instead of collapsing with self-pity, realize that her school is crawling with other guys – not to mention friendly girls, challenging extracurrics, fun sports. Why hang in for round ten of an on-again-off-again romance when she can start focusing her energy elsewhere? How come he gets to call all the shots anyway?

He might have new respect for her – and she for herself – if she stops behaving like a yo-yo on his string.

> I'm 15. Last summer a guy and I fell in love – real love. It was perfect until I had to go away. I went to Scotland but we wrote letters. One night after I got back, I called and he hung up without saying he loved me. It hurt very much. The next day I asked what was wrong and he wouldn't say. Later I called and his sister said, 'Okay, Tamara, I'll have him call you.' The only thing wrong is that my name isn't Tamara! I saw them together the next day and I broke up with him. But I thought, 'It can't end like this.' I called and we agreed to be friends. A few months later he and Tamara started having problems. Then he wrote me a letter saying he still loved me. I couldn't believe it. Of course, I was still in love with him. So we went out and it was a wonderful night, but the next day I called and he admitted that he likes another girl. That blew my mind! I haven't called since then, but today I got a UPS package with a teddy bear in it from him. I still love him – I don't know why, but I do. What should I do? My friends don't understand

me so I can't talk to them.

I hope she didn't spend her whole vacation in bonny Scotland mooning over this two-timer. It was sweet of him to send her the teddy bear (assuming he sent it because he still cares and not just to get rid of his guilt). But I doubt they are going to get back together any time soon. Just as he has gone out with other girls, she needs to open her eyes to other guys. If they can continue to be friends, fine. But if that friendship keeps her from getting over him, the price is too high. And her own friends? Do they really not understand her? Or are they just sick of watching her play the fool? Now is a good time to work on those friendships – and to find out what's new in their lives.

> *Steve and I went out for three weeks. We're both 13. he broke up with me a few weeks ago and started going out with Denise, a 16-year-old. Today, he walked me home from school and said, 'I want to give you a kiss.' I died.*
>
> *'What about Denise?'*
> *'I don't care about Denise.'*
>
> *We kissed and had our arms around each other and I finally said good-bye. That was about an hour ago. I'm so con-*

fused. I would hate it if a girl kissed my boyfriend. But if Steve wanted to kiss me again, I couldn't resist.

Must be some kisser, that Steve. I don't think she should torture herself over the forbidden embrace because it's not as if she were barging in on a two-year relationship. Steve is probably as confused as she is because everything is happening so fast: a three-week relationship, a breakup, another relationship, a stolen kiss. It takes time to sort things out. If I were her, I'd be friendly to Steve without being too forward and without getting my hopes too high.

My boyfriend and I have been going together for seven months. He dropped me over a year ago. A couple of months ago, I was baby-sitting and he was at the park across the street. I told the kids about him and they got all immature and ran over to get him. They let him in. (The parents weren't going to be back until 1:00 a.m.) He started giving me his sweet smile as he did when we were so in love. I had the chills just knowing he was there. I remember how he used to say he'd never use a girl. Well, he and I started kissing just like old times – almost to the point

269

of going all the way. I love him so much. But when he left, there were two weeks of school left and he wouldn't talk to me, call me, say hi or even smile. It hurt and hurt. He told a friend that he has feelings for me but doesn't want to go out.

I'm enclosing a dollar with my self-addressed envelope. You deserve it for helping me.

Post-breakup passion is not uncommon, but since this cad is willing to make out but unwilling to make conversation, he gets low marks from me. I returned the dollar and sympathized as best I could (even though I'm not at all in favour of making out on the job).

The real trouble with one-year-later kissing is that if the relationship doesn't take off anew, the more vulnerable person can go through heartache and withdrawal all over again. Things may have been different in the past, but this guy doesn't deserve her love any more, and she needs to talk herself out of caring so much for someone who has done so little lately to earn her affection.

TEN THINGS NOT TO DO
AFTER A BREAKUP

1. Crank call his house at 3:00 a.m. He'll know it's you and you'll wake his parents.

2. Polish off a quart of ice cream. You want love, not love handles.

3. Rush into someone else's arms. Heal your heart before giving it away again.

4. Cry yourself to sleep more than three nights in a row. Must you add exhaustion and puffy eyes to your list of woes?

5. Bicycle past his house. So you can see her bicycle in his driveway?

6. Play 'your song' over and over. Silence your song and turn off the radio. Try jazz, classical music or something new and upbeat that has no sappy lyrics to trip you up.

7. Dwell on the good times. Remember the bad times too: the squabbles, the fights.

8. Pore over his photos. Zero in on the one where his eyes are closed and his hair is sticking out.

9. Pray he'll come crawling back. If you must entertain such thoughts, finish the fantasy: Picture yourself laughing and saying, 'You, my dear, are history. Now get off your knees and run along.'

10. Boycott showers and makeup and live in a sweatshirt. Dressing your best will boost your spirits, and if he bicycles past *your* house, why shouldn't *he* eat his heart out?

GETTING OVER HIM?

When a romance ends, it takes a long time to put down the torch and pick up your spirits. Even if you are staying busy, you may feel that you're still grieving inside. And that's okay. In fact, it's a tribute to your love and your ability to care deeply about someone. So don't let your life come to a standstill after a breakup, but do be patient with yourself if time goes by and you still get misty-eyed.

> *I just read Chapter 3 of Girltalk – the one about love – and I cried all the way through it. About three months ago, I broke up with my first real boyfriend, Wes, and I haven't had another since. I thought I was over him but I guess I was just locking my feelings away.*
>
> *Last night I went to a dance and he was there. It hurt so much to see him dancing with other girls. Even though I*

danced with other guys, I had the most miserable feeling inside me.

We used to have something really special, but we just grew farther and farther apart. I miss him so much. We never really said good-bye. One night when we went skating I knew it was almost over. But we never officially broke up. He just said he'd call me, and he didn't. That was the last time I saw him before last night. Do you think it could have been our age difference? He's 20 and I'm 16.

I try to do things to get him off my mind, but whenever I do, he comes creeping back into my thoughts. It's been three months now and I'm not over him at all. Will it ever get any better? My mum says, 'There will be other people,' but who is she kidding? It took me almost 17 years to get Wes.

I have lots of guys who are 'just friends' and friends are nice, but it frustrates me that my friends are all dating and having a good time when I'm not.

Do you have any advice? Even if you don't write back, it has made me feel better to let someone know how I'm feeling.

Will it ever get any better? Yes. She's probably

closer to getting over Wes than she thinks, but may be having a 'relapse'. When you see your old boyfriend for the first time since breaking up, your tear ducts are bound to swing into action. There he is, looking as handsome and sweet as ever, but now you're not supposed to run up and slip your hand into his! It's awful to feel timid with someone you used to feel close to. Some exes don't see each other again for years (like my husband and Maggie), but others have to run into each other every time they walk down the school halls or swim in the local pool.

Did the age difference contribute to this break-up? Probably. Whether Wes has a job or is in college, his worries are very different from hers. Sometimes couples drift apart not because of lack of love but simply because they don't quite fit into each other's future.

She's already as concerned with replacing Wes as with getting him back – which is realistic. She even seems to realize that she doesn't miss just Wes, she misses dating and feeling loved. Will it take seventeen more years for her to find another guy? Oh, please! What do you think?

> *I'm trying to get over my last boyfriend, Jay. I put away all the things that remind me of him and I'm trying to remember only the fun we had, none of the bad times.*

It's working. I'm no longer depressed over him. Yes, there are times when I miss him so much that it's almost unbearable, but I think that's part of my healing.

After liking Jay for the past seven months, I'm finding it hard to like anyone else. Also when Jay broke up with me, he said that he knew some day we'd get back together. We ended things because we fought too much. We fought because our 'friend' would tell him things I never said or vice versa and everything would get so confusing until finally it was over.

Since then, Jay and I have talked a few times about getting back together. But so far we haven't. Do you think I should continue to wait for him? Or should I go out with other guys?

Go out with other guys! Jay may have meant well by saying that he knows they'll wind up together, but that just makes things harder for her. She may be thinking, 'Why get over him if he might call any minute?'

Sure, it would be convenient for him if she's sitting by the phone if and when he decides to dial her number. But that's not fair to her. And what if he doesn't call? Or what if they go out again only to break up again?

Instead of being at his beck and call, she should live her life. By the time he calls, she may find that she's outgrown him and is happy on her own or is involved with someone else.

There's a chance they'll walk into the sunset together. But the odds are against it. Was it really gossip that broke them up? Or were there other problems? While she's enjoying good memories, she can think about the bad times too. It will help her get over him.

> *In June my boyfriend and I had a big fight. It really bothered me because my fourteenth birthday came and he didn't call, come over, talk to me or anything.*
>
> *We finally made up. When school ended, he said he was going to Canada, but two days later he said he was already back. I had an urge to tell him I loved him but didn't get it out.*
>
> *I've written three times and called. One day I called and a recording said the number was disconnected. I haven't been the same since. I really love him – I always will. How will I get over him?*
>
> *My friends don't understand. They look up to me with their problems and don't realize I have problems too.*

She will get over him by deciding that enough is enough and that lines like 'I really love him – I always will' work best in romances. Why surrender your heart to a guy who lies and doesn't acknowledge birthdays, answer letters or return phone calls? If she and he had three kids and a twenty year marriage in common, I might understand her putting up with such treatment. But that's not the case. I hope her next crush is more worthy of her affection.

> *I turned 14 yesterday and I am involved in a deep relationship – too deep. I have loved a guy for about a year and I would do anything for him. About six months ago, I lost my virginity. We made love a second time about a month later and I thought I might be pregnant, but finally I found out I wasn't. I decided not to do that again until I was on the Pill. Now he hardly talks to me or calls me. Maybe he just lost interest – I don't know. When I call him, we really talk, but it doesn't last. Everyone says I should forget him, but I can't.*

She will never forget her first love and first lover. But she should turn the page on that chapter of her life. Hanging around and being available if he wants her back does nothing for her self-esteem and nothing to make her more attractive in his eyes. Neediness is not as appealing as self-confidence. Her not knowing why he lost interest and their having had sex make it harder to get over him, but she'll have to tell herself that while their relationship is over, her whole life is still ahead. And she's lucky her problem is not an unwanted pregnancy.

A guy and I started saying hi and talking. Then he started taking me home after school and calling. Finally he asked me out. Everything was fine until he suddenly started ignoring me and even avoiding me in school. I think some people found out I liked him and one girl in particular made fun of me.

Six months later, I have learned to cope with it, but it still bothers me. I see him once in a while now and I know he looks at me too. Sometimes I think this will be in the back of my mind for the rest of my life. What did I do?

Nothing. I wish I could say, 'You forgot to rinse with peppermint Scope,' but it's not that simple. Don't quote me on this, but boys can be total jerks at times. The nicest Prince Charmings sometimes turn into toads. New relationships are fragile and breakups rarely come complete with explanations. After a clean break, some girls can recover quickly, but when a breakup is mysterious, it's hard not to stew and stew about it.

She may be perplexed and hurt by his change of heart, but it won't lurk in the back of her mind forever. When she's interviewing for a future job or walking down the aisle with another man, she won't be wondering about this short-term sweetie. For now, her best bet is to try to push him out of her mind by letting other activities and people (male and female) in.

> *I never found out why my last boyfriend broke up with me. I'm slowly getting over him, but now I'm afraid to go with other guys because I'm afraid to go through the pain I had to endure this time.*

In *The Wizard of Oz*, the Wizard tells the Tinman, 'Hearts will never be practical until they are made unbreakable.' Too true. But then, if you protect yourself from heartache, you'll deprive yourself of joy. Love can make you feel happier and more alive than ever before. And yes, when it ends, it can leave you feeling sad and empty.

After you've been through a few romances, you gain some perspective. You still get ecstatic if he calls; you still despair if he leaves you. But since you've been there before, a breakup may not make you break down. You know the sun will keep rising and setting. And you know a morning will come, maybe when you've just sliced a banana on your raisin bran and are about to pour on the milk, when you'll say to yourself, 'Okay. I've cried. Now it's time to move forward.'

A relationship should leave you wiser. You may understand yourself and guys that much better. You may be more realistic, less ready to moan that you'll always love your ex or that you'd do anything for your boyfriend.

When you fall off a horse, you get back on the saddle. When a guy wounds your pride, you get back on the Rollercoaster of Romance. (But, hey, it's okay with me if you want to sit out a ride or two.)

In the words of Alfred, Lord Tennyson: ''Tis better to have loved and lost than never to have loved at all.'

In the words of a girl who signed her letter Happy in Hawaii:

> *Remember how obsessed I was with Ben? Now I'm totally over him. Like magic, I couldn't care less what he does or says. I'm really proud of myself.*

And in the words of Un-heartbroken:

> *Your book came along after a very bad breakup with my boyfriend. Reading it I understood that no matter how painful things are, life goes on and you just have to pick yourself up and start again. I'm starting to date another boy. I would have said no, but instead of sitting at home, I thought, 'Why not? I'll give it a go!' And now I like this boy very much and the other absent love seems almost forgotten.*

TEN THINGS TO DO AFTER A BREAKUP

1. **Call your friends.** Remember? All the girls you didn't neglect just because you had a guy? Plan movie dates, shopping sprees, a slumber party.

2. **Take a leisurely bath.** And when it cools off, don't hop out. Drain off some lukewarm water; add some hot. Ahh. A little self-indulgence never hurt anybody.

3. **Eat nutritiously, take vitamins and get**

enough sleep. You need your strength, so put away the Coke and chips.

4. Get some exercise and sunshine. A walk outside will lighten your mood, and if you're in good physical shape, you'll be in better emotional shape.

5. Add something to your life. Theatre, church choir, student council, basketball, field hockey, computer club, ballet classes, piano lessons, sewing, cooking, volunteer work, a part-time job – whatever!

6. Get a haircut, manicure, makeover or new look. Watch out world! There's a new girl in town.

7. Clean your room and organize your drawers and closet. Sounds dull, but throwing stuff out is therapeutic.

8. Write in a journal. Include a long list of your ex's worst traits: he smokes, he gets terrible grades, he adores Barry Manilow, he looks awful in orange, he gets jealous at the wink of an eye, his dog has fleas – anything.

9. Write your granddad, aunt or a friend who has moved. But don't badmouth your ex nonstop for four pages. It will just make them wonder why you thought he was so great.

10. Start noticing other guys. Love on the rebound can backfire and you shouldn't immediately recruit a replacement boyfriend. But there's no harm in window-shopping!

ARE YOU PINING AWAY?

Some girls spend more time getting over a guy than they did going out with him. It's natural to mourn when a romance dies. But after a while, you have to dry your eyes and tell yourself that, if nothing else, getting burnt builds character.

> *Last summer I went to Europe for two weeks with some friends. I met a man who was 26. I was 16. We shared one day together. It was the most wonderful time I have ever had in my life. I knew I was falling in love, and that it wasn't just a one-night stand. We both cared for each other a lot. He meant everything he said and wasn't playing with my feelings. I ended up having sex with him – I knew I was ready. I did it because I felt something very strong and so did he. The next morning, he dropped me off at the hotel and we kissed and hugged and cried and didn't want to let go. At least I didn't.*
>
> *He promised to write and at first he did – a lot. But then I started getting*

*letters only once a month. And then not
at all. A few weeks ago I telephoned him
and a lady answered and I hung up. I
called again later and the same thing
happened. It's now been nine months since
we've seen each other and I still feel very
strongly about him. I even cry myself to
sleep wishing I could be with him again.
When that woman answered the phone, I
just wanted to die. I would have died for
him, I loved him so much.*

*Now I'm 17 and I'm so heartbroken.
If you can't help me it's all right, I just
need someone to understand how I feel.*

On the one hand, I understand that she feels
sad, puzzled, rejected, betrayed, rotten, despond-
ent, gloomy and glum. She's been through a
terrible time. On the other hand, this sort of
letter makes me want to say, 'Okay, now pull
yourself together!'

She would have died for him, she loved him
so much? Nathan Hale died for his country,
but why die for a guy whose love is a lie?
That's a rhyme with no reason. I hate to be
so unsentimental, but they had one day, several
letters and a few phone calls – that's all. Granted,
a lot can happen in a short time. But c'mon. It's
time to file away the memory.

Intimacy makes breakups harder and I wish they hadn't had sex so soon. Plus, since her lover is older and lives an ocean away, it's easy to remember him as perfect. They weren't together long enough to discover each other's bad habits, short fuses and differing points of view. (Love at first sight often wilts under repeated examination.) Is she really crying for him anyway? Or is she crying for Love with a capital L and for lost innocence and a bruised ego? Was he really so enthralling? Or was she also under the spell of Europe's towering steeples, flowering countrysides and Old World charm?

She'll be 17 only once and it's too good a year to spend looking backward. She should throw herself into her school work, and spread her leftover love among family and friends. Maybe she can get an afterschool job or go college shopping. Just as there are attractive guys in Europe, there are attractive guys all over the world and in Canada, the Caribbean and all 50 states. Her first love will not be her last.

> *A boy named Zachary and I went out for about two months last year. We went places together, took walks, had mushy phone calls. Zak was a popular guy and any girl would kill to go with him. He said I was his love now and forever.*

285

But then there was Kim. She flirted with him at a party and he knew she liked him. The next week, his friend said he was going to break up with me. I was totally torn apart. When I couldn't stand the agony any more, I confronted him.

At first he denied it. I said if there was a problem, we needed to work it out. He said he needed something new. I cried my eyes out that night and I couldn't eat supper.

When he asked Kim to go with him, I felt like dirt. Zak was nice to me, but I was mad at the whole wide world. I felt like my life had fallen apart.

Summer came and I went away to camp. I wrote Zak two letters and he wrote me one. Now school's started and the obsession seems to be creeping up on me again. I've tried to notice other boys, but I just pretend to like them, while Zak still has my heart. I'm so obsessed it is unbearable.

Oh dear oh dear oh dear. What would we all do without waterproof mascara? Look, it's all very well for me to keep pointing out that life is long and that there are other fish in the sea and boys in the halls and malls, but when you are in the throes of an obsession, it's tough. I know. I've been obsessed too. And when you're obsessed, you lose sight of the Big Picture and you can't imagine that while you're consumed with Zak today, in two months you may have flipped over someone else. You can't imagine that while you couldn't eat supper, you'll probably be able to scoff down breakfast just fine.

This girl, like so many others, would do well to try to yank out Cupid's arrow, let the wound heal and leave the reminiscing for when she's old old old. Zak may have meant well, but he's too young to commit himself 'now and forever'. As far as whether any girl 'would kill' for him, girl friends often assume that, but it's not always true, and besides, what counts is how she feels about him, not the cheering crowds.

It's boring to spend more time crying over a guy than you did going out with him. It's boring to be one-track-minded and fixated. To tread water endlessly. Next time Zak creeps into her thoughts, she should change the channel.

> *My mother got your book for my 16-year-old sister, and here I am, 24 years old, writing to you. Recently I went back for my high school diploma and I'm now taking a typing class and working in a department store — so I feel like I'm*

making progress in terms of my career. But my social life is terrible.

I had a really good boyfriend last summer, but I took him for granted and I lost him. I tried to get him back, writing letters and stuff, but I never got a response. He was 20. When we were going out, he was head-over-heels for me. I don't know why I let him go – I must be crazy. Now it's too late. Maybe I'm just desperate and I'm not looking in the right place for a man. All my girl friends are married and I want someone to share my life with. I want to be in love again!

Even women in their twenties can feel confused about love. My hunch is that she let Mr. Head-Over-Heels go for a reason, and now that she's alone, she's looking back through rose-coloured contacts. (And if he was one in a million? Then there are at least 200 like him in the United States alone!) My advice is: learn from the past but get on with today. She'll meet other guys in her courses, in the department store, through friends and as she continues to develop her career. Matter of fact, advancing her career is exactly what she should be doing, so three cheers! Having a successful career can improve her life and self-esteem. And if she's not happy with herself, she can't be happy with anyone else.

All the words in the world can't talk someone out of hurting (people aren't robots, thank heavens), but time and words do help. Feeling down is a natural part of growing up. Spring always follows winter.

NOT SO LONG AGO . . .

Stop crying, When you're going through doubt and depression, you often feel alone. But your grandparents, aunts, uncles, parents, neighbours, teachers and friends have probably been through similar times. I know I have.

This is what I wrote about my boyfriend in my eleventh-grade diary.

> *Maybe I'll never be satisfied or maybe I'm too young or maybe I'm just in one of those moods, but sometimes I think we've lost the love – though other times, it's there. Even Mum said her love ebbs and flows. I guess it's mostly that I'm not ready to centre my life on one person when there are so many interesting people around. It's so screwed up. Often I think we should just call it quits. But the next*

week I'll be dying for him.

In the diary I kept during my senior year in France, I sometimes asked myself if I was lucky – or loony – to be committed to my boyfriend back home in New York.

> *I'm crying. He wrote and asked what I think about not exchanging Christmas gifts. I can't believe it. I've been knitting him a sweater ever since I got to France. I've put a lot of time, work and love into his gift. Am I losing him? I love him so much. I guess I'm afraid of growing apart, of going into the unknown without him. I wrote and told him to tell me if he's breaking away.*

No, he swore his love and I swore mine. But we ended up breaking up anyway after I returned and started college. Should we have set each other free earlier rather than postponing the pain? Didn't we know that the paths to our futures had already diverged?

This is from the diary of my freshman year at Yale, just after I'd spent a weekend at my boyfriend's college.

> *I'm in the bus and I'm crying. This morn-*

*ing he asked me if I wanted to break up.
We were both crying. I'd told him I was
starting to like a guy, Kyle, at school
and he said, 'Anyone who doesn't fall
in love with you is crazy.' We went out
for breakfast and he took me to the bus
stop in Albany and we kissed good-bye.
It was so sad. I know it's the right decision because we shouldn't limit each other
since we probably won't get married. But
I don't know when I'll find the true love
that he offers me. He loves me for me. (I
don't even know if Kyle likes me. Will I
regret this if he doesn't?)*

*I've bitten off all my nails. And I
just realized that I'm still wearing his
jean jacket.*

*I'm glad things are honest between us
and that we decided we're 'on very good
terms'. Stop crying, Carol!*

*I had to change buses at Springfield,
and I sent him the jacket. I sent it with a
note that said, 'Your coat kept me warm
during the last few hours as you have for
the last few years.'*

If you're wondering if Kyle, my college crush,
fell in love with me, he didn't. He didn't want
to have anything to do with me. But no, I

didn't regret breaking up with my high school boyfriend, much as I loved him. The time had come for us to say good-bye.

STILL MORE (PARTING IS SUCH SWEET SORROW) LOVELORN LETTERS

You really really will feel better soon. And you really really will find another guy out there. Maybe not now while you're spending your days watching *The Young and the Restless* reruns with bloodshot eyes. Maybe not even this year. But soon – perhaps when you've gotten so busy that you've forgotten how miserable and desperate you're supposed to be.

Is your old beau beginning to fade into the distant past? No?

> *I'm dating this guy. The problem is that he looks exactly like my ex, Rich. He even talks the same and dresses the same. A lot of times I look at him and think of Rich. Sometimes I think the only reason I even go out with Chris is because he looks so much like Rich. It's not fair to either of*

us. I think I like him but I'm not sure if it's for him or who he reminds me of. How can I clear this up?

If it's still a question, that's her answer. Unless she decides she's taken with Chris's charm, wit or chess game, it's time to bid him farewell. Sometimes a few dates with a nice guy can help a girl get over the end of a long-lasting relationship. But Chris isn't taking her mind off Rich. He's more crutch than crush. She may always be attracted to Rich's type, but it makes no sense to go out with a lookalike if she's not also drawn to whatever makes him different.

I have this ex-boyfriend – he broke up with me a couple of weeks ago – and he doesn't even talk to me or communicate with me. I don't understand why. He only says hi when I say hi. I go out of my way to be nice to him. I write him friendly notes like we did before, but he never writes back any more. When he sees me, he walks the other way. I keep letting him know that we are friends and that I respect that fact. But I don't get a response. My friends say he's still in love with me and that is why he isn't communicating.

Turning romance back into friendship can be as impossible as turning brownies back into batter. Many ex-couples have no desire to become friends or find it too painful even to try. Even couples who do salvage a friendship find that it takes time to redefine their relationship. This girl is rushing things. She may not have accepted the breakup in the first place.

If I were her, I'd stop going out of my way to be nice to the ex. He knows she's reaching out. She's made that clear. If she leans back, he may even lean forward. Or he may continue going about his business, in which case, sigh, she should get on with hers. What about her friends' theory that he's still in love with her? Nice, but I'm afraid I don't buy it.

> *I broke up with Ian. Now he won't stop bugging me!!! He asked if he could call me, and I said sure (dumb me). He called the next day and I said I was busy. He called every day and I kept saying I was busy, so finally he quit calling. I figure I p.o.ed him, but that's life, buddy! Ha ha! Since then, he wrote me and now he thinks I'm going to go with him when school begins. I can't stand him and he doesn't know it.*

Yoo hoo, Ian, wake up and smell the coffee.

Here you have it in reverse: the guy doesn't know when to give up. He should have guessed by the second unenthusiastic 'I'm busy' that his chances were slim. Instead, he put on blinkers and made a pest of himself. I hope this girl isn't mean to him and doesn't make fun of him to her friends. If necessary, she could say, 'Ian, you're a good guy, but my feelings have changed.' With any luck, he'll soon pick up on the news without her having to broadcast a special report. Some people don't know when they've been kindly rejected until they've been unkindly rejected.

> *I used to be popular with boys but now I'm just the opposite. Ever since my boyfriend and I broke up, we've been fighting. We can't stand each other. He's a real jerk. He hurts people's feelings like crazy. His friends take after him. Whoever he hates, they hate, so you know what that means. Life is so unfair. Help!*

> *P.S. He's really popular, so he has a lot of friends.*

If it makes anybody feel better, the tyranny of popularity is strictly junior high and high school stuff. It's much easier in college and as an adult! I don't envy this girl, but if I were her, I'd call a ceasefire. If she and her ex quit fighting, he'll eventually stop picking on her and his friends will accept the truce too.

> *My last boyfriend, Tray, broke up with me because he said he felt uncomfortable. I asked him why. Was it the way I act? The way I look? Who my friends are? He said no. I asked him if it was when we were at church, school or with his grandparents. He said it was church, so I haven't gone since. But now he is going with someone else and he may move to Las Vegas. Sometimes I think that if he doesn't like me, life isn't worth living.*

Bite your tongue, cupcake! What kind of a get-out-the-violins attitude is that? She's giving Tray way too much power. Her life is definitely worth living with or without him. And if she likes church, she should go – with or without his approval. My guess is that Tray doesn't even know exactly why he broke up with her. He may have simply realized that he wasn't in love and didn't want to be 'tied down'. I bet it had nothing to do with church – but he felt pressured to pinpoint something. I hope she'll keep developing her own interest and talents instead of limiting herself according to an ex's specifications.

> My guidance counsellor gave me your book because of all my problems. My problem now is really confusing, and you may have to read this more than once to get it, okay? Anyway, here goes. Last March I started to go with Tony. I was 15. In September I met Joe. I broke up with Tony and started going with Joe. Joe and I got along great but sometimes I wished he'd find another girl friend because Tony had started calling me again. Joe and I had sex. (I was protected.) My mum found my letters and made us break up. The day we broke up, I started to go back out with Tony. I saw Joe with another girl and I started crying. Meanwhile Tony asked what I wanted for Christmas and I said a ring. A few weeks later, Joe and I started going out again, but we broke up within a week. I was a mess. I didn't want anything to do with guys so I broke up with Tony on our one-year anniversary. He said, 'After a year, you tell me it's not working? You've just been leading me on.' Should I go back to Tony? Should I wait for Joe?

Ay yi yi. Tony, Joe, Tony, Joe. Neither relationship sounds ideal because she was often with one but thinking about the other. I suggest she concentrate on school, friends and herself for a while. As for asking Tony for a ring when she still cared about Joe, I think she did lead him on a bit, don't you?

If two guys took an interest in you, you might think it'd be crazy to put them both off. But if you aren't smitten, going out can be more confusing than exciting.

> *I am 15. I broke up two months ago with this guy Jon. We had a weird relationship of talking on the phone every night, sometimes three or four times a night, for two years. We met face to face only twice. I've been really depressed since our breakup. Yesterday I even cried in the bathroom at school when a teacher criticized me for something. Now when I know a guy likes me, I can't even look at him. I feel like I'm cheating on Jon. I trust you and whatever you say, I'm going to stick to it religiously. My friends have been getting the raw end of the deal because I'm so grouchy. Please help. If all this is normal, that's all you have to write back.*

The trouble with telephone romances is that it becomes too easy to turn a disembodied voice into a dream boyfriend. Sure it's normal to miss a guy after a breakup. But this girl needs to get busier, to be a better friend and to stop feeling that she is betraying Jon when she meets another guy's eyes. A flirtation or two might do her good.

But whoa, please don't accept whatever I say as gospel. Use my book as a guideline, but make your own decisions. You know yourself and your situation better than I ever can.

> *I wrote you about Sam (my ex). He's always talking about his bar mitzvah to get me jealous. What made Sam decide not to invite me? I might have a pool party and if I do – no Sam!!!*

Sam doesn't sound very mature. Many guys aren't at age 13. If she does have a pool party and insists on excluding Sam, I hope she won't tell him. Why stoop to that level? He'll hear about it anyway. Frankly, I hope she'll soon spend her time thinking about what she can do for her friends rather than how she can spite her enemies.

> *My boyfriend broke up with me. He's 14. He said the only reason he broke up*

with me is because I just got my braces on. Shelly, the girl he wants to go with, just got hers off. Please write back.

Just as many 13-year-old guys aren't the picture of maturity, so many 14-year-olds can also be pretty silly. His departure may be a blessing in disguise.

I recently broke up with my boyfriend of two months, Mark. Today I found out that he is going out with my friend April. Mark must not have liked me very much if he got over me that fast. How can I ever trust another guy? I feel like everything he told me about how pretty and funny I was was a lie.

If one guy turns on you, you can't discredit all mankind. So Mark was a plop. She can still trust other guys. So he hopped into another relationship. He did like her and she is as pretty and funny as ever.

My boyfriend just broke up with me. I am 11. I know it's young but please take me seriously. Some adults don't. Anyhow, I felt kind of relieved because there were things that bugged me about him. But I feel like I need to like someone. (Do you know any nice cute guys my age?) I'm bored if I don't have a boyfriend.

Do I know any cute 11-year-olds in Milwaukee? 'Fraid not. But I do empathize with her wanting to liven things up by liking a guy. When I reread my teen diaries, I'm amazed at how many quickie crushes I had. In junior high, I was in the mood to like a guy – any guy. Liking him was as important as his liking me.

But you know what? Friends, family, school, extracurrics, reading, cooking and sports are among many other worthwhile distractions. Why not become an expert on something? Go to the library and read up on frogs or Jane Austen or how to become a journalist, model, doctor or fashion designer. Find a hobby and run with it!

Now that you and what's-his-face are no longer two peas in a dinky little pod, make the most of your time, your independence, your freedom – your new beginning!

6

Thinking About Sex

Thinking about sex? Of course you're thinking about sex. You're a teenager, aren't you? Your hormones are on the rampage, aren't they?

So 'fess up. How many of you turned straight to this chapter? Can't fool me. I always used to flip through books looking for the 'dirty' parts.

Whether you started reading from the beginning or just opened to this page, I'm glad you're here. Sex is important. You should be thinking about it.

In the next two chapters, I want to answer all your questions about sex. I want to give you reasons to say no and ways to protect yourself if you decide to say yes. Sex can be meaningful or meaningless, responsible or reckless. The more armed you are with information, the better off you'll be.

HOW DO YOU FEEL
ABOUT SEX?

Anxious? Excited? Confused? There's a whole range of reactions. You'll probably recognize some of the ones here. (For those of you just joining us, yes, these letters are real, and yes, I have permission to use them.)

When it comes to sex, some girls are . . .

Overwhelmed:

> *My best friend and I are both trying to cope with stress and peer pressure. High school is coming up in one more year. You're almost required to have sex, drink, take drugs and do all the other stuff the 'in' crowd does.*

Overeager:

> *My problem is that my boyfriend is still a virgin and I have trouble not pressuring him. But forcing him to make love to me is the last thing I want to do. He thinks that because I'm not a virgin, I've done everything and I haven't.*

Sorry:

I am 13 and am involved with a 15½-year-old. Everyone tells me I act way too mature for my age. Boys think of me as a slut. But I just lost my virginity a few months ago. And believe me, I've felt bad about that ever since. I just feel so guilty.

Satisfied:

I am 16. My boyfriend and I had been going out for a year and a half when we finally made love. And that's exactly what it was. It was both of our first times which made it more meaningful. Instead of breaking up afterwards (which I've heard often happens), he and I were closer than ever before. Perhaps because we shared with each other something that we'll never be able to share with anyone else ever again: our first time. We always protected ourselves. A few months ago, we broke up for different reasons, but we are still close friends.

Afraid:

> I'm scared in a major way about my first
> time. My friend Camilla who 'did it' when
> she was 14 said (get this), 'Don't worry, it
> doesn't hurt THAT much!' Thanks Cam!
> I don't care about THAT much, I care
> about HOW much, and if it's painful or
> just uncomfortable. I think I'm scared to
> start any serious relationships because I'm
> hung up on the SEX SYNDROME.

Aghast: '

> I am 19½. I've never had a boyfriend
> and I don't intend to. I know everyone
> says sex expresses love, but I think that's
> a bunch of bull. I don't believe men ever
> love anything. And how could something
> so disgusting and embarrassing show love?
> All it does is let the guy get his thrills. I
> heard some guy in an interview say, 'Men
> are sexual creatures.' I wanted to throw
> my shoe at the TV. Are there any other
> girls who think sex is degrading and sick?
> Or am I alone?

It may be comforting to know that Overwhelmed is mistaken: you don't have to have sex,

drink and take drugs to be accepted. Overeager should slow down. Girls hate to be railroaded into sex and it's not fair to turn the tables on guys. Everyone feels peer pressure, but as Sorry found, having sex can sometimes make you feel less – not more – accepted. Truth is, most junior high and high school students are virgins, but they don't boast about it in the locker room.

And Afraid? For most women, the first time is neither as painful nor as pleasurable as they imagine. Sex with the wrong guy can be emotionally painful, so I'm glad she's not in a hurry to lose her virginity. But it's too bad her nervousness about intercourse is getting in the way of her love life. She could enjoy a boyfriend's company and kisses without going all the way.

The girl who is turned off by men and disgusted by sex signed her letter Alien. Might something have happened in her childhood that made her wary of the other gender? I won't play amateur psychologist, but I advised her – as delicately as possible – to get counselling to help her work through her hostility. No point in her spending another 19½ years angry, alone and alienated.

SEX? WHO, ME?

I remember when my high school boyfriend – the one I met at that fateful New Year's Eve party – first suggested we make love. I was stunned. I had thought about sex in the abstract. I had done my share of kissing. And I knew a few classmates who had gone all the way. But somehow I hadn't imagined that sex, real live stark naked get-down-to-it-intercourse, had anything to do with me, a 15-going-on-16-year-old, or my boyfriend who was weeks away from 17.

I was at a summer party at my friend Wendy's. My boyfriend called at nine to say his car was dead and he was going to have to hitch over and hoped to be there by ten-thirty. I wasn't thrilled about his hitching, but his best friend assured me that he had a golden thumb – that cars 'fought over him'. Sure enough, my boyfriend appeared just half an hour later, and soon escorted me out onto Wendy's lawn. It's all in my diary:

> We were lying down in the grass and
> he said, 'How long have I known you?'
> 'Six months. Ten days.'
> 'Loved every minute of it.'
> I kissed him and said, 'You're so nice.

Everything you say and do is nice.'

'Do you think making love to me would be nice?'

'Yes. Wait. What? No. What??'

'You didn't catch that, did you?'

'I guess not.'

'Why not?'

'I don't know.'

'You must have a reason.'

'I'm only 15. I'm not ready.'

'When will you be ready?'

'I don't know.'

'Best answer I've heard from you yet.'

I pushed him away and laughed.

He said, 'You're not serious, but I am.'

It left the evening with a question mark.
I am lucky. He is nice – but too fast. I'm
not that bitterly opposed to losing my vir-
ginity – but not at 15. And what about
pregnancy and VD? And what if he's not
a virgin?

Much much later, I found out that he was a
virgin. But in some ways, I lost my innocence
that night. Not earlier when I first learned the
facts of life. Not later when we finally made love.
But that June tenth at Wendy's when I realized
with a jolt that sex and I would not be strangers
forever.

ARE YOU REALLY READY TO
GO ALL THE WAY?

In the fifties, the ideal of girls was to be chased but chaste. By the late sixties and seventies, it was cool to be experienced. Nowadays, girls aren't expected to be pure as the driven snow or fast as Corvettes. They can make up their own minds about sex.

You may sometimes feel like the Last Virgin in the Western World, but you aren't, I promise. Over half of all 16-year-olds are virgins. Forty-seven percent of 17-year-old girls have never had sex. And the median age at first intercourse is just under 18. The pendulum has swung back towards chastity recently. New diseases have slowed couples down sexually and brought a return to romance. Even if you don't plan on waiting until marriage, I hope you won't have sex until you yourself really want to and until you have a loving and responsible relationship with a thoughtful caring boyfriend. Virginity isn't just accepted these days; it's respected.

Whatever happened to cuddling anyway? Remember back when you and your friends talked about going to first, second and third base? That stuff is fun. Couples can spend many months or even years getting to know each other and each other's bodies before going all the way. I got a letter today from a girl who had 'never kissed and never done it'. Why lump kissing and intercourse together? There's a whole world of intimate touching for couples to discover before they start worrying about stealing home base.

· So go slow. Sex is not a hurdle on the obstacle course of getting and keeping a boyfriend.

> *I bet you've heard this problem millions of times. My friend and I met some boys, Vince and Earl. I told Vince that I liked him, and that very same day his friend said Vince wants to do it with me. And now every time I see them, they ask if I want to do it with Vince. But I would like to know if Vince really likes me.*

Likes her? Vince doesn't really know her, let alone like her. She may be flattered that he finds her attractive, but Vince and Earl sound like show-offs at best, scuzzbags at worst. They're looking for a good time – and aren't worth her time.

> *A friend has been meeting me between classes and telling me to walk with him down the hall and then kissing me and slapping me on the butt. I am a senior*

and he is a freshman. I am getting a little worried what he thinks he can get from me.

He can't get anything from her that she isn't willing to give. Since she doesn't welcome his advances, she should say so.

My friend's boyfriend asked her if she wanted to go all the way and she doesn't really want to. But if she doesn't, he might drop her. She's considering it for his sake. They are 13.

Sex is not something you do for someone else's sake. If he can't be patient, he doesn't deserve her. At 13, does she really believe this is her last chance for romance? That she needs to compromise her values? If he drops her because of sex (or lack thereof), then good riddance.

My friend is 13 and she met a guy who is really into sex – not making love! They had sex because he is the type who, if you didn't do what he wanted, he would knock you around, so she had no choice.

This gorilla makes Vince and Earl look like Cub Scouts. You always have a choice. You

311

always have a right to say no. Don't lead guys on, but know that you are always in the driver's seat – even if you two are in the backseat. It's your body, right? If you ever feel you don't have a choice, that's not sex, that's rape or date rape (see the section on *Rape* in Chapter 7).

Listen, I like guys. I really do. But some of these fellows sound unsavoury. Why be within spitting distance of such impatient imbeciles? I'd rather go it alone than hang out with a guy who rates a −6 on the sensitivity scale. And I want you to think enough of yourself to feel the same way. Being manhandled by someone you scarcely know does not guarantee happiness or popularity.

As far as having sex goes, why rush it? It's better to have love without sex than sex without love. And you only have one first time. There's no such thing as a born-again virgin. Wait as long as you can before saying that final good-bye to girlhood. It's not that your life will change dramatically the moment you lose your virginity. It's not that virgins and nonvirgins are worlds apart. But your first time is special; you will remember it forever. And when you do, I want you to smile, not wince.

My boyfriend and I are in the seventh grade and I know positively that I'm in

love. I think he is too. I know it's awful
young and he's not fully developed and
I'm not either. But we're on our way!
We've French-kissed, hugged, held hands
and held each other. I have a feeling sex
is about to happen. What should I do?

Wait a sec! Hold your horses! Sex doesn't just happen. In seventh grade, a couple can enjoy long walks, telephone talks, Eskimo kisses and Eskimo pie . . . why start scheduling sex when you've scarcely reached puberty? He may be as nervous as she is. And childhood is short enough. Why take on adult responsibilities and complications? Why risk pregnancy or disease? Kissing and hugging are so much fun, don't rush the rest. Besides, if a couple has sex, it can become that much harder for them to sort out their true feelings for each other – and it can be that much more devastating if they do break up.

Many girls ask me about the appropriate age for having sex:

I am 13 and my boyfriend is 15. My
boyfriend has had sex a few times, and
this will be my first time. I love him very
much. My parents are against teenagers
having sex, but I will use contraception.
I'm just wondering, am I younger than

most girls having sex?

My boyfriend and I broke up for a while, but now that we're together again, everything is better than before. I love him and I know sooner or later we'll start having sex because we are so close now. He is 16 and I'm 14. Do you think I am too young?

You may think this is the wrong question for a 14-year-old to ask, but how far do you think a girl should go with a guy if she's only 14? A lot of my friends have gone all the way, but is that right? I'm so unsure about everything.

A lot of girls in my school have already had sex. I want to. I'm only 13, but I don't think age matters just as long as the two people are in love. I know if I asked you, you would probably tell me that at my age, I shouldn't even consider it.

She said it, not me. Do I think girls who are 13 and 14 are too young to be having sex? YES. About one out of ten 13- and 14-year-old girls has had sex, and every day around 25 American girls aged 13 and 14 have their first child. By age 15, one out of five girls has had sex (which means the other four are virgins). But why grow up so fast? 30,000 girls under 15 get pregnant each year. That's 30,000 too many in my book – and this is my book!

Boys should slow down too, but girls have more to lose. Everybody needs to worry about disease, but girls, not boys, risk getting pregnant. Girls, not boys, risk getting a reputation. A promiscuous guy is often called a stud; a promiscuous girl is often called a slut. And if a couple parts ways after having been intimate (young love has a nasty habit of disappearing), it's the girl who often feels most distraught.

I got a letter today from a seventh grader who had sex – without birth control – with a 17-year-old. Like too many other guys, he rushed from bed to megaphone and couldn't wait to make her private decision public news.

> *He tells people about what we did. I hate him for that. I feel ashamed of myself. See, I felt like a woman while I was doing it. But I'm not a woman yet. I'm only 13 and I'm scared.*

If you are considering having sex and wondering if you are too young, you probably are. Here are 10 better questions for you.

TEN QUESTIONS TO
ASK YOURSELF

1. **Do you feel free to say no?** If he's not giving you room to make up your own mind, he's not playing fair.

2. **Have you talked together about birth control and will you use contraceptives every time you have intercourse?** If not, you could find yourself among the more than 1,000,000 teenagers who get pregnant in the United States each year.

3. **Have you talked about what you'd do if you got pregnant?** If you are adult enough to consider having sex, you are adult enough to consider the possible consequences. Would he help you pay for an abortion, find an adoption agency or raise a child? If he's 13, I sincerely doubt it.

4. **Might he have sexually transmitted disease?** If there's any chance that he has a disease – he's been around, he shoots up drugs – don't have sex with him or insist that he wear a condom.

5. **Are you thinking about having sex because you think it will help you keep your boyfriend?** It doesn't usually work that way so ask yourself now if you'd feel cheated or used if you event-

ually broke up.

6. Is he taking this as seriously as you are? Do you feel committed to each other? Do you feel as much desire as he does? If you aren't both consumed with love and lust, why even consider getting so involved?

7. How long have you known each other and how long has it been since your first kiss? If you don't have a solid, ongoing, long-term relationship, why is sex even an issue? It's easy to say 'I love you', but do you love being together and love the way you treat each other? If not, why push the relationship forward?

8. Why don't you want to wait a little longer? Having sex is a big decision. Take your time. If you can wait, wait.

9. Would your father have a heart attack and your mother have a cow if they found out what you were up to? If so, could you handle either their disappointment or your guilt and secrecy?

10. Are you planning to be drunk or high when you have sex? I hope not, and if it would be 'having sex' rather than 'making love', I urge you again to reconsider your urges.

THE FIRST TIME COUNTS

Don't throw your virginity away. And don't let anyone else steal it.

Dear Carol,
  I am 13. Early last month I ran away from home. A friend said I could stay with her, but while I was waiting for her where she works, I met a guy named Tom. The real stud type. We hit it off and I told him I was 16 (I look about 18). I got his phone number and the next day, I called and he wanted me to come over. I was a virgin until that night. We slept together and I'm not gonna lie, it hurt, but after a while it was easy. Afterwards, Tom said I had to leave but we'd keep in touch. The next day I went to where Tom was working and when he saw me, he acted like he didn't even know me. I went home and my father grounded me. Tom called today but I'm very mixed up about my feelings. So far I've skipped my period the whole month. I'm really worried.
                    Desperately Confused

Dear Carol,

Hi! I'm 15. My best friend and next-door neighbour is 13. I'm writing to you because I am worried about her. She has a massive crush on a kid named Kevin (he's 15). She called him three times, and he wanted to see what she looked like. So we walked over to his house (she made me go with her). Now let me tell you what she looks like. She's 5'7", blond hair, green eyes – she could be a model. Kevin must have liked what he saw because he wanted to see her again, alone. They made plans the next night at Kevin's best friend's house (his parents were away). She told her mum she was out with me.

Later she told me that Kevin had wanted to have sex but that she said they didn't have time. Well, today Kevin invited her over (his parents weren't home) and she 'made love' to him. (I said 'made love' because I didn't want to write f----d but it was definitely not love.) When she told me, I couldn't believe it. I'm not a prude, I'm a virgin by choice, but when I have sex the first time, I'm going to make sure I really love the guy and he loves and respects me. She said she didn't want to do it but was afraid she'd lose

319

him. I don't think he gives a damn about her as a person and I told her so. I could kill Kevin!!

Here's my question. They had sex twice. The first time he used a rubber. The second time he didn't, but he didn't come. Could she be pregnant?

Sick Thinking About It

Both 13-year-olds could be pregnant, and I hope neither is. Having sex is not a shortcut to falling in love. If someone once took advantage of you, or if you once said yes because you didn't know how to say no, I hope you didn't get pregnant either. You live and you learn, and now you know more about your sexual rights and responsibilities than you did then.

Your first time counts. But you can always say no.

Dear Carol,

I started liking Clint as soon as I met him. It was like we were made for each other! We went to dances, parties, our houses and almost everywhere together. We went out for about two months and then he broke up with me. But we talked it out and he asked me to go back with him. Of course I said yes. Three days later, he said he wanted to break up again.

We were separated for two weeks (the longest two weeks of my life). During that time, he asked me in biology if I wanted to skip school one day. Of course I said yes.

The day we skipped, Clint wanted to do more than talk. I really loved him so I told him I didn't think it was right for a couple to do it unless they were going together and loved each other. He asked me to go with him again and of course I said yes.

Then we did it. It was in a field. The whole situation was nothing like I'd dreamed about. It was really disgusting, sort of. I don't regret it, but it just didn't happen the way I wanted it to.

> *Blind as a Bat About Love*
> *But Learning Fast*

Is Blind learning fast? Up until now she has been naive. At least she and Clint had had a relationship before she signed up for his extracurricular biology lesson. But what makes her so agreeable? She's not his marionette. And lusty sweet talk is – of course – not a good reason to do a guy's bidding or risk unwanted pregnancy.

Dear Carol,

I have a major, major problem. I've had a boyfriend named Dale for a little over a month now and he has been pressuring me into having sex. He is 17 and I am 14, but he thinks I'm 15. Lately he's been getting mad at me when I've been saying no, and that has made me mad and confused. I used to really love Dale but now that he has been so insensitive, I am having second thoughts. I think he is too.

When I've said no in the past, he's asked why. I told him I didn't want to get pregnant, and he's said, 'You won't. I have condoms.'

Yesterday I bought some contraceptive foam and today I said yes. I used the contraceptive foam, Dale didn't use a condom, it wasn't that great and now I think I'm pregnant. I am scared out of my mind. I plan to call Planned Parenthood for a pregnancy test. If I am pregnant, I'm really going to freak, but I will have an abortion.

Before Dale left this afternoon, he said that he didn't think we should see each other any more and that I was too young for him. When he said that, I almost passed out, but then he said he was just kidding.

Now I'm scared that he wasn't kidding and he was just afraid of being thought of as a jerk.

After we did it, there was a lot of blood and I'm still bleeding now. I'm wondering if I'm having my period (it's not regular yet). I was with someone like this once before but he didn't really penetrate and Dale did. Please help me. I am really confused and scared.

Desperate

With any luck, this girl doesn't have a 'major, major problem', but she could be pregnant. Foam alone is not an effective method of birth control, and Dale was a selfish jerk for not wearing a condom. The blood? I doubt it's her period. Dale probably tore her hymen – the thin skin covering a virgin's vaginal opening. (Many women bleed the first time they have intercourse.)

If Dale makes a quick exit from her life, I hope she won't grieve for him. I hope she'll remember that neither he nor the romance were 'that great' and that she'll at least have learned a lot from the experience.

While saying yes can be the start of a new phase of a solid relationship, it often marks the end of a shaky relationship.

Before you say yes, think things through. Be sure you are as ready as your boyfriend.

IF YOU WANT TO SAY NO

My problem is boys. Is sex all they have on their mind? Can't we be boyfriend-girl friend without sleeping together? Sometimes I don't think so.

How do you tell a guy no about sex without hurting his feelings? I need an answer. I sit up all night trying to find a way to say no and you are my only hope.

No is a very little word: two letters, one syllable. Yet girls who can rattle off mouthfuls like 'hypotenuse', 'paramecium', 'protagonist' and 'conjugation' often stumble over this oral contraceptive. Before I elaborate on how to say no, try simply saying it. (Sounds dumb, but humour me, okay?) Ready, set, go – NO.

I meant out loud, Try again.

Perfect! And easy, right?

'Cute,' you're thinking, 'but how am I going to say it to Jason?' I admit it's harder to say no to your boyfriend or to the girl who is passing you a joint or wants to borrow your new white blouse than it is to say no to a page in a book. But even though you've been brought up to be willing and able and eager to please, sometimes

you have to please yourself first and foremost. Learning to say no and draw the line where you want it drawn will make you a stronger individual
and will give you self-respect. Saying no to others often means saying yes to yourself.

That doesn't mean you have to be a cold-hearted bitch about it. You can say 'No, thanks,' and pass on the pot without hopping on a soapbox to deliver a holier-than-thou marijuana-leads-to-heroin lecture. You can say you'd rather not lend out your blouse but offer to lend your seashell earrings instead. You can soften a no without giving in.

And your boyfriend? Talk with him about your feelings and doubts long before he has a chance to wonder whether he should wriggle out of his clothes. If you have decided you aren't ready for sex, discuss your decision with him. (If you're uncomfortable talking about sex with him, why, I repeat, why would you consider having sex with him?) And if he's not really your boyfriend, if he's really just a horny guy, then don't lose sleep worrying about how not to hurt his feelings. Worry about your health and happiness and say no.

When should you and your boyfriend have The Talk? Not the first time he asks you out or kisses you. But if things are getting hot and heavy and you sort of like his touching you here but you don't want him touching you there, it may be time to speak up.

If you like, tell him how much you care about him and how handsome you think he is so he won't feel rejected. But tell him that you aren't ready to be more intimate and that you hope he understands. (He may be relieved. And he too may be a virgin. Some guys aren't in a hurry to have sex and some worry about their own 'performance', but think they are supposed to keep unzipping and unbuttoning until you yell, 'Stop!') You don't have to announce that you want to be a virgin bride (even if you do), but tell him that you are comfortable going only so fast and so far. If you talk this out ahead of time, you may both enjoy making out more because you'll know where you stand and every embrace won't turn into a tug-of-war.

> *I'm 14 and I just found out that my boy-friend, who is 15, is NOT a virgin. I was completely shocked! I thought I was 'out of it' or something because I'm a virgin (and proud of it). I also thought that if we held hands or kissed, it wouldn't mean as much to him as it meant to me. He informed me that all he wants to do is be with me and he's not going to push me to do anything.*

He just wants me around, not for sex, but for me.

Nice guy. Lucky girl. Some girls hope that their first lover will be a fellow virgin. Others hope their first lover will be experienced, a good teacher.

Think things through before getting into any awkward situations. If you don't fully trust yourself or your boyfriend, play it safe: don't meet in empty houses or park in secluded spots or get drunk alone together. (There's no reason to get drunk in a crowd either, but that's another bunch of grapes.)

Waiting makes lovemaking more special. Why not let sex be something to look forward to?

- If a guy says, 'Yeah, but we might all die tomorrow,' tell him you'll take your chances.
- If he says, 'You would if you loved me,' tell him he wouldn't insist if he loved you.
- If he says, 'Everybody else is doing it,' tell him you assumed he liked you because you're different.
- If he says, 'You're a tease,' remind him that sex isn't all or nothing, and remind yourself that nobody ever died of 'blueballs'.

(Uh oh. How much do you want to bet

your grandmother flips open to this page in the bookstore as she is trying to choose an appropriate gift for you, her pride and joy? 'Blueballs', Grandmum, is what boys call sexual frustration or unfulfilled desire. It is a vulgar expression – sorry! – but many girls don't realize that it doesn't hurt a guy to get an erection and then have it go away.)

Some guys collect lines but don't expect you to take them seriously. If a guy says, 'How can I love you if you won't lie down?' or 'If I said you had a terrific body, would you hold it against me?' or 'I think I can fall madly in bed with you,' all he really expects from you is a smile.

What if you and your boyfriend have been going out for ages – a month and a half is not ages – and you like fooling around, but you aren't ready for sex and he's climbing the walls? What then? If he says, 'I just can't take the frustration any more,' and you love him, maybe you two can put your X-rated imaginations to work. Consider rolling around with your clothes on or, if you're older, petting to orgasm or finding some other way to relieve the pressure without penetration. If you're creative, most guys will stop making such a fuss about your not wanting to go all the way. Because of new fears about sexually transmitted diseases, petting (sometimes called mutual masturbation) has been making a, ah-hem, comeback. And I have yet to meet a *technical virgin* ('We've done everything but –') with a bun in the oven (i.e., pregnant).

Even if you have had sex in the past, you can say no now. You don't have to feel guilty about your past, but you also don't have to stay sexually active if you don't want to. It may be harder to play mermaid with Marvin this week if you slept with him last week. Once you say yes, guys often push you to say it again. But others are willing to take a step back.

If you want to say no, say no. You are entitled. And it's just two letters, one syllable.

> *I bought* Girltalk *when I was 13. I read it but it wasn't until a few months later that I undertstood what it was all about. There was a guy in our school who was really popular. I was popular too, but since I was two years younger than he, I was very surprised when he asked me to his prom. He could have any girl he wanted and he picked me!*
>
> *Our relationship grew and we started to really care about each other. But it wasn't too long after that when he started pressuring me into having sex. I didn't feel I was ready so I kept pushing him away. For the first couple of months, he didn't*

seem to mind. But then he started to get mad. Well, I was together with this boy for over a year and we had lots of fun times together and we grew to love each other very much. He was still upset that I wouldn't have sex with him, but he knew it was my final decision.

It's been a couple of months since we broke up and he's not completely out of my life. I just wanted to say that I'm almost 15 now and I'm glad I said no when I did. I still have the memories of the fun times we had without sex. I'm really glad that I decided to wait until I myself know that I am ready - and not just my boyfriend. I could never thank you enough for your help and advice. I think I would have had sex with him if I didn't keep thinking of all the things you said in your book.

IF YOU WANT TO SAY YES

You get my point: if you ever want to say no, just say no. But what if you want to say yes? Do you just say yes? No! Not unless you'll be using contraceptives. And not unless you've done a lot of thinking.

> *I'm 17 years old and have been going with a guy for two years. During the past month, he and I have been talking about intercourse. We are very much in love and we are sure we want to do it. We have weighed the pros and cons and discussed birth control. The only thing holding us back are my mother and father. I've always been the 'perfect child' and I'm afraid of what my parents would do. They might lose confidence in me or not trust me or something. Please advise me.*

What advice is there? It's not easy to be one man's darling daughter and another man's sexy lover. It's not easy to be both child and woman. Teenagers might want their parents' approval, but most mums and dads aren't willing to give their kids a go-ahead on sex. Girls have to make up their own minds and then choose whether to tell the parents and risk their wrath or to be discreet and accept the new independence.

For the record, most teenagers don't sashay into their parents' bedrooms to announce, 'Guess what? Tad and I are having it off!' Most remain close to their parents, but keep their sexual activities under wraps – so to speak. You don't know every detail about your parents' sex life and, so long as you're being responsible, they'd probably just as soon not know every detail about yours. If you and your single mother both have boyfriends you may become more candid together. But when it comes to sex, most girls are mum to Mum.

> *Can you help me? I am 16 and I am afraid to have sex with my boyfriend. He and I broke up over this, but we love each other a lot and we started going back out again. I don't want to lose him. Can you tell me what to do?*

No I can't. I can tell her to think about the emotional and physical risks of having sex, but whether to say yes or no is her decision. Not her boyfriend's. And not mine.

> *Where does the penis go when you have sex?*

> *What is it like to have sex? What happens if I goof up? My mum won't tell me what to do during sex.*

Before saying yes to sex, it's helpful if couples know more or less what they're doing and if they have realistic expectations. The penis goes in the vagina, but my hunch is that these letter writers are young and should wait wait wait. When the time comes, they won't 'goof up'. Nobody is born an expert and nobody should expect anyone else to be. Some couples may find intercourse a bit of a letdown in the beginning – although it helps a lot if they are wildly in love. Sharing your first time with your boyfriend may seem momentous and poignant even if it's also clumsy and awkward. Sensitive lovers soon learn how to be responsive and generous and to give each other and themselves more pleasure.

I'd like to know how to prevent pregnancy but still be able to have sex.

Birth control. I thought you'd never ask. And you probably think I'll never get to it. I will. Honest. In the very next chapter.

But first a word (give or take a couple of thousand) about two taboo topics: masturbation and homosexuality.

DO-IT-YOURSELF ORGASM

Dear Carol,
I feel a little embarrassed asking this,

333

but here goes: can a gynaecologist tell if one has masturbated?

Just Wondering

I remember going to an orthodontist once when I was in grade school. I plunked into his chair. He peered into my mouth. And then he announced, 'You're a thumbsucker, aren't you?' I thought I'd die of shame. I wished Scotty could beam me up. And I decided it was time to kick the habit.

So much for true confession. Do gynaecologists have a similar sixth sense? Nope. Besides, though masturbation may still be impolite table talk, it's normal and common and needn't be a source of guilt. Rest assured, it's okay to touch yourself and it's okay not to.

What does 'to come' mean? I'd feel really stupid asking any of my friends.

What is 'orgasm'?

I know it's hard to say no to sex because I know it feels good to have an intercourse.

Whoops! 'Intercourse' is when a man's penis is inside a woman's vagina. She may mean to 'have an orgasm' or to 'come'. And what does that mean? Many girls and guys first find out by touching themselves during masturbation. More boys than girls masturbate, but many girls do engage in solo sex. While some people think self-stimulation is wrong, most educators and sex therapists disagree. Many think that exploring one's body and acquainting oneself with one's sensuality can do more good than harm.

A person has an orgasm when he or she experiences the peak of sexual excitement either during masturbation or with a partner. When a boy 'comes', he ejaculates – wet sperm-filled semen shoots out of his penis. When a girl 'comes', she feels a pleasurable rhythmic throbbing in her clitoral area. In guys and girls, this sensation of pleasure and relief after the buildup of sexual tension is called 'orgasm'.

Orgasms vary in intensity and are harder to describe. (Try describing sneezing to someone!) Girls and women don't always have an orgasm every time they make love. And they usually take longer to come, or 'climax', than guys do. Some girls and women never experience orgasm and yet enjoy intercourse. A girl or woman who is comfortable with her own body and has learned to bring herself to orgasm may be more sexually satisfied in the future because she can show her partner how to arouse her and she knows how best to position herself during intercourse. Girls and women who have masturbated and whose partners stroke the clitoral area while petting or before, during or after intercourse are more likely to climax than girls or women who have never masturbated and whose partners are insensitive or impatient.

Masturbation can help a guy learn to delay orgasm so he won't ejaculate immediately upon penetration. Have you seen the movie *Love And Death* in which a countess tells Woody Allen that he's the best lover she's ever had? His response? 'I practise a lot when I'm alone.' In *Annie Hall*, he says of masturbation, 'Don't knock it, it's sex with someone you love.'

HOMOSEXUALITY

I just saw a TV show about AIDS. They were talking about gay people and at the end they showed two men walking side by side with their backs to the camera. Each man had his arm around the other, but how do they know these men are gay? I go to an all-girls' school. Our class is very close and affectionate. We are always hugging and occasionally, in a semi-joking way, kissing each other on the cheek. But

*we aren't gay. So how come the media is
so sure those men are?*

Homosexuals are adults who are consistently
more attracted to members of their own sex than
to members of the opposite sex. No one knows
why people are gay or straight, but an individual's
sexual orientation is now believed to be given, not
a decision. It's more a question of chance than
choice.

Although it's not always possible to guess
whether someone is homosexual or bisexual,
I think the camera crew was probably right
to assume that the two men were gay. Why?
Straight men don't express same-sex affection as
readily as women and gay men do. Women often
greet each other with a hug or peck on the cheek
whereas straight men usually exchange hugs or
walk arm in arm only if they haven't seen each
other for a long time or if one is comforting or
congratulating the other. And up to 10 percent
of the male population is gay. Of course, a man's
sexual preference is his own business – unless you
happen to be thinking of getting involved with
him.

You've probably heard a classmate use the
words 'faggot', 'queer', 'flamer', or 'dyke' to
describe gay men or lesbian women. I hope
you are more tolerant and less judgmental of

other people's life-styles and that you don't feel so insecure or threatened that you put others down to build yourself up. Needless to say, gay people are just as able to love, care, respect and feel hurt as straight people.

Do you think you might be gay? Many girls have 'played doctor' or experimented with their female friends as children but are not lesbians. No one should assume tomboys, feminists or girls who have occasional crushes on women or fantasies about women are automatically gay either. Some girls go through brief lesbian phases but then get married, have children and lead heterosexual lives.

If you think you are gay, you are not alone. From 3 to 5 percent of women are lesbian. If you think you are gay, you are also not abnormal – although some small-minded people would have you feel otherwise. Should you make your private life public? I see no reason to rush 'out of the closet'. And when you do, brace yourself: your friends and parents may not be immediately comfortable with your news. It gets easier. Most colleges and cities have social and political groups where gay men and lesbian women can meet and talk.

If you are anxious or confused about your feelings, confide in a trusted adult or contact the organizations listed in the *Information* section of this book. If you are at ease with your homosexuality but your parents can't handle it, they can advise you on this too.

And if it's the other way around?

> Dear Carol,
>
> I am 13. My mother is a lesbian. I have tried my best but I can't cope with it. If you write a new book, can you include this topic telling me and other teenagers what to do?
>
> If you were going to suggest a counsellor, it won't help. My mother, not knowing I was mad that she was gay, sent me to one. I am not the type to tell people my problems, so it didn't work out. Besides, when she did that, it really made me mad!
>
> I have another question. What should I say when my friends (or their mothers) say, 'Where does Gwen sleep?' (Gwen is the other lady who lives with us.) They know there are only two bedrooms in the house! I am faced with that question a lot. I usually ignore it, but after a while, they ask again. I also thought of telling the truth. I suppose I could tell my closest friends – but most people are prejudiced against gays.
>
> Actually I can't blame them. I am too. I

guess because it affects my life. I can't talk about boys on the phone otherwise I get teased until the day I die. If a boy called me (which one never has, but my mum is a real jerk and thinks that every time the phone rings, it's a boy), she would have a spaz!

This started out to be a very short letter but I guess I got carried away! Thank you for reading it.

Hopeless

Dear Hopeless,

Thank you for writing me and please don't stay hopeless for long!

You aren't the only teenager with a gay parent, but that doesn't make your home situation any easier. Frankly, I don't think your mum's idea to have you see a counsellor was so bad. You say she sent you 'not knowing' you were mad. I bet she sent you because she does know you are upset and are, understandably, having trouble dealing with her homosexuality. You wrote a long letter because you have a lot to get off your chest. Although you didn't hit it off with the counsellor your mother chose, a different counsellor might be better able to help you deal with your

340

mixed emotions: love, anger, humiliation, guilt, rejection.

Talking to a counsellor doesn't mean you are crazy or have insurmountable problems or anything like that. I talked to a counsellor after my father died and the sessions were extremely helpful. You can get by without counselling, but consider it again. You and your mother might even go together. If you decide you still don't want to talk to a counsellor, confide in an adult you trust.

When people ask where Gwen sleeps, they're being rude. You can be rude back, you can be silent or evasive, or you can be truthful. Ask your mother for advice. Or how about: 'What an odd question,' or 'She's never asked where you sleep!' or 'Why does it matter?' 'Gwen respects my privacy and I like to respect hers,' or 'In my mother's room – they let me have a room to myself so I can study.' There's nothing wrong with just telling the truth, but choose your confidante or confidantes carefully. You know how the high school grapevine can be.

Even girls with straight parents get teased when they talk about boys – and it bugs them too! Any chance you could *get a phone in your bedroom? Or would it do any good to have a heart-to-heart with your mother (or write her a note) and ask her to please respect your personal life as you are trying to respect hers? Tell her it hurts when she teases you – she may stop.*

You can't change your mum. But you can try to change your relationship. And you can learn to become less prejudiced against gays. If you work at accepting your mother's life-style, and if she works harder at being supportive and giving you room to grow, you may find that you two can have as close and caring a mother-daughter bond as some of your friends and their mothers do. I hope so.

By the way, whenever I answered a teenager's questions about parents and sex, I'd feel funny about blithely sending it off to her home address. So I'd usually try to 'tamper-proof' the letter by sticking a Snoopy or holiday sticker on the back of the envelope. Then I'd pop it in the mailbox, cross my fingers and hope my response would reach the girl's eyes only.

7

Protecting Yourself

Sex is serious and this chapter is about how to protect yourself from pregnancy, disease, rape and incest.

Wait! Hang on! Time out! Are you beginning to think that I'm purposely making sex sound like more trouble than it could possibly be worth? That's not my aim. Really. I'm not trying to scare you into being celibate forever.

Sex should be a loving, pleasurable and meaningful part of your life some day. Sex should be something you'll feel good about.

It's sex too soon, sex without contraception or sex with the wrong person that can spell trouble and can leave you feeling guilty, worried or wistful. Which is why I want you to know what you're getting into. It's not that hard to protect yourself. And nothing is more important than your safety and your health.

Nowadays school children are learning about AIDS before they learn about lovemaking. Paranoia is not the answer and I don't want to contribute to it. But today more than ever, it's crucial to be cautious.

QUIZ: HOW MUCH DO YOU KNOW ABOUT BIRTH CONTROL?

One out of five teenage pregnancies happens in the *first* month after a girl loses her virginity. Half of all teenage pregnancies happen in the first six months. And 40 percent of sexually active teenage girls get pregnant each year. Take this quiz. And read the next sections. I don't want you to become a statistic.

1. If you go on the Pill today, how long will it be before you are fully protected and don't need to use a backup method of contraception?
   (a) One week.
   (b) Two weeks.
   (c) One month.

2. Of the following contraceptives, which also provides the best protection against sexually

transmitted diseases?
(a) The condom.
(b) The diaphragm.
(c) The Pill.

3. In terms of getting pregnant, when is the most dangerous time to have sex.
(a) During your period.
(b) Two weeks after your period starts.
(c) Two weeks after your period ends.

True or False

4. T F The condom alone prevents pregnancy 99 percent of the time.
5. T F Vaseline is recommended for couples who use condoms and need extra lubrication.
6. T F Taking one of your friend's pills before having sex is better than taking no precautions at all.
7. T F Smokers should not go on the Pill.
8. T F If you forgot to take your pill yesterday, you should take two today.
9. T F Your parents must always be notified before you can go on the Pill or be fitted for a diaphragm.
10. T F Your diaphragm size can change.

11. T F If you use the diaphragm and have sex twice in the same day, you should reapply spermicide before the second round.

12. T F You can get pregnant even if your partner withdraws before ejaculating.

13. T F Douching with Coke is an effective method of birth control.

14. T F The IUD is recommended for young women.

And the answers are . . .

1. c The Pill is the most popular method of birth control among teenagers and women in their twenties. It's easy, it's not messy and it doesn't interrupt intercourse. But beware – when you first go on the Pill, you aren't fully protected until one month goes by. Can't wait that long? Use a backup method such as the condom and foam combination. When you go on the Pill, especially at first, you may have some side effects such as slight weight gain, headaches, nausea, depression and breast tenderness. On the plus side, your periods will be lighter, shorter, more regular and less painful.

2. a Condoms (also called rubbers) are the

second most common method of birth control used by teenagers. Why? Latex condoms provide some protection against AIDS and STDs (sexually transmitted diseases). They're convenient and can be bought without a prescription at any chemist. And they enable guys to participate in the responsibility of birth control.

Never let a guy argue you out of being protected by saying that condoms cut down on his pleasure. Worrying about pregnancy and disease would cut down on your pleasure too. Besides, some guys find that the diminished sensation is actually an advantage because it keeps them from ejaculating too quickly.

3. b Attention everybody: the most 'dangerous' time to have sex is around two weeks after the first day of your period. (Most teenagers don't know this. Please spread the word.) If you have a 28-day menstrual cycle and you get your period on day one, then you ovulate around day 14 – an egg drops down from one of your ovaries and hangs out waiting for sperm. While it's wise to be extra careful mid-cycle (days 10-18), don't kid yourself. You can get pregnant any time, even during your period. That's why the rhythm method (abstaining from sex several days before, during and after ovulation) is unreliable. Since many girls' cycles are irregular, it can be particularly hard to calculate which times are riskiest. And did you know sperm can live inside your body for several days?

4. F Used with contraceptive foam, condoms are 99 percent effective. Used alone, they are only 90 percent effective. Be smart. When you go to that chemist three towns away and buy a toothbrush, Kleenex, a nail file, dental floss and, ah-hem, a packet of condoms, blush a little redder and buy contraceptive foam too.

Before intercourse, the foam is inserted into the vagina (follow the directions – it's like inserting a tampon), and the condom is rolled onto the erect penis, leaving a ½-inch space at the tip to trap the sperm-filled semen. If the condom should happen to rip (accidents do happen), the sperm-killing foam comes to the rescue by acting as a roadblock and preventing any sperm from swimming up towards your egg. After ejaculation, the rim of the condom is grasped during withdrawal and the condom is removed before it can slip off.

5. F Vaseline, petroleum jelly or any oil-based lubricant can weaken the rubber of a condom. If penetration is a problem despite slow and tender foreplay (and it is for many girls), buy prelubricated condoms or use K-Y jelly. Vaginal foam will also add moisture – and protection.

6. F Taking one pill at random does no good at all and also leaves your friend unprotected. Only when taken day by day according to directions does the Pill suppress ovulation – preventing your ovaries from releasing eggs. With no egg around for sperm to fertilize, you can't get pregnant.

7. T Smokers shouldn't be on the Pill – it increases their chances of developing cardio-vascular disease. But for most nonsmokers under 35, the Pill's health benefits are thought to out-weigh its risks. The Pill has been around since 1960, and the new low-dosage pills are considered much safer than the original pills. But the Pill is not recommended for girls who smoke, girls who are forgetful or girls who are quite underweight, have very irregular periods, high blood pressure or blood clots.

8. T If you miss a pill, double up the next day. If you miss two pills in a row, take two a day for the next two days and use a backup method of birth control until your next period. If you consistently forget your pills and get off track, the Pill may not be the best method for you.

9. F If you are having a sexual relationship you need advice on contraception. If you are under 16 your doctor or clinic will advise you and prescribe contraception without your parents being told or asked for their permission if the doctor feels that your case is 'unusual'. Your case will be considered 'unusual' if:

● you really don't feel able to tell your parents/guardians

● it's best for you to get advice and treatment although your parents/guardians don't know

● you understand the advice you're asking for

● you're likely to have sex without contraception

● you're likely to suffer physically and mentally if you don't get advice and treatment

The doctor will decide whether you can consent to the treatment (this means she/he thinks you capable of understanding it) and whether it is in your interest to prescribe contraception.

If you are 16 or over, you are entitled to advice on contraception and treatment and it's up to you whether you tell your parents/guardians or not. There is no law that they should know. Contraceptives from Family Planning Clinics or on prescription are free.

None of this applies in the Republic of Ireland, where it is illegal to advise or prescribe contraception for unmarried people.

10. T If you gain or lose 10 pounds, or if you have a baby or an abortion, your diaphragm size may change. It may also change during the first few months of becoming sexually active. Check your diaphragm periodically for tiny rips or holes; replace it, no matter what, every two years. A diaphragm used with cream or jelly works by physically and chemically preventing sperm from reaching the egg – but if you are using a diaphragm that is torn or too small, determined sperm could zip on through.

11. T Several hours (or even just several minutes) before having sex, squeeze sperm-killing cream or jelly into the diaphragm bowl and around its rim and insert it into your vagina bowl-side up. If you are going to have sex again in the same time period, use a plastic applicator to insert more spermicide into your vagina. You won't be able to feel the diaphragm up there, but don't forget about it. Leave it in for at least six to eight hours after the last intercourse but *never* for more than 24 hours. That could be toxic.

12. T Like it or not, droplets of semen containing sperm can escape into the vagina even before a man has an orgasm. Worse, a guy may intend to pull out before ejaculation but be so aroused

351

that at the last moment he fails to do so. If he's a novice to sex, he may find it especially difficult to be in complete control. Withdrawal is better than nothing but prevents pregnancy only 70 to 75 percent of the time.

13. F Think about contraception before, not after, sex. Douching with Coke does no good at all. Neither does jumping up and down or standing on your head after intercourse. Other myths? That you can't get pregnant if you don't have an orgasm. That you can't get pregnant if you have sex standing up. That you can't get pregnant the first time.

14. F Because there are questions about the IUD's link to infertility and pelvic inflammatory disease, IUDs are not recommended for women under 25, women who have not been pregnant or women who are not involved in a stable mutually monogamous relationship.

The birth control methods of choice among teenagers are the condom and the Pill. But according to the 1986 Planned Parenthood poll of 1000 teenagers aged 12 to 17, only one-third of sexually active teenagers use contraceptives all the time. Despite the high stakes involved, over one-quarter never do. And only 41 percent of sexually active teenagers polled had used birth control the first time they had intercourse.

Why aren't more teenagers sexually responsible? Many say that intercourse is unexpected and just happens. (Spare me. Either say no to spur-of-the-moment just-lust sex, or at least remember what you learned in Girl Guides and 'Be prepared!') Many believe pregnancy couldn't happen to them. (Guess again. Four out of ten girls who are 14 this year will become pregnant at least once before turning 20.) And many don't realize that condoms and foam are safe, effective and easy to obtain, or that the Pill is considered safe, effective and easy to use.

It may seem romantic to be swept away by the moment. But all it takes for you to get pregnant is for one sperm cell from his body to meet one egg cell in yours. If you have unprotected sex, his sperm and your egg are going to try their hardest to hook up and really won't care if you two are in love or if you can even afford a baby buggy, Pampers and Gerber Strained Bananas.

Promise yourself that until you're ready to start a family, you will use birth control every single time you have sex. Got that? Every single time. Even the first time.

Bonus: sex is more fun when it's worry-free.

TALKING WITH PARENTS ABOUT CONTRACEPTION

How do you ask your mum about birth control?

I hear that question a lot. And mums want to know how to broach the subject with you. Why are parents reluctant to talk to daughters about birth control? Because they are afraid their daughters might think they approve of teenage hanky-panky. Why are daughters reluctant to talk to parents about birth control? Because they are afraid their parents might think they are promiscuous or pregnant. It's not easy being the parent of a teenage daughter. They say parents of a son worry about their boy while parents of a daughter worry – rightly or wrongly – about every boy in town.

If you're thinking about having sex, you don't need your parents' permission and you shouldn't expect their blessing. So it's up to you whether you try to stage a Family Talk. It could bring you all closer. Or it could set off World War III.

Don't assume your parents are up on every new finding about birth control or STDs. But don't assume they are hopelessly naive about sex either – you didn't exactly get here by immaculate conception, you know.

When I went to college, I went on the Pill. My period was still unpredictable, and I decided it would be good for me to take the Pill to regulate my cycles. My mother and I knew that that wasn't the only thing the Pill could offer me, but there was no need to elaborate.

About two-thirds of American teenagers have talked to their parents at some point about sex and pregnancy. But only one-third have discussed birth control. The ideal time to talk to your mother or father about sex is long before you're even involved with anybody. If you come home with a necklace of love-bites and say, 'Dad, what kind of rubber do you think is better?' you'll probably get your mouth washed out with soap and be grounded until you're 30.

You may have better luck if you are (or at least sound) inexperienced and if you are (or at least sound) just curious about their thoughts. Wait until you and your parents are relaxed and doing dishes together or going for a drive. Or wait until you're watching TV together and there's a bedroom scene or news about AIDS or a condom commercial. Then, instead of cringing, seize the opportunity to test the waters. Don't ask, 'Would you ever let me go on the Pill?'

Open the conversation less directly. Try:

- 'Can you believe how much sex there is on TV? You hear a lot more about sex than birth control.' OR
- 'It's really scary about AIDS, isn't it?' OR
- 'Did you hear that a 15-year-old American girl is five times as likely to have a baby than a girl from another developed country?' OR
- 'Did anybody in your school drop out because she was pregnant?' OR
- 'Do you remember your first kiss?' OR
- 'A girl in my school went on the Pill so her periods would be less painful.' OR
- 'I'm reading a book about boys and there are a few things in the sex chapter that I don't understand.'

It's okay to tell your parents that you feel awkward – they probably do too. And do reassure them that you are responsible (which I hope you are) and that you don't even have a boyfriend (if you don't). Tell them you value their opinion and appreciate their openness. Such a conversation may pave the way for future talks, or, alas, may make you realize that your parents will never be comfortable talking about The Big S. If they say, 'A book about boys? A chapter on sex? Gimme that!' and wing this into the fireplace, then please forgive me for the dumb suggestion and it was nice to have had you aboard up to this page.

TO BE ON THE PILL OR NOT
TO BE ON THE PILL
AND OTHER QUESTIONS

Still here? Good. I got worried there for a sec.

Some girls took a pass on mum and dad and mailed questions to yours truly instead.

> *The thought of getting pregnant scares the hell out of me. I don't want to rely on store-bought contraceptives, but do you think I'm too young to go on the Pill? I'll be 15 in a few months. Do I have to go to a doctor for a prescription? They scare the hell out of me too.*

Getting pregnant is scary, but doctors shouldn't be. Girls need to visit their doctor or a family planning clinic to get a pelvic exam before they can get oral contraceptives. But it's not that big a deal. For the record (and I know I'm sounding like a broken one), I think this girl sounds too young – and too scared – for sex.

A doctor might ask her, 'Have you had regular periods for at least two years?' If so, the doctor might ask about her medical history and whether she smokes (pills and cigarettes don't mix, remember?) before writing out a prescription.

But wait, what's wrong with store-bought birth control? If used responsibly, the condom and foam combination is very reliable – and offers some protection against STDs. Besides, why have full-time protection if you may be having only once-in-a-while sex? You wouldn't take an aspirin every day for once-a-month headaches, would you? Oral contraceptives should be taken only by girls and women with consistently active sex lives or girls who are sexually active and are sure they wouldn't have the discipline to use the barrier (condoms, diaphragm) methods of birth control.

> *It's about the Pill. How long before and after sex do you take it? What if you have sex two nights in a row?*

Before sex? During sex? Instead of sex? Allow me to clear up the confusion. You take the Pill at the same time each day, ideally after a meal (to prevent possible nausea). Pills are made of a combination of synthetic hormones. If you have a

28-day packet, you take a pill each day; the seven pills you take during your period are do-nothing placebos that simply help you stay on track. If you have a 21-day packet, you take a pill each day and skip the week of your period. If you take the Pill properly, you'll be fully protected after the first month and it won't matter how many times in a row you have sex.

If you've been on the Pill a long time and then go off it, can you get pregnant?

Millions of mums used to be on the Pill. The Pill does not affect fertility – so don't believe the myth that it makes you sterile. When a grown woman goes off the Pill, however, she should wait to complete two or three periods before trying to conceive. Women who become pregnant immediately after being on the Pill are more likely to miscarry.

Good news: condoms and diaphragms used with spermicide can actually decrease a woman's risk of some types of infertility because while they block sperm, they also block infection. So not only do they prevent pregnancy now, but they can help to preserve fertility for later.

Be careful. It's sad when a girl gets a venereal disease from casual sex, lets the infection go unchecked and ruins her chances of becoming pregnant years later when she may want to raise a family.

> *My boyfriend found some of his dad's old condoms. How do we know if they're still okay to use?*

While unopened, lubricated condoms that are a few years old may be okay, they also may have dried out. Condoms should be stored in a cool dry place and used within two years of purchase. (Some are marked with expiration dates.) A condom carried in a wallet for a year should be replaced since the warmth and wear and tear on it can age it faster. A condom kept in a warm glove compartment could age faster still. Spend a few bucks, use 'condom sense' and buy new ones. It's better to be safe than sorry, protected than pregnant.

> *I moved this year and was surprised to find that some of my friends who are boys have condoms. I'm only in the eighth grade. The boys were giving odds on whether I'd 'do it' this year. And what really scares me is that they use the condoms over and over and let their friends use them.*

That would scare me too. But you know

what? I don't believe it. I think the boys are just mouthing off – as eighth-grade boys are wont to do. It might be possible to rinse, reroll and reuse a condom just as it might be possible to wash, dry and reuse a tampon. Both ideas are equally repugnant and unsanitary. A condom should never be reused even by the same guy. After ejaculation, the condom's reservoir tip fills up with semen – leaving no room for more. A used condom would also be weaker and more likely to rip than a new one.

> *I once came close to having sex. We were in a camper. He tried to get it in but it wouldn't go in. Is that normal and am I still a virgin? Also, if we had oral sex, am I still a virgin?*

A girl is a virgin until she experiences penis-inside-vagina intercourse. And if anyone is wondering, oral sex doesn't mean just talking about it. Fellatio is when a woman stimulates the penis with her mouth. Cunnilingus is when a man stimulates the woman's genitals with his lips and tongue. Oral sex cannot make you pregnant, but STDs can be spread through fellatio or cunnilingus. If oral sex does not appeal to a couple, neither the man nor woman should feel pressured to do it.

Many couples have trouble having intercourse the first time. Some virgins have difficulty at first because the girl's hymen (the thin piece of skin across the vaginal opening) is intact. When this is torn by the boy's penis, some girls bleed a little, although many don't.

Other couples have trouble because they are in such a hurry that they don't give the girl's body time to respond sexually. Spermicidally treated lubricated condoms can help provide necessary lubrication – and can also help prevent pregnancy and disease.

> *My friend has been with three different guys and has done it dozens of times. Because of your book, she knows about the stuff she should have known about before. She now thinks she might be pregnant but doesn't understand why she hasn't been before.*

Luck can run out. Every year, 90 percent of girls who have regular sex without birth control get pregnant. Unless you're infertile, you can't beat the odds forever. Having a so-many-men-so-little-time attitude is a good way to get pregnant or get a disease. A girl's first appointment at a family planning clinic should be for information, a checkup or birth control

– not for a pregnancy or STD test.

> *Why do parents get upset about their kids having sex?*

Why do bears tinkle in the woods?

Parents get upset because some kids get pregnant and get diseases and get hurt when they have sex too soon. Most parents are protective because they love their kids.

I remember going with my boyfriend and his parents to his college. We were all standing around his dorm room and he started unpacking. He flipped his suitcase upside down on his bed and out spilled T-shirts, dental floss, notebooks, socks, condoms. Condoms?! A twelve-pack no less. Oops! And I had to drive back alone with his parents.

It's natural to have a zillion questions about sex and birth control. And it's too bad there's still no perfect contraceptive. New methods are being developed all the time and some day contraceptive implants, cervical caps and pills for men may be safe, effective and available.

But these contraceptives may be years away – or may never be marketed. If you're having sex now, go on the Pill, get a diaphragm or use condoms and foam. Birth control may sound intimidating, but it really isn't all that complicated. And if you're sexually active, it's worth the hassle. Believe me. There's a lot to be said for being sweet-sixteen-and-never-been-pregnant.

WHAT IF YOU ARE PREGNANT?

How do you tell your parents if you're pregnant?

If you think it's hard to talk to your parents about birth control, imagine telling them you're pregnant. There's no easy way to break that sort of news.

Some parents turn out to be very supportive. Others lash out. Others are angry or disappointed at first but then do all they can to help their daughters through the crisis. And some girls end their pregnancies without ever telling mum or dad.

If you are pregnant, you aren't alone. Every thirty seconds a teenager gets pregnant. Each year, about one out of ten American teenagers gets pregnant. Each year over 400,000 teenage girls have abortions, about 100,000 miscarry, and some half a million girls have babies – which most keep and relatively few give up for adoption.

Who are these pregnant girls? Whites. Blacks. Hispanics. Many are economically disadvantaged (which is a roundabout way of saying poor) and many feel they have little to lose. Studies show that girls who get good grades, have career aspirations and are involved in sports and extracurrics tend to see beyond the moment and therefore use birth control more regularly and get pregnant less often.

If you have sex without protection and your period is late, don't waste time worrying about whether you are pregnant. Find out. Get a urine test or blood test at a clinic or at your doctor's. Or at least buy a home pregnancy test at a chemist.

> *My boyfriend and I had sex about a month ago. The rubber broke and we were really scared. We waited for a couple weeks and then got a home pregnancy test. The test was negative. In two days I got my period. A couple days later I was in school and I had severe stomach cramps. Then I fainted. The school nurse said it could have been caused by stress, a bladder infection or pregnancy. I went to the doctor and he said it was something to do with my blood pressure. The nurse there took a urinalysis. She asked me if I was pregnant and I*

said, 'No, I have my period.' She said that sometimes girls will be pregnant and still bleed. I told her I wasn't pregnant. Lately I have been feeling sort of sick to my stomach. I also feel as if my stomach is swelling. It could be my imagination about the swelling, though.

My questions are: when they give you a urinalysis, do they check for pregnancy too? The doctor said nothing about it when he got my results. Also, if you have your period, does that mean for sure that you're not pregnant?

I'm only 14 and my mum could never understand. I don't have anyone else to answer these questions. So please answer quickly.

I answered quickly and I tried to be reassuring, but it's a shame she didn't ask her doctor or nurse to give her a pregnancy test. Doctors do not routinely test for pregnancy. If she was worried about her parents' finding out, she could have asked the doctor about confidentiality or she could have gone to a hospital or clinic and gotten a test there. She could have telephoned and asked if she could be tested anonymously or without parental notification.

Some pregnant women bleed or spot a little

at first, but this is not actually a period. Fainting and severe cramps are not typical tell-tale signs of pregnancy, but in the worse-case scenario, this girl could have an ectopic (outside the womb) or tubal pregnancy. What about that swelling stomach? Most women gain only two to four pounds during the first three months of pregnancy. The bottom line is that since this girl is still worried, she should get tested and set her mind at ease once and for all.

What are the more common symptoms of pregnancy? Many, but not all, pregnant women experience fatigue, nausea, frequent urination, tingling swollen breasts and nipples and food aversions (a girl who has always loved Chinese food, for instance, may find it unappetizing for a few months).

What if you skipped your period and are feeling tired and queasy, not to mention upset and frightened? What if you *are* pregnant? Do some soul-searching. Talk to someone you can trust (an older friend, teacher, relative, guidance counsellor, clergy member) and, as soon as possible, try to decide what is best for you. Think of the pros and cons of ending your pregnancy versus having a baby.

Abortion

Teenagers have about one-third of all abortions performed in the United States. Women aged 18 to 19 have the highest abortion rate of any age group. If you decide to have an abortion, it's best to have it as early as possible during your pregnancy, ideally within the first three months. Early abortions are cheaper, safer and simpler than later abortions. They can usually be performed in less than half an hour (although you may need to rest for a few hours afterwards) and don't require general anaesthesia (which would make you temporarily unconscious). Later abortions are somewhat more complicated and often involve an overnight stay at the hospital or clinic.

In Britain an abortion needs the consent of two doctors, which can cause delays, so go to your doctor at once if you think you may be pregnant and may need an abortion. If your doctor is against abortion (e.g. she/he may be Roman Catholic) you should immediately contact one of the advice agencies listed in the *Information* section of this book. If you are under 16, the law now requires your doctor to inform your parents. *Do not let this deter you from seeking early advice*. Your doctor will have dealt with many young people in your situation and be able to advise you.

As most teenagers recognize, abortion is not a method of birth control or an easy way out. It is a last resort. After the abortion, you may feel sad, guilty, wistful, but you may also feel very relieved – and ready to be as careful as possible about contraception in the future.

I'm 17 and my boyfriend Ray is 19. He is also my best friend and we've always had a great relationship – until last month.

Six weeks ago, I found out I was pregnant. We spent the next day crying together. I decided the only thing I could do was have an abortion. We couldn't afford a baby and I didn't want to graduate pregnant. He's in college and I plan on going to college in the fall. A baby would have made things impossible.

Ray was totally against the abortion. He said I was being selfish. Then he gave me a choice: me, him and the baby or just me. After a million tears, I chose just me.

He was against it, but he paid for half the abortion and took me. He also said he didn't love me any more, would never forgive me and that we had no future together. I was so hurt, I wanted to die. I trusted him and couldn't believe he turned on me.

Well, the other night, he called me crying and said he was really sorry and still loved me and wanted me back. We're back together now, but I feel so guilty for having the abortion. I know it hurt him terribly. And he hurt me with all those awful thing he said. Every time I see a baby, I cry. I can't remember the last time Ray and I smiled together.

What I need to know is: how can I make things better between us? Was I being selfish by having the abortion?

I don't think so. She thought about it long and hard. And frankly, sometimes people have to be selfish. Neither Ray nor she are cold-hearted and I feel for them both.

It's natural that she is still upset; the abortion is barely behind her. But it *is* behind her. If she doesn't start feeling better in another month or so, she may want to call the clinic and talk to someone there about her feelings. Or they may be able to recommend a counsellor.

Will she and Ray recover as a couple? Crises can bring couples closer together or drive them farther apart. These two have hurt each other and have been through a lot. They can remain together if they both want to, or they may drift apart – as most teenage couples do, even those with a less painful history. For now, they both need to forgive each other and to forgive themselves. They've learned a lot the hard way.

Abortion is never easy, but it's not always this difficult. Matter of fact, some boyfriends don't get involved at all and many teenagers are too cavalier about abortion. Ethical questions aside, a girl who has several abortions may have more difficulty carrying a pregnancy to term later when she wants to have a family.

Having the Baby

If you choose to have the baby, you should make that decision as promptly as possible too. If you are going to have a baby, make it a healthy baby. Don't smoke, take drugs or drink alcohol. Even medication for acne or headaches should be avoided. Cut out junk food and start downing more milk and juice, eating more healthful balanced meals and taking special prenatal vitamins. Since you and your baby are growing – and competing for nutrients – this is no time to diet or fill up on pretzels and caramels. Counsellors at family planning clinics can advise you about nutrition and prenatal care. They can also help you decide whether to give up the baby or keep it.

Adoption

If you decide to have the baby adopted you can feel confident that it will be well loved and cared for. These days there is a shortage of babies for adoption by people unable to have children of their own. Remember though that although adopted children now have the legal right to information about their biological parents, you do not have the legal right to information about a child you have given up for adoption. This can be very painful. Some parents who have given their children up for adoption have deposited letters and information with the Adoption Society so that the adopted child can easily trace them if she/he ever wants to. Your Adoption Society and social worker should be able to advise you on all this.

Here is a letter I received from an adopted girl who hopes to meet her birth mother.

> *I was adopted and I'm very curious about my natural mother. I love my real (adoptive) mother very much and would never hurt her. But I'm curious about my natural mother. All I know is that she was a teenager when she had me. Do you know how to help me get started?*

Her curiosity is natural, and I'm glad she's being sensitive to the feelings of the mother who raised her. The agency or intermediary that handled her adoption may be able to provide her with information – if they have any. Or she could leave a letter or photo there in case her birth mother ever returns with questions. I wished her luck in her search, but warned her not to get her hopes too high. Some adoption files are closed, some birth mothers are not welcoming and some experts caution that adolescence is not the ideal time for an actual reunion because a teenager's emotional swings and quest for self-discovery are already complicated and overwhelming enough.

Keeping the Baby

Do you want to keep the baby? Think ahead and be realistic about the commitment. Will you have to drop out of school? (Less than one-fifth of brides and grooms who marry under age 18 finish high school.) Will your parents or your boyfriend help raise your child? (What makes you think so?) Will the baby's father marry you? (After ten years, women who got married when they were 14 to 17 were three times as likely to get a divorce as women who married in their early twenties, one study found.) Will the baby's father be able to support you? (Teenage mothers earn less than half of what mothers in their twenties earn. If he foots the bills, will he have to throw his career plans out the window?) Where will you and your baby live three years from now? (Five years from now?) Will you have to go on social security?

It's hard having a baby with no money, no husband, no qualifications. Child abuse and suicide are more common among teenage mothers than among older mothers. And you can't become a veterinarian, teacher, psychologist, pilot or politician without continuing your studies and having enough time to pursue your dreams. Having a baby too soon can stunt your growth.

Many determined young women overcome the odds, have their babies and raise them well. Homes and schools for pregnant women can also help. Ask your clinic for addresses.

I am 14 years old and I like to have my way – like dating and smoking. Neither my mum nor my grandma likes that. They're afraid I might get pregnant. I don't use birth control and I do love this boy who is 17. He wants a baby and so do I. My parents are too protective of me and I'm scared to sit down and talk to them.

If I were her mother, I'd be protective too.

She and her boyfriend may want to have a baby, but are they really mature enough to be good parents? Even her mentioning smoking and pregnancy in the same paragraph worries me – babies of smokers are likely to be born smaller and weaker than babies of nonsmokers.

Perhaps she thinks having a baby will make her more grown-up. Having a baby may make her more dependent on adults than ever, and may land her on the path to permanent poverty. Perhaps she thinks a baby will provide her with someone to love and who will love her. Babies are lovable, but they also require a lot of care. They get hungry at 3:00 a.m., aren't toilet trained for over a year or two and can't be left totally alone for nearly a decade. As teenagers, many follow their mother's example and have babies of their own. (Do you want to be a grandmother by 30?)

You're only young once: why saddle yourself with so much responsibility? Finish being a kid before having a kid. Figure out what you want to make of your life before bringing another life into the world. I want you to be proud of yourself. To finish high school. To have a goal – not a baby. (Bear with me. I'm about to get off the podium, but this stuff is important.) Too many babies are born out of wedlock and into welfare. And too many young mothers have to sacrifice their own hopes for a better life in order to raise a child.

Yes, the girl who likes to date and smoke can have a baby at 14. But she can also have a baby at 24. Or 34. And by then, she may have more to offer the baby and be a better mother. I'm glad I spent my youth going to college and dating different guys and travelling and becoming a writer. Now that I have a husband and a home and a career – now that I know where my life is going – I'm ready to have a baby. At 14 I wasn't ready. Is she? Are you?

AIDS, HERPES AND OTHER BAD NEWS

Sex can be risky business. Reduce the risk by abstaining from sex, going out with just one faithful uninfected guy or insisting that your sexual partner wear a condom. And learn all you can about STDs: sexually transmitted diseases. Two and a half million teenagers contract STDs each year, and sexually active teenagers have the highest rates of STDs among heterosexuals of any age group.

Here are a dozen questions to help you separate myth from fact. (Okay, so this is not the most cheery quiz in the book. It's not a bad way for you to test your knowledge, is it?)

True or False

– **1.** A girl who has no symptoms could have a sexually transmitted disease.

– **2.** There is still no cure for herpes.

– **3.** STDs can lead to sterility.

– **4.** You can't have more than one STD at a time.

– **5.** If you have gonorrhea once, you can't get it again.

– **6.** A pregnant woman with an STD can give it to her baby.

– **7.** You can get tested for STDs without parental consent.

– **8.** Gynaecologists routinely test for all forms of STDs.

– **9.** Symptoms of some STDs can take months, even years, to appear.

–**10.** If you are not gay, you can't get AIDS.

11. The most prevalent STD among teens is
(a) gonorrhea.
(b) AIDS.
(c) syphilis
(d) chlamydia.

12. People with genital herpes typically
(a) Get genital sores once then never again.
(b) Get genital warts.
(c) Get sores that come back periodically.

(d) Get crabs.

Answers:
1. T
2. T
3. T
4. F
5. F
6. T
7. T
8. F
9. T
10. F
11. d
12. c

How'd you score? When it comes to STDs, what you don't know *can* hurt you. AIDS kills. Herpes lasts a lifetime. And many girls haven't even heard of chlamydia, the most widespread sexually transmitted disease of all.

Knowing about STDs can – and should – influence your choice of sexual partner and of birth control. Not only should you be looking for Mr. Right, you should be looking for Mr. Clean. When you have sex with a guy, you aren't having sex just with him, you're having it with his previous lovers. Symptoms in guys are usually more apparent than in girls, but since some guys find it embarrassing to own up to an STD, they may go for treatment without encouraging their ex-girlfriends (much less one-night stands) to do the same.

In the case of STDs, people should kiss and tell. That's one reason why this letter bothers me.

> *I'm 16 and I feel I am ready to become sex-*
> *ually active. Curiosity is about to drive me*
> *out of my mind. Should I ignore my pas-*
> *sionate feelings for my boyfriend? Should*
> *I wait for some other girl to do for him*
> *what I couldn't do for him? He has told*
> *me he has been to bed with other young*
> *ladies while we have been involved with*
> *one another.*

Let's get this straight. While she's sitting around wondering whether to wait for some other girl to do for him what she has not, he's out getting things done for him by other young ladies. Who needs it? STDs are reason enough to steer clear of playboys like him.

It's not enough any more for a girl not to be promiscuous. She also has to be selective – she has to avoid guys who are indiscriminate. If you suspect your partner has slept with lots of other girls (who have slept with lots of other guys who have slept with lots of other girls who . . .), don't risk your health. If you suspect he has slept with prostitutes or with other men or that he has used intravenous drugs say no. If you think he might not know he has an STD or might choose not to tell, say no. (It's been said that an erection has no conscience.)

If you're going to say yes to someone you feel uneasy about, at least insist that he wear a condom. You don't have to come up with some witticism like 'No glove, no love,' but do get your point across. Condoms can prevent pregnancy, prevent STDs and save lives. Ideally they should be used with a spermicide containing nonoxynol-9 for extra protection.

How can you ask your partner to wear a condom? Say, 'Let's not give each other the third degree. If you wear a condom, we'll both be safe.' Some guys might say, 'Forget it! I don't take showers in my raincoat or baths with my boots on.' But if he says no to a condom, you can say no to him. When given the choice between sex with a condom or no sex at all, most guys stop protesting.

The next letter was signed Itchy.

Are sex diseases running rampant amongst teenagers and what do you do if your boy-friend gives you VD when you believed

You drop the bum and go straight to a doctor or to a clinic for treatment.

Are venereal diseases rampant? Yes. Many are easy to treat but hard to detect. Certain diseases can compromise a woman's health or fertility.

If you are a virgin and you also have not engaged in oral sex, relax. It is extremely unlikely that you could have contracted an STD. If you have one steady boyfriend and your first time was also his first time, it's also extremely unlikely that you could have an STD. So don't worry needlessly. But if you are more sexually experienced, be sure to have regular checkups at a clinic.

STDs do not go away by themselves. Your checkups will be confidential. Don't be embarrassed – doctors see cases all the time. If a doctor gives you medicine, take it all as prescribed because your symptoms may disappear before the disease does. If you are pregnant, be especially cautious and ask your doctor about possible complications during delivery or any hazards to the newborn.

This is the most embarrassing letter I've ever written. I hope you don't think anything bad of me after you read this. I also hope that you read this and not some secretary. Girltalk is my survival kit; definitely one of the best purchases I ever made. This is so embarrassing, but I'm extremely worried. Okay. In your book you said masturbation couldn't get you pregnant or give you a disease. But you also said if you touch a cold sore and then another part of your body without washing your hands first, you could spread herpes.

What I'm worried about is this: If you touched a cold sore and then 'm'd' (with panties on), could you get genital herpes? I'm sorry to be so graphic but I'm really terrified. I remember one time when I might have done what I asked you about. That was about a year ago. Lately, I've had this itch 'down there' and I've always had a discharge. I don't think I've ever had a sore, though. I'm probably being silly, but I've always been a worrier. If I have herpes that's the only way I could have gotten it. I'm still a virgin and I've never even kissed a boy although I'm 16. (I'm not gay – I'm just extremely shy. But that's another story.) Please help me. I'm going crazy.

I read this letter myself and I certainly don't

think anything bad of her. What about the $64,000 question: can you give yourself genital herpes? Technically, yes. But you'd practically have to be trying. And I bet it rarely ever happens. (So don't you start worrying. Bad enough that the letter writer is in such a state.) Since she says she 'm'd' (as it were) with panties on, I'm especially inclined to give her a clean bill of health. If she had herpes, she would surely know it. She'd have recurrent sores, not a discharge or itch.

She could have a vaginal infection that has nothing to do with cold sores or masturbation. If so, she might want to avoid bubble baths, scented toilet paper and nylon-crotch underwear (cotton is better). If she has an unusual discharge, or persistent burning, itching or irritation, she should get it checked out – without embarrassment! About five million women (many of whom are virgins) get vaginitis each year; there are three types and only a doctor can prescribe the right treatment for each.

> I'm 12. I've never had sex with anyone, but I have a sort of pimple between my vagina and my rectum. It was sore and swollen for two days but now it's just a small bump. Please write me. It will really take a load off my mind.

I wonder what the postman would think of my mail if he had x-ray vision.

Just as people get blemishes on their faces, they can sometimes get them elsewhere. I'm not a doctor and I encouraged her to go to a clinic. See the *Information* section at the back of this book.

Do you know about the most talked-about STDs?

Acquired Immune Deficiency Syndrome (AIDS)

You've heard the slogan 'If you think you can't get AIDS, you're dead wrong'? AIDS is alarming people around the world. With reason. It is fatal and as of this writing, there is no cure. But that doesn't mean you should panic or be afraid to go near a person with AIDS.

AIDS was not officially diagnosed until 1981. It is an affliction that cripples the body's immune system making it unable to resist and ward off certain infections and cancers. People can come down with AIDS from several months to many years after exposure to HIV (the human immunodeficiency virus). On average, a person who contracts AIDS develops symptoms such as weight loss, fatigue, fever and sometimes lesions, and may die within a year or two.

Although AIDS is a nightmarish epidemic, it is not particularly prevalent among children and teenagers, and it is not a cinch to catch. Most children with AIDS got it from infected mothers or from a very unlucky blood transfusion (before hospitals began routinely screening blood donors in early 1985). AIDS is usually spread when someone has unprotected vaginal or anal sex with an infected person or when a drug user shares an infected person's contaminated needle or syringe. You can't get AIDS by donating blood because a new needle is used for each donor. And there have been no documented cases of AIDS spreading via swimming pools, hot tubs or toilet seats.

So far in America, most people with AIDS have been gay or bisexual men, intravenous drug users who share needles and their sexual partners. And you? Don't worry. But do avoid having unprotected sex with bisexuals, intravenous drug users, their partners and promiscuous people in general. Avoid anal sex (it probably wasn't on your to-do list today anyway). If you aren't going to abstain, and you aren't sure that your partner is free of infection, have him use a condom together with a spermicide containing nonoxynol-9, during intercourse or fellatio (oral sex). (I know it doesn't sound sexy.)

Although more Americans have died of AIDS than have died in some wars, the average girl in your high school has no reason to suspect that she might be infected with HIV or might eventually contract AIDS or ARC (AIDS-related complex). It is also not certain that everyone who has tested positive for AIDS antibodies will eventually get the deadly disease.

For more information on AIDS/HIV see the *Information* section at the back of this book.

Genital Herpes

The good news: people aren't as paranoid about herpes as they used to be. The stigma has lessened and many victims consider herpes a periodic annoyance rather than a social leprosy. There is a new antiviral drug which provides some relief to sufferers who have outbreaks of genital sores, blisters and ulcers.

The bad news: there is still no cure for herpes. And the virus is more common than ever.

Many millions of Americans have herpes. Some rarely get sores. Others get flare-ups several times a year. Herpes is especially contagious during intercourse with a sufferer who has a cluster of open sores. (And if a herpes sufferer with open sores has sex with a person with AIDS, the herpes sufferer runs an added risk of being infected with the HIV virus.)

Beware. Genital herpes can also be contracted during oral sex with someone with a cold sore in the mouth. And oral (mouth) herpes can become ocular (eye) herpes as well as genital herpes. A person who touches a no-big-deal cold sore in the mouth should wash her hands before tinkering with a contact lens. (Now, don't freak out. Just be cautious.)

After exposure, it can take days or weeks for genital herpes symptoms to appear. These include genital sores, painful urination and fever. Some carriers never have herpes outbreaks. Herpes is particularly dangerous in pregnant women since a newborn who catches herpes during delivery could die or suffer brain damage. (If a woman knows she has herpes, she can deliver by Ceasarean section.)

Herpes is no fun, but it doesn't have to ruin your life. For more information see the *Information* section at the back of this book.

Chlamydia

You may not be able to pronounce it (kla-mid-ee-a), but chlamydia is the most prevalent STD in America today. Some five million new cases are reported each year. Chlamydia is easy to cure with antibiotics. But it's hard to detect. Up to 80 percent of infected women have no symptoms. Those who do may have genital burning, unusual discharge, between-periods-bleeding and pelvic pain.

And if a chlamydia infection is not treated? In women, it can cause pelvic inflammatory disease (PID) which in turn can be the cause of sterility or of ectopic pregnancy (when the fertilized egg grows in the fallopian tube instead of the uterus). The babies of pregnant women with chlamydia sometimes have pneumonia or eye infections and are sometimes stillborn.

Gonorrhea

The 'clap' is another widespread STD, also harder to detect in women than in men. Gonorrhea can usually be cured with penicillin, although some types of gonorrhea are resistant and must be treated with other antibiotics. When left untreated, the disease can result in complications including PID and sterility as well as arthritis, meningitis, blindness in newborns and other problems. Symptoms include puslike discharge, painful urination, and soreness, and may appear within ten days of contact. Many women who have gonorrhea also have chlamydia – but each requires its own separate treatment. If you have gonorrhea, ask for a chlamydia test.

Syphilis

Syphilis is less common than chlamydia or gonorrhea but at least as serious. A chancre (sore or blister) may appear on the genitals or lips several weeks after infection. It then disappears on its own and is followed by a rash, warts, hair loss, sore throat and/or swollen glands. Untreated, syphilis can ravage its victim and cause brain damage, degeneration of bones and nerve tissue, insanity, paralysis, heart disease or death. It can also be devastating to newborns.

Venereal Warts

(Can you stand to read any more about all this charming stuff? Hang on – I'm just finishing up.) Genital warts usually appear one to three months after a person has had direct contact with someone else's venereal warts – although the incubation period may be longer. They are caused by a virus and are highly contagious. The tiny flat or cauliflowerlike warts can be removed through medication, burning, freezing or surgery, but this may require several treatments. Infection is correlated with cancer of the cervix.

Crabs

Crabs are little six-legged lice that hide out in the pubic hair and itch, itch, itch. They can appear one week or one month after contact. Kill them with a special lotion available from a chemist. Then wash and dry all your clothes and sheets on the HOT setting.

Bleahh! Enough said about STDs! The point is to abstain or to be prudent. If you ever have a troubling discharge, irritation or itching, go to your doctor or any STD clinic. Girls can get scabies (itch mites), cystitis (bladder infection) or vaginitis (there are several types) without having intercourse and those should be treated with drugs too. It's better to be embarrassed and inconvenienced now than to ignore a problem and let it get out of hand.

I really like the chapter on sex in Girltalk. *I'm a virgin and have been wondering a lot lately if it was time to change that status. The sections on birth control and STDs helped me realize the responsibilities involved. I've decided I'm not ready for sex yet and I feel really good about that decision. Thank you.*

RAPE AND DATE RAPE

Most women will never be victims of sexual assault. But all women should know how to avoid dangerous situations and defend themselves in case of emergency.

How cautious are you? Here are a dozen questions. Mark 'Yes' 'Depends' or 'No' after each.

1. Would you walk or jog alone at night?
2. Would you hitchhike?
3. Would you enter an elevator if the only person inside were a suspicious-looking man?
4. If you arrived at your parked car or door-step alone, would you have your key ready to use (rather than have to fish for it)?
5. If you had a gut feeling that you were being watched or followed, would you take the feeling seriously (rather than dismiss it)?
6. Would you agree to baby-sit if asked by someone you've never met or heard of?
7. Would you let a plumber or meter reader into your home if you weren't expecting the visit?
8. If driving alone in a dangerous neighbour-hood, would you put up the windows and lock all the doors?
9. If lost, would you ask a strange man for

directions?

10. Would you park on a secluded road with a guy you didn't know that well?

11. Would you let a stranger on the phone know that you were home alone?

12. Would you work in an empty schoolroom or hang out alone in a business building after hours?

How'd you do? A perfect score would be 'Yes' for nos 4, 5, 8, and 'No' for the other nine. If you wrote many more yesses, you're taking too many chances. But if you wrote 'Depends' now and again, that's okay. I don't want you to go around being unnecessarily scared or paranoid.

The point is, rapists look for easy targets. So don't amble down the street when you can walk briskly; don't look frightened when you can look confident; don't hang out in deserted areas where no one could even hear you cry for help.

'Fair enough. Starting now,' you promise yourself, 'I'm going to quit strolling down dark alleyways and stop befriending drunken strangers.' Then you realize you haven't been striking up conversations with many alley bums lately anyway. But you know what? Most rapes don't occur between strangers in alleyways.

About half of all reported rapists are acquaintances, 'friends' and relatives – and many incidents of date rape and incest go unreported. Over half of all rapes occur at home – in most cases, the abuser was invited or allowed in. Most rapes occur between members of the same race. And most victims are young women, although children, older women and even boys are vulnerable and are victims.

What should you do if, God forbid, you are assaulted by a stranger? Run like blazes and try to escape. If you have a whistle blow it like mad. And scream bloody murder using a deep yell that will carry. Shout 'Rape!' (or 'Police!' or 'Help!') so that people within earshot know you're not crying wolf. If you're inside, try to get to a phone and dial 999 to summon the police.

What else to do depends on the circumstances and your instincts. Does the man have a weapon? Where are you located? Can you seize an opportunity to get away? If you're going to get physical by biting, scratching, gouging his eyes, bending back his pinky or beating his face with your keys or the heels of your shoes, don't be halfhearted about it. Why not take a self-defence course now?

Experts also suggest talking to the rapist sympathetically or trying to outsmart or surprise him. They say to show that you refuse to be intimidated. Another idea is to ask him concerned questions about his life, or tell him your mother is dying of cancer, or cry and beg release. Other alternatives? Tell him you have AIDS. Gross him out by urinating, vomiting or saying you have your period. Or go absolutely limp. Try to keep your wits about you.

If you are raped and you think the rapist may hurt you to keep you quiet, lie and say that you'd die if anyone found out and that you won't tell a soul. Then, when he's gone and the coast is clear, call a rape crisis hotline and go straight to the police and tell them what happened. Go even before bathing so that the police can collect useful evidence (hair samples, etc.). A doctor may be able to prescribe hormone therapy to avert the possibility of pregnancy, and can follow up weeks later with STD tests.

Around 80,000 rapes are reported each year, and rape crisis centres can offer medical, emotional and legal help. By reporting a rape, you're not only regaining control of your life, you're helping other victims too because most rapists rape again.

What about date rape? What about men who force their dates to have sex without their consent? Some boyfriends are bullies who play rough and have frightening tempers. Are you ever afraid of your boyfriend or do you ever feel that he doesn't respect you? Does he have violent tendencies? If so, are you positive you want to go out with him? Why?

Sometimes, a woman says no but a man hears yes. She might willingly kiss a guy but not want to go all the way with him. A woman shouldn't lead a man on, but if she says no assertively, leaving no room for doubt, and is nonetheless forced against her will to have sex, that is rape. Make no mistake – it is rape even if the rapist was her friend or boyfriend. She may feel ambivalent about reporting him and the case won't be easy since it will be her word against his. But date rape and acquaintance rape are realities that are being recognized in more and more courts across the country. Even if a girl doesn't want to prosecute, she should know if she has been raped so that she can deal with it emotionally.

> *I wish I had had* Girltalk *when I was growing up. I am 18 years old. When I was about 10, I got raped by my best friend's older brother. No, I didn't report it because I didn't know what was happening. I got over it, but not completely. Sometimes I wake up crying and it scares me.*

Many rape victims feel numb, depressed,

angry, nervous and guilty. Many benefit from counselling and from being reminded that while the rapist was abusive, not all men are. And that while the rapist is to blame, the victim is not. If you were violated, it is not your fault. If you were raped, stop blaming yourself for succumbing and start applauding yourself for surviving.

> *You are the first person I have consulted about my problem. I was riding home in the bus from kindergarten one day and a boy asked if I would undress for him. I wasn't so sure at first, then after he told me it was okay, I did. I think it was the biggest mistake of my life. Anyway, something happened that I don't wish to say. Now when I'm around boys, I'm very squeamish. I don't know what to do. I know this probably sounds like just another love problem, but it took a lot of guts to write this letter.*

This girl may not have been raped, but she was violated. Since the incident colours her feelings towards guys, she should talk it out with a counsellor. She should not be ashamed at having been intimidated when she was just five years old. If she feels too embarrassed to talk to a counsellor, she should remind herself that she was so young that it's almost as if she'd be talking about someone else. It will help her to tell the whole story and to realize that despite that episode, most guys are not out to take advantage of her.

For more information, look up the section on *Rape/Sexual Assault* at the back of this book.

INCEST

I hope this section doesn't hit home for you. Incest is when a family member – parent, stepparent, sibling, uncle, grandparent, cousin – has sex with a relative. In some cases, the girl is too young to understand what is going on or to realize that she is being abused. Other times she wants to report the situation but is afraid that her mother won't believe her or that the offender will be tossed into jail. She may also worry that if she doesn't tell, her younger sisters could be the next victims. Or perhaps deep down, she thinks she is to blame because she used to flirt with her daddy, or because she didn't tell her uncle 'no' the first time.

If you are a victim of incest, it is not your fault. It is the offender's fault. You are also not alone. Incest is much more common than people like to believe. There are many individuals and agencies ready to help you. And you may need help to end the abuse and to recover emotionally. It can be hard for an incest victim to learn to trust and love other men. But talking to a social worker or counsellor about your anger, humiliation and guilt can help you sort out your feelings. If you are a victim, it will take courage to seek help, but it has also taken courage to live with the secret and put up with the abuse. See the *Information* section at the back of this book for organisations that will help and support you.

As you'll see from some of these letters, incest can also leave girls with worries about homosexuality, sexually transmitted disease and pregnancy.

> *When I was about 7 or so, my grandfather molested me. He didn't go all the way but came very close. I was afraid to tell anyone for years. I finally told my mother when I was 12. She was very upset (it was her father), but also glad I told her. What I didn't tell her was that after my grandfather molested me, I really didn't think much of it.*
>
> *After a while I started to do the same things to my friends (girls) that my grandfather did to me (like feeling and kissing).*

I didn't know what a lesbian was or what a lesbian did when I was younger. I found out when I was 11. I quit doing those things with my friends immediately. So between the ages of 7 and 11, I was a lesbian, right?

What I'm afraid of now is this: could I have AIDS? I'm 14 and I'm really worried about it. I couldn't ask my mother or ask any other relatives. There's no way I can go to a doctor without my parents knowing. So I'm asking you, could I have AIDS?

Scared

It's not fair. A disturbed man makes unwelcome advances and years later an innocent girl suffers the consequences. It's highly unlikely that her grandfather had AIDS or that she contracted it, but I wish she had known how to end her worrying sooner. She could have anonymously called an AIDS hotline or gone to a clinic.

Was she a lesbian? No. Same-sex kissing and hugging before puberty is not all that unusual. Her activity with her friends was probably more exploratory and playful than sexual – and was no doubt inspired by her grandfather. Her own sexual orientation will probably be clear to her soon if it isn't already.

Will she be scarred? Many incest victims find that they have difficulties respecting or becoming intimate with men. Many become secretive or compulsive or develop phobias or simply hate themselves. Some block out the traumatic experience while others suffer flashback and can't seem to put down the baggage of shame, rage or fear.

Fortunately, this girl's mother believed her and was sympathetic. The girl now says she doesn't think much about the incident and she may be just fine. If her past *does* get in the way of her future, she may want to talk to a professional counsellor about her rude sexual awakening. Counselling (alone or in a group) could help her accept that she was and is a good person – it's her grandfather who has the problem.

I have a cousin who is 15. I am 12. It happened last summer, but I just can't get it off my mind. My cousin and I were in my room talking and taking turns giving each other backrubs. I was under my covers on my bed and he was on top of them. I had a nightgown on with no underwear, but I lifted it over my head because I wanted to get the full effect of the backrub.

Did I get an effect all right! After

*a while, my cousin started massaging
my bottom and I kind of pretended I
was asleep. He also was trying to feel
at my breasts. I let him do that knowing
I should stop him, but it felt so good. Then
he tried to get around my bottom and into
the front, but by squeezing my leg muscles
together, I didn't let him – thank God.*

*Finally I pulled myself together enough
so he got the point and after a while he
said, 'Do you know why I did that?' and
I pretended I was half-asleep and said,
'Mmmmwhaat?' I then felt some sticky
stuff coming out of my vagina. Is that
what happens when you're going to have
sex so that the vagina is lubricated? I just
want to forget that night with my cousin
because I love him a lot and he's my friend.
Is there any way to forget without facing
up to him? HELP? I feel like such a slut
for not stopping him.*

She *did* stop him. Granted, she could have
stopped him earlier, but hitting herself over the
head for a year is penance enough. It's time for
her to let herself off the hook, to forgive herself.
The mere fact that it's been weighing on her conscience shows that she's not a 'slut'. It's natural
that the forbidden backrub was exciting and it's

good that she's learned from the whole incident. It might help her to get over it faster if she talked with her cousin. She could say, 'I'm glad we're still good friends because I felt pretty stupid and guilty about that night in my room a year ago.' Maybe he has too.

About that sticky stuff. Yes. Her body was responding to sexual stimulation.

> *My second best friend has a problem. Her older cousin asked her to do it with him and nearly forced her to. What should she do if he makes her have sex? She hasn't told her parents because they are strict and they would be ashamed of her.*

If he forces her to 'do it', that's not sex. That's rape. She could threaten the kissing cousin that she would report him to the family or the police. She should definitely avoid being alone with him at family get-togethers. If she doesn't go off with him and doesn't lead him on, she should be okay. Perhaps the letter writer could rôle-play with her: she could pretend to be the jerky cousin and say something like, 'C'mon, you know you want it,' and her friend could see that it isn't hard to say, 'No, I don't. Leave me alone' or 'Keep your hands to yourself.'

She should also know that so long as she

says no, she has no reason to be ashamed. It is her cousin who should feel ashamed of taking advantage of her.

> *My mum remarried about three years ago. My stepdad has a brother, so he is my stepuncle. He has a son who is my stepcousin. Now my questions: 1) If we got married, would our kids be retarded? 2) How can I get something to happen between us? We are both 13.*

One reason incest is taboo is because when blood relatives marry, their children have an increased risk of birth defects or genetic problems. Since stepcousins are not blood relatives, their children would not be genetically at risk. The only risk these steps run is that if they strike up a short-lived romance, they may feel awkward at future Thanksgiving dinners!

The most poignant letters I received about incest were from a girl I'll call Susan. For her, incest wasn't a nagging worry or a troubling memory, but an all-too-vivid reality.

> *I have no one to talk to about my problems about sex. I just wanted to know what can I do about being pregnant. My mum said she don't care at all and I would like to*

know what you think. Being pregnant is not fun at all. It is upsetting. The baby is from my stepfather and my mother knows that I am pregnant from him. She drinks – that's her problem. He has been doing it to me when I was smaller too. Thank you.

I felt so sad when I read this letter. How could I help? How many months pregnant was she – too many to safely consider abortion? If I called the authorities, would her family be split apart? And if so, would that be a welcome improvement?

There was no listing under Susan's name in her hometown, so I wrote and urged her to call Childline right away. Legally, when an adult knows that a minor is being abused, the adult is obliged to report the crime. But I told Susan that I'd prefer that she set the wheels of change in motion and that I'd be in touch very soon to be sure that she did.

A few days later, I got another letter.

Hello? You know why I am writing to you, right? Because Carol they are still hurting me very badly and I just don't know what to do any more. I am 5½ months pregnant and I just don't like it at all. It hurts a lot. My insides are killing me and at night, I just can't sleep at all.

My stepfather go to bed with me every night and one night this week he went to bed with me and made me bleed very heavy, yes, I was very upset about it because I am still bleeding and it still hurts me very badly. And when this happened I was thinking that my baby came out of me. And my mother just don't care what go on in the house at all. I hate to say this but I hate my mother and stepfather a lot. I don't say anything to no one and I feel like I can't talk any more. I don't have no friends to talk to at all. So one day I went to a book store and I saw this book and I got it. The girl talk. I read it and I said to myself I can write to you as a friend. I need one, I feel like I am going crazy in the head. I need a friend to talk to and write to. I will talk to you.

Some friend I was. I'd done virtually nothing. I wondered if she'd called the child abuse number and decided, now that a week had gone by, that I had better do so myself.

Fortunately, right about then, the phone rang.

'Carol?'

'Yes.'

'Are you the one who wrote the book?'

'Yes.'

'This is Susan.'

'Susan! What's going on?' Susan began by telling me that she had gone to a Family Planning clinic. 'They said I should have come in earlier,' she said, because it was already too late for her to have an abortion. At the clinic, she learned about the adoption option and how to care for her unborn baby.

'Did you call Childline?' I asked.

'Yes.' Social workers were already helping her and her siblings move into her grandmother's house. (Susan's father was dead.) Turns out the stepfather had also been abusing her sisters and was now even approaching her brother.

'My brother has a knife,' Susan said. 'He wanted to kill my stepfather but I told him not to.'

'That was good advice.'

'And my mother won't let me go to school. She says that if I don't do what she says, I'll get in trouble.'

'Susan, you are already in trouble,' I said, but I assured her that the worst was almost over – that she would get through this and things would get better from here on. The social workers helped me keep my word. Susan and her siblings moved into her grandmother's home – where the kids could attend school by day and sleep safely at night.

One evening a few months later, Susan called me from a hospital. 'I had my baby,' she said. 'And I held her. But I'm not going to keep her. I'm going to give her up.'

'How do you feel?' I asked.

'Tired,' she answered.

I told her I thought she made the right decision.

Already, less than a year later, Susan is back in school and doing well. She is also holding down a part-time job in a shoe store. I'm proud of her for having reached out when she needed help and for being brave enough to make a better life for herself. And I'm grateful to the social workers without whom there would be far fewer happy endings to awful stories like these.

Good-bye

I just read the chapter on breasts in Girl-talk. *Remember how you said yours took so long to grow? Mine are too. I'm 11 years old and I just need a little advice. Did yours ever grow? I know it's a very embarrassing question and you don't have to answer, but it would help me a lot if you would.*

I love this letter. And I'm including it here because I want to end with a point about patience. Yes, my breasts finally grew, but I had to wait longer than I wished.

You too may have to wait longer than you'd like for your figure to fill out and your grades to go up and your love life to take off. You too may be losing patience with being patient. But try not to be in a mad rush to give your heart away.

Love comes at its own pace. And love and sex are worth waiting for. Meantime if you make yourself as wonderful and interesting and attractive as possible, you'll catch the eye of some wonderful and interesting and attractive guys. Really.

Forget fleeting flirtations. Forget four-year crushes. I'm hoping you'll soon be sharing your triumphs and setbacks with someone who deserves you. He'll have to be pretty terrific.

Love,

Carol Weston

Information: Hotlines and Helpful Addresses

When you need help, try to talk to someone you trust – perhaps your parents/guardians, your teacher or your doctor. If you don't have anyone you can talk to, contact the organisations listed here. Many of them are in London, but some have branches in different parts of the country that they can put you in touch with. Most will deal with callers from outside London. London numbers start with 01. If you are in London do not dial the 01, just the rest of the number.

Abortion – see Contraception

Abuse of Care - see Incest

AIDS/HIV Infection

For information and advice on all aspects of AIDS/HIV infection contact:

The Terence Higgins Trust
BM/AIDS
London WC1N 3XX
which has a wide range of leaflets free on request.
The Terence Higgins Trust Helpline:
(01) 833 2971 7pm - 10pm weekdays
3 pm - 10 pm weekends

The National Advisory Service on AIDS
Helpline: 0800 567123 Freecall 24 hrs

Welsh AIDS Campaign
Helpline: 0222 223443

Northern Ireland AIDS line
Helpline: 0332 226117

Scottish AIDS Monitor
Helpline: 031 557 1757

Your local STD (VD) clinic. Advice is free and confidential. Look in the phone book under Sexually Transmitted Diseases (STDs) or Venereal Disease (VD) for the phone number and address of your nearest clinic. You don't have to be referred by your doctor, you can just turn up.

Lesbian and Gay switchboard will discuss AIDS/HIV infection and put you in touch with local support groups
(01) 837 7324

The Health Education Authority
Hamilton House
Mabledon Place,
London WC1H 9TX
(01) 631 0930
produces booklets on AIDS and has a reference library of all such publications

Body Positive Group
PO Box 493
London W14 0TF
(01) 373 9124 eves (7-10)
offers advice to those who have HIV infection

FACT (Facilitators for AIDS Co-ordination and Training)
9 Branksome Road
London SW2 5JP
(01) 274 2289
offers training on AIDS/HIV infection to youth workers and teachers on issues to do with young

people and AIDS/HIV.

AIDS/HIV infection Helplines in Australia:
Sydney - AIDS Hotline: (02) 332 4000
Melbourne - AIDS line: (03) 419 3166

AIDS/HIV infection Helplines in Canada:
Toronto – AIDS Hotline: (416) 926 1626

AIDS/HIV infection Helplines in New Zealand:
Auckland - AIDS Foundation New Zealand:
(9) 395560

Alcoholism – see **Drugs/Alcohol**

Battering
For information on refuges for women and
children, how to leave violent men, sympathetic
solicitors etc,
contact:
London Women's Aid,
52-54 Featherstone Street,
London EC1Y 8RT
(01) 251 6537

Outside London, information on local refuges
can be obtained through social services, Citizens
Advice Bureaux or the police.

Childline

This is a national help and advice service for children and young people.

Childline
Freepost 1111 (no stamp needed)
London EC4 4BB
phone number 0800 1111 (the number is the same wherever you live; the service is free and open 24 hrs)

The Childline phone service is so busy that it's often difficult to get through. For some problems Childline cannot help you directly but will refer you to some of the other specialist organisations listed here.

Contraception

For advice on contraception, abortion or pregnancy counselling contact:

British Pregnancy Advisory Service (BPAS)
7 Belgrave Road
London SW1V 1QB
(01) 222 0985

Brook Advisory Centres
153a East Street

London SE17 2SD
(01) 708 1234

Family Planning Association
27 Mortimer Street
London W1N 7RJ
(01) 636 7866

Counselling
The following organisations offer sympathetic and impartial counselling on family and other problems:

Family Network Services
National Children's Home (NCH)
Stephenson Hall
85c Highbury Park
London N5 1UD

Regional telephone numbers for this organisation:
Birmingham (021) 440 5970
Cardiff (0222) 29461
Glasgow (041) 2216722
Glenrothes (0592) 759651
Gloucester (0452) 24019
Leeds (0532) 456456

Ilford (01) 514 1177
Luton (0582) 422751
Maidstone (0622) 56677
Manchester (061) 2369873
Norwich (0603) 660679
Preston (0772) 24006
Taunton (0823) 333191

National Association of Young People's
Counselling and Advisory Services
(NAYPCAS)
17-23 Albion Street
Leicester LE1 6GD
(0533) 471200

Teenage Information Network (TIN)
102 Harper Road
London SE1 6AQ
(01) 403 2444 (London only)

Depression and Despair
Contact the organisations listed in **Counselling**.
If things are really bad ring the Samaritans. You
will find the local number in the phone book or
you can ask the operator to put you through
directly. This is a 24hr service.

Drugs/Alcohol
For help with a drugs problem contact:

Standing Conference on Drug Abuse
(SCODA)
1-4 Hatton Place
Hatton Garden
London EC1N 8ND
(01) 430 2341

Community Drug Project
30 Manor Place
London SE17 3BB
(01) 703 0559 (London only)

Families Anonymous
88 Caledonian Road
London N1 9ND
(01) 278 8060 (London only)

For help with an alcohol problem contact:
Al-anon (Groups in the UK and Eire)
61 Great Dover Street
London SE1 4YF
(01) 403 0888

Alcohol Counselling Service (ACS)
34 Electric Lane
London SW9 8JJ
(01) 737 3579/3570

Gay and Lesbian Advice Organisations

For information and advice on being gay, lesbian or bisexual contact:

Lesbian and Gay Switchboard
BM Switchboard
London WC1N 3XX
(01) 837 7324

Lesbian and Gay Switchboard can put you in touch with organisations which specialise in helping young gay and lesbian people 'come out' to their parents, and can put parents in touch with support groups such as:

Parents Anonymous
(01) 668 4805 24hrs

National Friend
BM National Friend
London WC1N 3XX
(01) 837 3337
will also advise young people on bi-sexuality

Lesbian and Gay Youth Movement
LGYM BM GYM
London WC1N 3XX
(01) 319 9690

This is a national organisation for young people which provides advice and help, runs a penfriends scheme and annual festivals and publishes a Gay Youth magazine.

Lesbian Line
BM Box 1514
London WC1N 3XX
(01) 251 6911

Haemophilia
For help and advice for people with haemophilia and on haemophilia and HIV infection/AIDS;

The Haemophilia Society
16 Trinity Street
London SE1 1DE
(01) 407 1010

Health Education
The Health Education Authority produces leaflets on all aspects of health education and has an extensive reference library:

The Health Education Authority,
Hamilton House
Mabledon Place

London WC1H 9TX
(01) 631 0930

Herpes
For help and advice for people with herpes:

The Herpes Association
41 North Road
London N7
(01) 609 9061

Advice can also be obtained from your nearest STD (VD) clinic.

HIV Infection - see AIDS

Incest/Abuse of Care
The following organisations will be able to contact someone in your area who will help you to deal with the situation and find you a place of safety:

The National Society for the Prevention of Cruelty to Children (NSPCC)
(branches in England, Wales and Northern Ireland)

67 Saffron Hill
London EC1N 8RS
(01) 242 1626

Royal Scottish Society for the Prevention of
Cruelty to Children
Melville House
41 Polworth Terrace
Edinburgh EH11 1NU
(031) 337 8539/8530

The Church of England Children's Society
Edward Rudolf House
Margery Street
London WC1X 0JL
(01) 837 4299
(You don't have to be Church of England
to contact this organisation)

Touchline (for people in the Yorkshire area)
(0532) 457777

Incest Crisis Line
32 Newbury Close
Northolt
Middlesex UB5 4JF
This service is run by incest survivors:
Richard (01) 422 5100
Shirley (01) 890 4732

Kate (01) 593 9428

Incest Survivors Campaign
London: (01) 852 7432
         (01) 737 1354
Manchester (061) 236 1712
Dundee (0382) 21545
Belfast (0232) 249 696

Avon Sexual Abuse Centre (for people in the Avon area)
39 Jamaica Street
Stokes Croft
Bristol BS2 8JP
(0272) 428331

Taboo (for people in the Manchester area)
PO Box 38
Manchester M60 1HG
(061) 236 1323

Choices (for people in the Cambridge area)
(0223) 314438

Australia
Sydney
Child Protection and Family Crisis – (02) 818 5555 (24 hours)
2UE Kids Careline – (02) 929 7799 (9am to

5pm, Mon-Fri)
Darwin
Department for Community Development –
(089) 814 733
Brisbane
Crisis Care – (07) 224 6855 (24 hours)
Adelaide
Crisis Care – (08) 272 1222 (24 hours)
Hobart
Department of Community Welfare, Crisis Inter-
vention (002) 302 529 (24 hours)
Melbourne
Protective Services for Children – (03) 309 5700
(9am to 5pm)
Perth
Crisis Care – (09) 321 4144 (24 hours) or
(008) 199 008 (toll free)

You can also contact through your local direc-
tory:
The Police
Lifeline
Rape Crisis Centres

New Zealand
Auckland
Help – 399 185 (24 hours)

Canada

The emergency number in Canada is 911.

For help and/or advice:

- Look in the telephone directory on the first page under Child Abuse
- Ring the police or social services

or

- Contact: National Clearinghouse on Family Violence

Health & Welfare Canada

Ottawa

Ontario K1A 1B5

(613) 9572938

who will refer you to someone in your area.

Legal Rights

The Children's Legal Centre
20 Compton Terrace
London N1 2UN
(01) 359 6251

National Council for Civil Liberties (NCCL)
21 Tabard Street
London SE1 4LA
(01) 403 3888

Release
169 Commercial Street
London E1 6BW
Emergency (24 hrs): (01) 603 8654
for information and help in dealing with the
Police, the Criminal Courts or drugs problems.

Lesbianism - see Gay and Lesbian

Pregnancy - see Contraception

Prostitution

At the time of writing there is only one organisation which specialises in helping young people caught up in prostitution:
Streetwise
3b Langham Mansions
Earl's Court Square
London SW5
(01) 373 8860
but the organisations listed under **Counselling**
will also offer help and advice.

Rape/Sexual Assault
For girls and women:

The Rape Crisis Centre
PO Box 69
London WC1N 9NJ
(01) 837 1600 (24 hrs)
The number of your nearest Rape Crisis Centre
should be in the phone book.

For gay men and boys there is no equivalent to
the Rape Crisis Centre but help and advice can
be obtained from:

Lesbian and Gay Switchboard
BM Switchboard
London WC1N 3XX
(01) 837 7324

National Friend
BM National Friend
London WC1N 3XX
(01) 837 3337

For heterosexual men and boys there is no
equivalent to the Rape Crisis Centre. Help and
advice can be obtained from the organisations
listed under **Counselling**.

If you want to contact the police ring 999 or your local police station (number in the phone book).

For support and counselling in the long term:
The Victim Aid Scheme
(01) 729 1252

Sexual Assault - see Rape

Sexually Transmitted Diseases
If you suspect that you have a sexually transmitted disease it's important to get help as soon as possible. Ring your local hospital or look in the phone book under Sexually Transmitted Diseases (STDs) or Venereal Disease (VD) for the address of your nearest clinic. See also **AIDS/HIV Infection**.

Index